Born To Hunt

QUEEN ELIZABETH ISLANDS
BANKS ISLAND
BEAUFORT SEA
VICTORIA ISLAND
BAFFIN BAY
BAFFIN ISLAND
GREENLAND (DENMARK)
ARCTIC CIRCLE (66°33')
U. S.
GREAT BEAR LAKE
GREAT SLAVE LAKE
DAVIS STRAIT
DENMARK STRAIT
ICELAND
GULF OF ALASKA
HUDSON BAY
CANADA
LABRADOR SEA
ROCKALL (U.K.)
LAKE WINNIPEG
ISLAND OF NEWFOUNDLAND
IRELAND
CELTIC SEA
LAKE SUPERIOR
LAKE HURON
LAKE MICHIGAN
LAKE ONTARIO

CIFIC
CEAN
FALKLAND ISLANDS (ISLAS MALVINAS) (ADMINISTERED BY U.K., CLAIMED BY ARGENTINA)
SCOTIA SEA
SOUTH GEORGIA AND THE SOUTH SANDWICH ISLANDS (ADMINISTERED BY U.K., CLAIMED BY ARGENTINA)
DRAKE PASSAGE
SOUTH ORKNEY ISLANDS
SOUTHERN OCEAN
ANTARCTIC CIRCLE (66°33')
BELLINGSHAUSEN SEA
WEDDELL SEA
AMUNDSEN SEA

Born To Hunt

Forty Years and Six Continents

by

Gary R. Ingersoll

Safari Press

Ingersoll, Gary R.

Second edition

Safari Press

2010 Long Beach, California

ISBN 978-1-57157-349-0

Library of Congress Catalog Card Number: 2009928088

10 9 8 7 6 5 4 3 2 1

Printed in China

Readers wishing to receive the Safari Press catalog, featuring many fine books on big-game hunting, wingshooting, and sporting firearms, should write to Safari Press Inc., P.O. Box 3095, Long Beach, CA 90803, USA. Tel: (714) 894-9080 or visit our Web site at www.safaripress.com.

Dedication

To my wife, Elizabeth,
and my family

Table of Contents

Foreword by Rex Baker ix
Introduction xi

Part 1 **North America Is Tough** 1
Chapter 1 The Silver Bear of Yakutat (Alaska, 1987) 2
Chapter 2 We Thought We Were in Heaven (Colorado and Alaska, 1960s) 10
Chapter 3 Giants of the Arctic (Alaska, 1970s) 18
Chapter 4 Counting the Days for Sheep (Alberta, 1975) 32
Chapter 5 Phantom Mountain Caribou (British Columbia, 1981) 42
Chapter 6 The Old Seven and the Twenty-Seven (North American 27, 1980) 48

Part 2 **Classic Africa** 60
Chapter 7 Thirty-Five Days Living the Dream (Kenya, 1976) 62
Chapter 8 Stand By for Rebellion (Sudan, 1977) 74
Chapter 9 Quest for a Hundred-Pounder (Central African Republic, 1978) 86
Chapter 10 Close Call Leopard (Zambia and Zimbabwe, 1983) 98
Chapter 11 Ancient Nation, Modern Anguish (Ethiopia, 1985) 106
Chapter 12 Three Prime Hunting Countries (Namibia, 1981; South Africa, 1986, 2008; Tanzania, 1990; and the Weatherby Award 1991) 116

Part 3 **Asian Sheep Beckon** 128
Chapter 13 Afghan Urial with James Bond (Tajikistan, 1985) 130
Chapter 14 Compromise Pays Off for Blanford Urial (Pakistan, 1986) 138
Chapter 15 Super Slam Blue Sheep (Nepal, 1984, 1985; China, 1991) 144
Chapter 16 From Gobi Argali to Snow Sheep (Mongolia, 1981, 1984, 1985; Kamchatka, 1993–2004) 152
Chapter 17 A Gracious Reception (Iran, 2002) 166
Chapter 18 Three Tries for Marco Polo (Kyrgyzstan, 1995; Tajikistan, 2003, 2005) 176

Part 4 **Fine Times in Other Regions** 184
Chapter 19 Wild Man of the Chaco (Venezuela and Argentina, 1980s and 1990s) 186
Chapter 20 The Far, Far South (Australia and New Zealand, 1980s, 2004) 200
Chapter 21 Loyalty Pays Off (Europe, 1982–2006) 212
Chapter 22 Wrap Up (SCI International Hunter Award, 2001; Conklin Award, 2003) 228

Part 5: **Odds and Ends** 234
Chapter 23 Hunting Chronology 236
Chapter 24 Biography 240
Chapter 25 Bibliography 242

Foreword

It is an honor to be asked to write the foreword for such a good friend, especially if that friend has led a life few have enjoyed. I have known Gary for nearly three decades, and over the years we have fished, vacationed, socialized, and worked together as directors of various conservation/award organizations.

We became friends while fishing in Alaska in the 1980s. It was during that time I learned that Gary is a wonderful storyteller. Part of the adventure of hunting is that we all have stories to tell, and it was a great pleasure to listen to Gary's stories of adventures and misadventures around the world. These are the same stories he is now sharing with you in this book.

He has always seemed to be one step ahead of the times, which shows in the prescient choices he has made in his hunting career: He saw the tide shifting and was one of the last to hunt in Kenya, and he took a polar bear while they were still legal to hunt. He also took advantage of a thirty-day "cancellation" hunt in Ethiopia with Tom Mattanovich and collected around thirty species, including at least one world record. Some may say that Gary is lucky that way, but perhaps saying that he is a prescient hunter describes him better.

Even before the "ethical revolution" in the late 1980s, Gary always exhibited high ethical standards in the field. He is an honorable hunter. In my opinion the Anatolian chamois is the toughest of the eight huntable chamois to get, and no one is guaranteed success. Only rugged hunters attempt to go after this species. Gary had been hunting the Anatolian chamois hard in steep, snow-covered mountains in northeastern Turkey without success. On the last day, the locals spotted a good male way back up the mountain and wanted to go after it. Gary said to them, "I can't make it." One of the guides said, "Give me your gun, and we'll get it." Gary then said what any true sportsman would say: "No, I have never done that and I'm not going to start now." I didn't learn this from Gary, but from the next hunter into that camp. That is Gary—an ethical, honorable man of integrity.

Luckily, he has always collected above-average trophies. Any hunter who has collected over three hundred species, as Gary has, is going to be lucky some of the time: a) The law of averages works in the favor of any hunter who has spent that much time collecting such a large number of critters. b) With that type of resume and species count, a hunter has gotten good at picking outfitters and the correct time to hunt, and he has learned to climb and shoot. I watched Dr. Jim Conklin miss a world-record Blanford urial in Pakistan in the 1980s. Gary later collected this trophy, and it has been the world's record for many years.

We serve together on several boards of directors, and these are meetings of peers in the hunting world. Gary always checks his ego at the door. He is respectful, thoughtful, and often the last word before a vote—in other words, the ideal director. One particularly fine trait of Gary's is that he rarely says derogatory things about other people; he really is a nice guy.

He has won just about every hunting award there is, including the Weatherby Award, the Conklin Award, the International Hunting Award from Safari Club International, and many awards from the Houston chapter of Safari Club International.

He has done this while working full time, being a husband, father, and grandfather. He is complemented in his personal life by Elizabeth, his beautiful wife. She maintains the *casa* and cares for Gary's rare pigeons while he is away on business during the week. Gary is mild mannered while Elizabeth is at the other end of the scale in a funny, extroverted, highly intellectual way. They are lucky to have each other.

Gary is a self-made man; he has made the best of his opportunities both in the hunting world and the business world through skill, intelligence, and hard work, not inheritance. For those of you who do not know Gary, he is trim, fit, has a full head of hair, and looks twenty years younger than his age. Let us hope his Scandinavian genes help him to live a long time.

Gary, it is a pleasure and honor to be your buddy.

Rex Baker
Marietta, Georgia
June 25, 2009

Acknowledgments

Special gratitude goes to my family. My wife, Elizabeth, has been endlessly understanding about the amount of time and resources required for hunting, and about the imposition a large trophy collection makes on our home. She cheerfully undertakes airport runs and manages the homestead without me. By now, she may even prefer the peace of not having me underfoot all the time. My son Jason and daughter-in-law Jan, my daughter Traci, my stepdaughter Tiffany, and my three grandchildren, JR, Kyle, and Reed, who will soon be hunters, have forgiven me for missing key events. I thank them all for joining me when they can and for tolerating my frequent hunting absences.

I am grateful to Ludo Wurfbain of Safari Press for encouraging me to develop a book about what big-game hunting has meant to me. I want to thank Sally Antrobus, former editor of *Safari* magazine and longtime Houston Safari Club publications editor, for being my ghostwriter. She listened to my stories, reviewed my hunting journals, and drew material from previously published articles. Sally interviewed me to fill in the gaps and then wove all the threads into a cohesive memoir. I appreciate her ability to render my experience in my "voice." We enjoyed working on this project together.

Sally has adapted magazine articles by Tom Tischler, David Byford, and Frank Nicholson for use in this book. I want to thank these authors for their skill in portraying my hunts in print.

Introduction

I'd like to say a word about luck.

People often tell me I'm one of the luckiest hunters around, and I agree. I consider myself especially fortunate to have started hunting when I did. The small Minnesota farm of my youth in the 1940s and '50s was a modest start, a long way from the great game destinations of the world. We never had money to spare, but I learned self-reliance and also learned to shoot, ride a horse, and value a few close companions. The lessons would serve me well.

I grew up daydreaming of cowboys, and my early hunts were in that style. I would ride out on horseback for a couple of weeks. The guide and I would each have a packhorse, and we would make fly camps and sleep on the ground. In many ways the experience was quite close to hunting in Theodore Roosevelt's day.

At that time there were no booking agents or organized groups, no fancy camps, and no operations selling designer camouflage hunting attire, like Cabela's, Bass Pro Shops, or Gander Mountain. If you went on safari in Africa, you wore old clothes and left them there—I called them one-way outfits. I have pictures of myself hunting elephant in plaid Bermuda shorts! Food was basic; I ate lots of Spam. If you wanted a good meal, it could wait until you stopped at a restaurant or got home. No one worried about gourmet meals or cases of wine in the hunting camps. Our energy was devoted to the hunt itself. In fact, I lost five or ten pounds on all my North American hunts.

Hunting pioneer and consultant Bert Klineburger has often said that the heyday of hunting is now, and on some level I would agree. Today it's much easier to arrange big-game hunts than it once was. The field is large and growing. Outfitters, professional hunters, guides, and booking agents have flourished; they come to sporting conventions, where we can meet them and get a good sense of what they have to offer. We need not rely on word of mouth or plunge into the great unknown.

Places like South Africa and New Zealand have seen a great expansion of big-game hunting operations. Mongolia, Russia, and China have opened up to visiting hunters, and new hunting areas still open up from time to time. The long-forgotten tradition of beginning your safari by visiting a custom tailor in Nairobi seems downright picturesque, now that safari clothing is available on sales floors across the globe. You can buy your own satellite phone at any sportsmen's fund-raising auction, so it's easy to stay connected to home. My hometown of Houston has numerous booking agents; I recall only one in the 1970s. He booked safaris to Africa. The late Frank Green of Sporting International pioneered safari consulting some forty years ago, and if anyone was booking clients on North American hunts before that, I didn't know about it.

On the other hand, many kinds of hunting and destinations have receded or vanished altogether. We simply cannot experience them today, which is one reason I consider myself lucky. For example, things were much more flexible and less tightly organized when I first hunted Alaska in the 1960s. I missed out on going to India, but I did hunt in Kenya just before it closed all big-game hunting. My thirty-five-day safari bore little resemblance to the ten-day hunts now available in Africa for the younger generation in a hurry. Elephant hunting closed in the Central African Republic just months after I'd been there. My polar bear and walrus hunts took place during windows of an on-again, off-again situation. After long years of civil strife, my Sudan hunt occurred during a short-lived lull before a rebellion resumed.

These hunting stories appear in loose chronology. I generally hunted North America in the 1960s, Africa in the 1970s, and Asia in the 1980s and 1990s, with plenty of crossover. I have tried to include stories that are interesting in themselves, instead of aiming for completeness. The nuts and bolts of my hunts appear in

a chronology at the back of the book, along with a short hunting biography.

Awards are gratifying as acknowledgment of a goal-directed effort. They also serve to recognize all the hard work invested by outfitters, guides, professional hunters, and booking agents to make hunts and hunters successful. Yet no award can capture the joy of visiting faraway places and interacting closely with all types of people, sometimes in intense and hectic ways. These are the deeper rewards of hunting worlds away from home. I've been in camps with all kinds of people, and we got along fine. In the hunting fraternity, doctors, lawyers, and businessmen all have the common experience of hunting. This shared interest seems to bridge all divides, even though each hunter is trying to outdo the other. Hunting creates a type of alliance among us that we could never experience in ordinary international travel.

I firmly believe that successful hunting of big game requires a certain amount of luck. I also believe our actions have bearing on our luck. As I tell the salespeople I teach, the harder you work, the luckier you become. I am a firm believer in goal setting. No matter how small your beginnings, you can still shoot for big goals. And it helps to start young. My son Jason came with me to Africa in 1976 when he was five years old, and in turn, we took his son JR to Africa in 2008 at the age of five.

I hope this book is entertaining, and I intend it as a tribute to all those who have helped me in the hunting world.

North America Is Tough

Part 1

ARCTIC OCEAN
GREENLAND SEA
SVALBARD (NORWAY)
BARENTS SEA
GREENLAND (DENMARK)
JAN MAYEN (NORWAY)
NORWEGIAN SEA
DENMARK STRAIT
ICELAND
FAROE ISLANDS (DEN.)
NORWAY
SWEDEN
FINLAND
GULF OF BOTHNIA
WHITE SEA
ROCKALL (U.K.)
UNITED KINGDOM
NORTH SEA
DENMARK
BALTIC SEA
EST.
LAT.
LITH.
RUSSIA
IRELAND
POLAND
BELARUS
NETH.
GERMANY
CELTIC SEA
BELGIUM
LUX.
CZECH REP.
SLOVAKIA
UKRAINE
MOLDOVA
FRANCE
SWITZ.
LIECH.
AUSTRIA
HUNGARY
ROMANIA
BAY OF BISCAY
SLOVENIA
CROATIA
SAN MARINO
YUGO.
SEA OF AZOV
MONACO
BLACK SEA
ANDORRA
CORSICA (FR.)
ITALY
VATICAN CITY
BULGARIA
ALB.
PORTUGAL
SPAIN
BALEARIC ISLANDS (SP.)
SARDINIA (IT.)
GREECE
TURKEY
NORTH ATLANTIC OCEAN
AZORES (PORT.)
SICILY (IT.)
MALTA
GIBRALTAR (U.K.)
CEUTA (SP.)
MELILLA (SP.)
TUNISIA
MEDITERRANEAN SEA
CRETE (GR.)
CYPRUS
LEB.
SYRIA
MADEIRA ISLANDS (PORT.)
ISRAEL
JORDAN
MOROCCO
CANARY ISLANDS (SP.)
ALGERIA
LIBYA
EGYPT
WESTERN SAHARA
RED SEA
MAURITANIA
MALI
NIGER
CAPE VERDE
CHAD
SENEGAL
BURKINA FASO
THE GAMBIA
SUDAN
GUINEA-BISSAU
GUINEA
BENIN
NIGERIA
CÔTE D'IVOIRE
GHANA
TOGO
SIERRA LEONE
CENTRAL AFRICAN REPUBLIC
LIBERIA
CAMEROON
EQUATORIAL GUINEA
GULF OF GUINEA
SAO TOME AND PRINCIPE
UGANDA
EQUATOR
REP. OF THE CONGO
GABON
DEMOCRATIC REPUBLIC OF THE CONGO
RWANDA
BURUNDI
TANZANIA

Gary, the old 7mm magnum, and the "Silver Bear of the Yakutat."

Alaska, 1987

I could barely hear the rifle's report over the roar of falling water on the western slopes of Alaska's wilderness. The slug from the old 7mm pierced the silver hair just behind the bear's shoulder and ranged up through the heart and out into the daylight. The silver bear slumped on the steep, wet slope, slid down six feet, and came to rest at the base of a large alder.

I chambered another round and took another bead, but there was no need. I had my glacier bear, or blue bear. The coats of black bear in the glacier country of Alaska sport a beautiful, silvery-blue sheen. I call it "grandma blue," the hair color women of a certain age tend to favor. It was 6:30 A.M. on the sixth day of the hunt.

I kept the carcass covered while my guide, Ken Fanning, slid down through the rugged wetness of the canyon, climbed up the other side to the bear, and, with the cold steel of his muzzle, confirmed that the pale bear slumped around the base of the tree was dead.

This bear is considered one of the world's rarest trophies. It is found only in a restricted area around the Yakutat Glacier. Forty glacier bear had made it into the Alaska Department of Fish and Game records at that time. The glacier bear is a lighter color phase of the wide-ranging black bear, evidently an adaptation to life in the glacier country.

This hunt had a successful conclusion but a rocky beginning. It began in the dust and frustration of foiled plans, far from Ken Fanning's exclusive hunting area on the wet slopes of the Tongass National Forest. I had reached the Yakutat Glacier by a winding path of disappointments, and by the time I got there I was a bit nervous about the general state of my luck.

I had been booked to hunt with Bert Klineburger in the Central African Republic in January. A week before the departure date I received a telex (remember those?) saying, "Don't come; problems in the area," and so forth. That hunt was canceled. In February Beth Levitz Jones had booked me a trip to Pakistan for an Afghan urial, which would complete my Super Slam of sheep. Two days before I was supposed to leave on that hunt, I got another telex: "Don't come; utter chaos in Pakistan." It turned out that "chaos" meant torrential rains were paralyzing the country.

We dined like kings on scallops and halibut the first night in Ken Fanning's camp.

Things always happen in threes, right? And the third hunt in the pipeline was my spring trip for glacier bear. Knowing how tough it is to get these bears, it was hard to shake off the idea that if bad things come in threes, I was in real trouble. I was rattled.

Three times I called Ken's Alaska Guide Service to confirm.

"I'm not saying we're going to get the bear, but we are not canceling," he assured me.

I was booked for only a seven-day hunt, which had the distinct potential of allowing too little time. People have failed even to see a glacier bear on longer hunts than that.

The day before the hunt began I was scheduled to fly from Houston to Salt Lake City, on to Anchorage, and finally to Yakutat, all on the same day. The next day we were to backpack to camp and start hunting. My plane was to leave Houston at 8 A.M. But when I arrived at the Delta counter to check my luggage, I was greeted by a sign announcing: "Salt Lake flight canceled." The next flight was the following afternoon. A suitable interval of cussing followed. How was I to get to Yakutat in a day if I couldn't even get as far as Salt Lake?

It was time for Plan B. I flew into Seattle and called the Klineburgers. They had booked many hunts for me, and we had become close friends. Kent Klineburger picked me up and not only took me to their world-famous taxidermy operation but also to enjoy a fresh seafood dinner. In the morning I caught a 7 A.M. flight to Yakutat, figuring I could salvage half a day, at least. But this fallback plan would not be so straightforward, either. Would you believe the plane had "mechanical difficulties"? It looked as if there would be a half-hour delay.

Two hours later, I was still sitting in Seattle, worried I would never get going. Finally, the plane was ready for takeoff, and I arrived in Yakutat at 2:30 P.M., instead of noon. Ken was waiting for me and calmly declared, "I knew you'd get here sooner or later."

We dashed down to the sporting-goods store to buy my hunting and fishing licenses, then ran over to the grocery store to get my requisite two six-packs of Dr

Pepper. I figured a ration of two a day for six days would keep me going; you don't want to be toting too many canned drinks on a backpacking hunt. Food was ungodly expensive in that far outpost of a place, but we got a few staples, jumped into the truck, and drove to the end of the road, where Ron Warren was waiting for us.

He was what they referred to as a packer. He was only sixteen years old, but I hesitate to use the word boy because he could carry more than most men I know. His job was to pack the freight in. You could load a hundred pounds or more on that boy's back, and you still couldn't keep up with him. He had already made two trips that day—seven miles in and seven miles back—and he was to make one more with us.

I loaded him with my gear, and I carried just a light pack consisting of my cameras, my trusty cassette player, and my country-and-western tapes by Merle Haggard, Randy Travis, the Judds, and Willie Nelson—all the good stuff. I shoved an extra package of twelve tapes into Fanning's pack. He said we were going light and didn't need a lot of stuff. Conveniently, it didn't get dark until 11 P.M., which was just about the time we got to our camp.

I now had just six days, but at least I was there and tired enough to know I would sleep well. I broke open a Dr Pepper, and we dined like kings on fresh scallops and halibut. Our game plan for the next day was to cross the river in an Avon raft, hike up the other side of the mountain to the snowline, then go over the top to see if there was any sign of bear up there.

There was indeed a sign; we could see where a bear had come down out of the snow to feed. After this discovery, we spent a few hours glassing. We followed a creek back down the mountain, and around 3 P.M. we found what we were looking for. On the side of the mountain to our left, near the bottom and only about one hundred and fifty yards away, Ken spotted a glacier bear.

I admit I was excited. Here we were on the very first day of the hunt, with a bear at the bottom of a mountain, just across the creek at one hundred and fifty yards. We didn't have to climb or crawl. But I had to shoot fast because the bear was feeding toward some heavy brush. I grabbed Ken's backpack, ran to the edge of the creek, laid the backpack on a rock, and laid the rifle on the backpack.

Just as I was about to shoot, the backpack slipped. I shot high, over the back of the bear. It turned and hauled off as fast as it could up the mountain. I shot three more times, but all I succeeded in doing was blowing some branches off the trees. The bear disappeared.

I replayed the stories I knew of people who had returned here seven, eight, or ten times before they even saw a glacier bear. Here I was, having seen a bear on the very first day out and finding a good opportunity for a shot at only one hundred and fifty yards. And I had missed! The third bit of bad luck seemed to have arrived, after all. I was almost ready to pack up and go home, but I collected myself enough to give myself a little lecture.

I've got five more days. He won't go over to the other side because there isn't anything over there for him. I'm almost positive this bear has never seen a human before. He didn't see us. He just heard this loud noise and ran up into the brush. He might go up there and stay on that mountainside.

It was a miserable hike home. I pulled out a Dr Pepper and some country-and-western tapes to console myself.

Ken tried to make me feel better. "Well, you know, things like that happen; we'll still get him. . . ."

He was convinced that the trouble lay with the rifle, but I wasn't.

"That seven doesn't miss," I told him. "When I put it over there, it shoots. To make you happy I'll shoot it in the morning, but I'm telling you, it ain't the gun, it's me."

In the morning we drew a circle on a paper plate. The old seven shot true. There was no arguing: The miss lay with the hunter.

Second Try

We launched a new game plan for day two. Ron and Ken would make their way toward the top of the slope where we had seen the bear the day before. I would stay at the bottom so that if the bear was spooked, I could cut it off. This was an all-day program. Even with all of us wearing hip boots, it would still take Ron and Ken about three hours to get to the top through the tangle and brush.

After lunch Ken came back down to tell me they had found where the bear had gone up into the snow. Luckily, it hadn't gone over the top of the mountain. The bear had traveled only some fifty yards in the snow before turning to go back down into the brush. The three of us spent the rest of the day glassing that mountainside. On the way home I caught three Dolly Varden trout for supper.

The next morning's hunt would prove frustrating. We climbed and glassed and climbed and glassed for much of the day, and then it started raining. Wet and tired, we struggled back to the inflatable raft. We turned it over to use as a lean-to and cooked moose hotdogs and beans. After the meal I started glassing the mountain slopes again, and suddenly I spotted the bear, halfway up.

Leaving Ron at the bottom, Ken and I re-crossed the creek in the raft and climbed the waterfall. The brush in that area is hell to work through, and visibility is low, so Ron would signal to us where the bear was located. Ken climbed one of the few substantial trees, trying for a view. He couldn't see the bear, but he could see Ron, and Ron was waving his arms. We couldn't quite get his signals straight.

I began working my way through the heavy brush toward another waterfall. I was about three-quarters of the way there when Ken started hollering: "There's the bear! He's coming up the other side of the canyon. Quick, there's a tree over there. Get up that tree and see if you can see him."

Climbing trees isn't something I'm used to doing. The tree was too big for me to get my arms around, but, with Ken shouting, I somehow managed to climb high enough to find a branch to hang onto. Just then, I spotted the bear. It was about to top out and disappear.

"Shoot!" said Ken.

I can't tell you exactly what, if anything, I said to Ken, but here's what I thought. *Shoot? If I shoot, I'm going to fall out of this tree because I can't hold on and shoot at the same time, and if I fall out of this tree, I'm going to bust my ass when I hit the ground.*

I leaned into the tree, knowing full well that when I pulled the trigger, the recoil was probably going to knock me right off. I shot. I missed the bear. And I almost fell out of the tree. Clutching the gun in one hand, I grabbed a branch with the other to keep from falling.

"You missed him," said Ken.

"I know, but I didn't fall out of the tree," was my lame comeback.

Talk about two people stating the obvious!

I was utterly disillusioned now. Two sightings, two missed shots. The odds of getting a glacier bear seemed to be diminishing.

I revisited the idea of things happening in threes. Forget the bad things that happened before, Gary. Get your act together. If you spot the bear again, this will be the third time. This is it.

Is It a Rock?

Day four. The game plan was to go all the way back to where we had seen the bear the first day, crawl up a rock slide most of the way up the mountain, and glass the mountainside where I had taken the last shot. By 10:30 A.M. all three of us were glassing the slopes.

At the base of a tree about halfway up the slope, I noticed an odd, pale shape. It looked like a big rock or part of the tree's root structure, but, on the other hand, the color was right for our bear. I glassed the still shape for five minutes before announcing, "Ken, you're not going to believe what I'm looking at."

He had found it, too.

"I think you're looking at the same thing I'm looking at," he said, "the prettiest rock you ever saw?"

We agreed that the rock looked as if it had hair. If it was the bear, it was upside down.

Ken thought it might be the bear, and perhaps it was

Sixteen-year-old Ron Warren getting our Avon raft ready to take us hunting. He was a tireless packer and a useful third set of eyes on the hunt.

dead. I was thinking I couldn't possibly be that lucky when both of us saw movement. Up rose a paw. The bear turned, and Ken declared: "There's our bear!"

This was not easy to believe. Here was our third bear sighting, and the bear was lying there fast asleep.

We took a space blanket and folded it into a square to represent the bear. The backpack would represent Ken and me. Ron would stay and watch the bear, using these items to indicate our relative position. He would move the backpack until we were flush with the bear, so that when we looked across at Ron, we would see where the backpack was in relation to the space blanket. If the bear moved, Ron would move the space blanket. Very scientific.

We hauled off. Two hours later, we had gotten down, across, and up the other side. We were looking at the space blanket, and it hadn't moved, which meant the bear was still asleep at the base of the tree. Ron was moving the backpack. Then, as we moved above the bear, Ron started to move the space blanket. The bear was up.

We moved a little higher, and Ron moved the space blanket some more. We thought we were close, but we couldn't see much on our own side of the mountain. Ken climbed a tree and announced that the bear had moved off to one side and up the slope. Then he saw it.

"There he is! I can see him! Can you see him?"

I could see nothing through all that brush. Ken described a small ravine and told me the bear was on the other side of it, feeding upward.

"If he keeps going like he's going, he's going to come right out into the open," he said.

I moved forward to a blown-down tree and caught a glimpse of the bear through the thick brush. It was only about seventy-five yards away. I laid the gun down on the tree and tried to clear some branches so I wouldn't have to shoot through brush.

All of a sudden the bear stopped, turned around to look right at us, and then lay down. When it lay down, I had a perfect shot, but all I could see were the head, ears, and a little of the shoulder. I had a perfect rest on the log.

This is number three, I thought. *If I blow this deal, it is definitely over with.*

I was getting so gun-shy that I didn't know whether to shoot or not. If I didn't shoot, I might not get another chance at the bear, but I hated to shoot the animal in the

I caught three Dolly Varden trout for supper—and then a fourth as an offering for better hunting luck. We placed the last fish at the base of a tree where bald eagles were nesting.

head, and I didn't have enough target. If it stood up, I might get a broadside shot. I decided to wait.

Time passed, testing my patience. One of the rarest of trophies was just barely in sight at seventy-five yards. I thought about the time in Ethiopia when I sat for hours while a mountain nyala just lay there, until it finally stood up and I shot it in the throat. I was there from noon until dark; the sun blistered my hands. This could be like that, I thought.

I knew where I would shoot the bear. I'd shoot it in the neck. I had to shoot it.

Just then the bear stood up, and when it stood up, all I could see were its legs.

"Ken, I can't see him," I said.

"I can see him perfectly," said Ken from his tree roost, as the bear started to walk off. "There he goes. He's going up over the top."

I caught a glimpse of the top of the bear's back; all I could really see was some fur moving. I shot and missed. The bear took off like a rocket, went over the crest, and was gone.

"Did you get him?" Ken asked.

His next remark suggested he probably knew better. "Man, he took off up that mountain doing two hundred miles an hour."

Three times, and I could not hit this bear. It seemed to be charmed, letting us spot it, but when we crawled and climbed and sneaked up close enough, it got up and moved off. I felt as if the bear were playing with us—"Here I am, guys, come on"—but when we got there, we couldn't get it. I was seriously thinking I was not meant to get this bear.

Ken was trying to crawl a tree in hip boots. Most of the trees had few low branches, so they were the devil to climb under any conditions, and this made it even more difficult. It turned out he cracked a rib during his tree-climbing adventures.

Understandably, he grew rather disgruntled. He was trying to be a good sport about it, but you know as well as I do that he was thinking: *OK, this guy is supposed to be a big-game hunter, and he's been on a glacier bear three times, and he can't even hit it.*

I was doing some thinking of my own. I figured the bullets had to be hitting the brush. It wasn't the gun, and although the shots had not been the easiest, they hadn't been the most difficult, either. I was getting pretty spooked over the whole thing.

Walking back miles and having another lunch in the rain under the overturned Avon raft gave us time to tell old hunting stories, aiming to fend off dismay. I don't remember what we had for lunch; I was too depressed to notice. The atmosphere did improve slightly with a bellyful of food. When I caught three Dolly Varden for our supper that evening, I decided to try for a fourth to use as a sacrifice, like the goat my Muslim guide had once used as a sacrifice in Kenya (see chapter 7).

Each time we had made the raft crossing, we had seen two pairs of nesting bald eagles watching over the water from tall trees. This time I paused ceremonially before I tossed my spinner into the water again. I caught another trout, dispatched it, and placed it at the base of the eagles' tree as a hunting sacrifice for better luck with the bear the following day.

The next morning, the last day of the hunt, Ron ran over to check the base of the tree.

"The fish is gone," he declared.

Today we would get the bear.

We deployed and glassed for the same bear we had been hunting all along. Ken and Ron climbed high up the slope, while I stayed lower down, near the creek. Positioned on a rock slide, I waited for three hours without seeing anything.

But Ron and Ken had found the bear. Ron came down to tell me the bear was up there and had been eating and resting for several hours. Around 5 P.M. Ken returned with the news that the bear was on the move. In our soggy hip boots Ken and I climbed through the tearing tangles to the waterfall.

In the roar of the waterfall we made yet another approach. Ken urged me closer to where the bear was feeding on shoots of new growth. In the mist of the waterfall, our approach disguised by its noise, we spotted the bear at seventy-five yards. We moved closer—fifty yards. We moved even closer. We sneaked and crawled within twenty-five yards of the bear; it was a beautiful setup.

There was a big rock I could use as a rest; I didn't even have to kneel. I walked up and stood with the rifle resting on the rock, aiming straight across the water. I waited until the bear took one more step, which would give me a clear shot at its shoulder. It took the step, and I took the bear.

We photographed, measured, and skinned the glacier bear. Then we packed it down and across the stream and finally out to the camp. Time moved quickly now. We struck camp. The seven-mile trek and truck ride to Yakutat whirled by. Word spread like wildfire. Local people were photographed next to the bear's hide as it hung briefly on the wall of Ken Fanning's cabin at the Yakutat airport. It measured 6 feet, 3 inches squared.

The game department official said this specimen was one of the prettiest glacier bears he had ever seen. I agree with that assessment, though I haven't seen a lot of others. Over the intervening years, my own hair has taken on a kind of glacier bear patina, too. And I'll consider it quite a compliment if anyone should ever refer to me as the old silver bear.

Chapter 2

We Thought We Were in Heaven

Alaska and Colorado, 1960s

Picture two men settling down to sleep high in a Rocky Mountain meadow. I suppose the altitude was around nine thousand feet. We were not in your traditional heavy-canvas wall tent with a comforting woodstove, mind you. And there was no cook tent nearby. We just put down our sleeping bags under a tarpaulin in the open meadow and wriggled inside them.

The stars shone down on our project as we settled in for the night. We were going to be the most successful elk hunters in the mountains. Our horses were grazing peacefully nearby. They would be the ones to carry out the meat in the morning, after the elk discovered that the meadow they favored for their breakfast buffet had become Ambush Central.

The chill that came on with nightfall at our high elevation in Colorado was no cause for alarm. If you grow up on a Minnesota farm with horses, as I did, you learn to ride. You also learn a little about coping with the cold.

Lying there, enjoying the stars, we listened to the rhythmic *crrrt, crrrt, crrrt* of horses cropping the lush mountain grass that drew the elk to this meadow in the mornings. It could have been the 1860s as well as the 1960s. Heaven seemed much closer than usual—or perhaps we were already there.

Ironically, looking back on that 1960s elk hunt, I can see that I enjoyed a childhood that was much closer to frontier life than I realized at the time.

I loved horses, and I wanted to be a cowboy, of course. It seemed the Midwest heartland had trapped me in a life that was far from the romance and wild frontiers of the high country, desert, or far north. Everyone we knew was poor, and all anyone did was work. The movies provided our one great escape. Westerns with Roy Rogers and his horse, Trigger, seem corny today, but they filled youngsters like me with a sense of possibility. I had a Roy Rogers lunch bucket, and my horse was also named Trigger.

My trusty 7mm in its scabbard went with me to the high country for elk. Colorado outfitter Don Dilley favored surefooted mules for mountain hunting.

Watching Tarzan movies nurtured fantasies of the jungle and gave a generation of boys a powerful hankering for even more exotic places and animals.

I especially loved the story of elephant taking themselves to a giant elephant graveyard to die. Whoever could find that burial ground and collect all that ivory would be a wealthy man. How was I going to get there from a 120-acre farm in Pine Island, near Austin, Minnesota? Later, I learned that C. J. McElroy, the founder of Safari Club International, had similar fantasies sparked by watching Tarzan movies. He grew up in the Big Thicket of Texas, where he learned to shoot small game efficiently and economically with his .22. He had to; his mother gave him only one bullet. Like McElroy, I was burning to leave home and find adventure.

Growing up, we went barefoot all summer. My mother required us to wash our feet before we went to bed because we only had a bath once a week. There was no indoor plumbing. Six of us—four kids and two adults—took turns bathing in a metal tub. We each had two sets of decent clothes: the one we were wearing and the one that was in the wash. Our drinking water stood in a bucket in the kitchen, and we all drank from one dipper. Our mother did her best to keep us healthy by telling us to throw out what we didn't drink, and not put it back in the bucket.

We didn't run dairy cattle; my dad ran boarding kennels. He was in the business of training bird dogs, so we hunted pheasant in southern Minnesota. I learned to shoot and developed a lasting love for hunting both waterfowl and pheasant. Deer numbers were still rebounding from historic lows, and we didn't have enough whitetail in the area to hunt them. When I was old enough, I joined the fall deer-hunting expeditions to northern Minnesota; in those days we still proudly showed off our deer on the front of the truck on the way home.

Unknown to me, my life in Minnesota was preparing me for other kinds of big-

On early Alaskan and Canadian hunts, I was out for two weeks on horseback with a guide, a tent, and some packhorses.

game hunting. I felt at ease on a horse, and I knew how to beat the cold. As I became a respectable shot, I began to dream of hunting in Alaska or of packing into the western mountains on horseback to hunt for elk.

The Draw of the North

After finishing college in May 1962, I signed up for arctic survival training with the Army Reserve. It was the easiest way I could think of to get up north. I reasoned that once I got there, I could poke around a little and find people who knew about hunting the back country. They weren't hard to find.

My first guided big-game hunt was a two-week horseback trip in Alaska in 1963. There was no plane involved. I booked with an outfitter based in Palmer, and the license included moose, caribou, Dall sheep, black bear, and mountain goat. My guide, I soon realized, was not an experienced hunting guide—we were more or less setting out on a mission of discovery together. All either of us really knew about wild sheep was that they occupied the higher terrain. Most of the sheep we saw were nothing but faraway white dots on the open slopes. We got our feet blistered trying to get to them.

I shot my first black bear. We did not connect on moose or caribou, but the experience showed me a style of hunting that was right up my alley: two weeks in the middle of nowhere with just one other person, a pup tent, a couple of horses, and a few packhorses. It's not the right formula for everyone, but it helps a lot that I enjoy riding horses. Many of the Alaskan guides at that time were Native Americans. I would think, *What if we don't get along?* Plenty of hunters preferred not to learn about cultural differences while stuck out on a long hunt in the wilds of Alaska with only a horse for transportation. No one else was standing by to help fend off disaster or help skin out the trophy. No one served us cocktails at sundown. In most of those camps, no alcohol even accompanied us.

I shot my first black bear on a horseback trip in Alaska in the 1960s and booked to return for moose, caribou, and sheep.

Later, I came to understand that sometimes the business of getting to know someone from another culture can itself be the key to a memorable hunt. Over the years I would return again and again to the formula of my first Alaskan hunt. Almost every hunt I took in Canada would be a two-week horseback trip with a small tent and a guide, just the two of us. Being at ease on a horse would also prove quite an asset when hunting in the high mountains of Asia, though in the 1960s I had no idea I would ever wind up doing that.

I booked to go hunting in Alaska with the same outfitter in 1964, aiming to try again for moose, caribou, and sheep. This time he would guide me himself, and we chartered a plane to extend our reach. That was the trip we busted a strut on the Super Cub as we were flying into our camp. The bush landing area was short—too short for landing with a tailwind, and in patches the snow was deep. We were coming in with the wind right up our tail, and we dumped the Super Cub on its nose.

Yes, we were lucky the spill wasn't worse. Plane crashes in the wilderness offer a hundred ways to meet your maker, and they provoke some desperate thoughts until you know whether it's your moment to live or die. Still, it can definitely loosen your personal rivets to be stuck in the wilderness with a plane that needs a new wing strut. We were going to need a parts drop in order to get out of there. Rainy weather and fog then socked us in for several days. I read every magazine in my pack three times. When the weather lifted and a replacement part for our plane was delivered, we had just two hunting days left. We made the best of those days and got a Dall sheep while the plane was being repaired.

The Usual Cast of Suspects

Soon after I first hunted Alaska, some close friends and I decided to try our luck in the Rocky Mountain West. We booked an elk hunt in the high country of Colorado with outfitter Don Dilley, out of Del Norte. It

My first sheep was a Dall, and for added excitement on this same hunt we busted the wing strut of our chartered Super Cub.

proved to be so much fun that we soon booked a repeat performance with the same outfitter. The elk were as wild as could be. The scenery up on the Continental Divide was magnificent, there was no one else around, and we got all this for the modest price of something like one hundred and twenty-five dollars for the group permit. The whole hunt cost us about two hundred dollars apiece. A horseback elk hunt in Colorado became an annual tradition for us.

We would pack into the mountains on a Friday, so that when the season opened on Saturday, we were all ready to go. Don usually took out six or seven hunters, three or four guides, and about fifteen horses and mules for a week. Don was a real cowboy; besides being a hunting outfitter, he also broke and trained horses. He favored mules as pack animals because they were surefooted in the mountains. We would connect with Don and his horse trailer in Del Norte and go in a convoy to the point where we would set out on horseback, taking the trail deep into the mountains.

In those days everybody helped. We did have a camp cook, but we were all expected to help set up the tents and saddle our own horses. These were not trophy hunts so much as a chance for a bunch of friends to get away from the world of work and enjoy the mountains and the wilderness. The outfitter took us out on a group license that allowed a certain number of elk, including spikes; it didn't matter which of us shot them. The best I did in the trophy department was two four-by-four bulls in one season.

Among the usual cast of suspects was my childhood friend Richard Hawkins. Richard's father drove a milk truck. Every morning he picked up milk cans from a series of farms near ours and hauled them to the creamery. The drawback of my school bus route was that our place lay on the outbound leg—I had to board very early and then take a long, roundabout ride to get to school in the town of Pine Island. The milk truck went the opposite way. I could see it approaching down the hill, and when it passed us, it was heading straight into town. I negotiated a much more direct daily ride to school with Richard's dad in the milk truck, and I got to know Richard through his dad.

When I got out of high school, I moved to Rochester, where Richard was already married and working for IBM. His mother-in-law, Louise Miller, and her son, Larry, more or less adopted several of us. While I was in college, she provided me with room and board and employed me, among others, to maintain a "route" of vending machines. In due course Richard would take over the business from his mother-in-law and expand it greatly. After completing junior college, I moved to Mankato to finish my degree. To pay my tuition I worked nights as a hospital orderly, sold blood, and earned as much as I could between semesters to supplement the twenty dollars a week my grandparents were sending.

Richard Hawkins and I are standing in front of Don Dilley's horse trailer in Del Norte, Colorado, loading up for the trip to the base of the mountains.

Two other elk hunters were Tom "Ruby" Rubenstein and Bob DeWitz. Ruby owned a twenty-lane bowling alley, bar, and nightclub. In later years some of these friends joined me on other kinds of hunts—to Wyoming for antelope and to Canada for Quebec-Labrador caribou. Richard, Ruby, and Bob would all travel to Russia and China with me; Ruby and I went to Namibia together; and Richard accompanied me to the Sudan and to Tanzania. The routine of the Colorado elk hunts was especially valuable to me because I moved so much during those years. I left Rochester for Denton, Texas, then went to California and on to Mississippi. I was constantly in a state of being new somewhere, which made the bonds of friendship on the annual retreat to Colorado even more important to me.

We noticed that the elk usually came out of the wooded country into the meadows to feed early in the mornings, and this gave us an idea. What if we slept in the meadow so we would already be there when the elk arrived? The first time we tried this, it worked like a charm. First thing in the morning we collected two good bulls right off the bat. It was obviously a useful tactic.

The second time we set out to trick the elk by sleeping in their meadow, we were not quite so lucky. As Ruby and I lay in our sleeping bags under a tarpaulin in our makeshift fly camp, snow began to fall. It snowed and it snowed and it snowed. Should we get up and try to catch the horses in the dark in a snowstorm? Not a smart idea. We had little choice but to lie there all night as the snow piled up. Surely you know what I'm going to tell you next: No elk appeared in the meadow that morning. As dawn came on, we struggled to load our gear and limped back to our base camp.

The snow continued to fall. We waited and hoped, trying to persuade one another that snow would make it easier to track the elk. But the white stuff just kept coming down for five solid days. For eighteen hours a day we played untold games of gin rummy, using up every scrap of paper and cardboard we had for

A 4x4 elk bull was one reward. Another was having good friends along and having miles of the Rocky Mountains all to ourselves.

Once in Colorado it snowed on us for five days. We played endlessgames of gin rummy, stopping only to sweep snow off the tent, as the camp cook was doing here.

scorekeeping. We only stopped playing cards to step outside to sweep snow off the top of the tent. When the storm ended, Don declared he had never seen a buildup of snow like that before.

Neither had the elk. They all cleared out of the high country, trying to escape the deep drifts and get to lower elevations, where they had a better shot at scraping away enough snow to find green things to eat. We were beginning to run low on hay for our horses, and Don decided we had better move out. We set off, struggling through chest-deep snow to the horses, our feet in the stirrups dragging through it. Whichever animal was breaking trail with its chest soon needed to be spelled from that heavy work. All day we took turns at it. We left the heavy canvas tents in place; there was no sense having the pack animals carry such loads under those conditions. Getting out of the mountains was a long and difficult slog.

When at last we got into town, we could hardly believe it. The elk were already there. While we had been sitting in the mountains talking about tracking the elk, they had abandoned the high valleys early and waltzed right into town. It was a bizarre season. Hunters were shooting elk off restaurant porches and in parking lots until the game department closed the season in response to the chaos. As the winter advanced, volunteers began hauling in hay to save the elk from starvation. The animals simply couldn't find enough to eat in all that deep snow.

Our plan to ambush elk at dawn from a makeshift fly camp was undone by a night of steady snowfall. No elk appeared in the meadow that morning.

There are easier ways to get top-quality elk and sheep trophies than the kinds of hunts we took more than forty years ago. But for top-quality friendship and the satisfaction of having enormous tracts of country all to ourselves, I'm not sure we could have done any better. I used to think I was born about a hundred years too late, but I've changed my mind. The truth is, I had a fine time on those early trips. I established my confidence as a hunter, even if not as a master of the art of ambush. I have no complaints.

Chapter 3

Giants of the Arctic

Alaska, 1970s

Hopelessly hooked on Alaska after my visits in 1963 and '64, I found its wildness drawing me back for a third hunt in 1965. This time I hunted moose and caribou on the Alaska Peninsula with Denny Thompson and Bill Simms. I collected a good caribou and a moose that scored more than sixty inches. Seeing that I was coming up north each year, Denny and Bill began encouraging me to consider species I had hardly even thought about. What about trying for a Grand Slam of North American wild sheep?

They also believed the writing was on the wall for polar-bear hunting in the United States. It would likely be closed soon, they told me.

There was a broad range of hunting opportunities in Alaska, with significantly fewer restrictions on visiting sportsmen than there are today. At that time it was still legal to fly and hunt on the same day. Pressures against this had begun to build in the boom years following World War II, as the state's population expanded and people used airplanes to reach more and more remote places. Something would eventually have to give. Before it did, I would find myself way out on the sea ice, learning something about what airplanes can and cannot do in extreme conditions.

Bear on the Sea Ice

Polar-bear hunting in Alaska had never been a large-scale affair. In the 1960s the state issued about forty permits per year. Denny and Bill proposed that I apply for one of these. There was nothing to lose—if you weren't drawn, you got your money back. I was drawn the first time I applied. The price of the hunt was twenty-five hundred dollars, which also included two wolves.

The term spring is relative when you're talking about going out for miles on the sea ice when the temperature is twenty or thirty degrees below zero. The elements could kill you in a hurry.

Guides encouraged me to try for a polar bear permit, as it seemed likely that Alaskan hunts for the species would soon close. I drew a permit the first time I applied, and took a bear measuring more than ten feet.

Denny Thompson was my guide for an Alaskan moose that proved up at more than sixty inches.

We took two important precautions to minimize our chances of dying out on the ice. First, I was equipped with a custom snowsuit made of caribou hide so that if I were out there for several hours, I could avoid dying of exposure, which otherwise would be a likely prospect.

In 1971 you couldn't simply go to an outdoor-gear superstore and buy clothing to protect you from extreme cold. I had to have a caribou-hide suit custom made when we reached the hamlet of Kotzebue. The seamstress took my measurements and created it for me in a day or so. The outfit consisted of heavy, extra-long pants, a parka, mittens, and a pair of mukluks to keep my hands and feet from freezing. The suit was too bulky and awkward to wear in the seat of the tiny Super Cub, and the plane did have a modest heating system. The idea was to don the new gear once we got out onto the ice. In theory, once you're wearing your caribou ensemble, you can survive at forty below.

The second precaution was that the guides used not one airplane but two. If anything went wrong, it was possible to squeeze three people into the other plane and get out. The small planes parked at the Kotzebue airstrip on the frozen shoreline were equipped with skis. Using skis makes it possible to fly into places where you simply could not land on wheels. The problem with skis is that you have no brakes, which distinctly raises your chances of getting into trouble.

Temperature also presented a problem for the planes. Each one on the strip was plugged into a head bolt heater to keep the engine oil from freezing. Quartered at the local hotel, we also washed off our guns with gasoline so there would be no risk that remnants of gun oil would freeze.

I found it exciting to be able to fly over the ice pack. Flying close to the Bering Strait, we could see the coast of Russia. This Alaskan hunt was not like the surface-bound, native-guided style of polar-bear hunting that has since become the norm for visiting hunters in Canada. The far greater reach of an airplane meant that we could look at a lot of bear. Soon I learned that you can tell some important things about a bear by looking at its tracks from the air. The front paws of a big boar, for example, turn inward more than those of other bear because of the weight of the animal's torso.

When we found a suitably large male, we landed the plane. This was a scary and risky business in itself. Big pressure ridges in the sea ice can create visible topography, but under the snow it was not always possible to see smaller land areas that were rough enough to trip up a ski plane. Coming down on the sea ice can definitely raise your heart rate. Denny landed safely and covered the plane's nose with a blanket to conserve the warmth of the engine. One of the pressure ridges would provide us with cover as we approached the bear across the ice. We crawled up behind the ridge, Denny with a .375 and I with a .300, and peeked over the top. My first shot was too far back, and it took two more shots to drop the great white bear. It measured ten feet plus.

Now we faced the considerable task of skinning out the bear at twenty degrees below zero, and we needed to be quick. Blanketing the engine was a help, but if the plane stood too long at those temperatures, we might not be able to take off again. Bill landed our recovery plane, helped us complete the skinning, and got airborne again, just in case we had trouble.

While I was in Kotzebue, one of the other hunting parties failed to return before sundown. Even though the planes had radios, it was still possible to get so far out on the ice that there was no radio contact. Finally, they got through on the radio, indicating they were safe and were coming in. How in the world those men found their way home in the darkness over that featureless world I can scarcely imagine. There were no lights on the ice of the landing strip. People hastily lighted smudge fires along the strip to guide the approaching plane.

It turned out that both skis on their other plane had been broken when they landed to pursue a bear. Efforts to repair the skis had failed. Eventually, they salvaged the crippled plane's radio and flew back in the second Super Cub, three of them crammed into the two-seater. The client in that plane was one scared

The price of my polar bear hunt included two wolves. One had a gorgeous pale coat.

The bustling transportation hub of Kotzebue is shown here. Small planes equipped with skis were lined up along the frozen shoreline, and dog teams took over the hauling once the supplies were off-loaded from the planes.

hunter. His experience clearly illustrated the benefit of using two planes.

The next day people went out searching for the abandoned plane, but they never found it. Nobody was carrying handy little GPS units for pinpointing locations in those days. I suppose the plane sank to the bottom of the sea some weeks later, when the ice broke up. Every visiting hunter in Kotzebue was silently giving thanks that night. The party in the crippled plane had been doing just what the rest of us had been doing, except that we missed the ice ridges and they hit one. What if their second plane had also gotten into trouble while landing? What if their combined weight had proven too much for the Super Cub to take off again?

When we took off with my bear cape in our plane, it was as if we also had a third person aboard. The plane was laboring because the bear cape weighed almost as much as I did. The next step in processing was a return visit to the woman who had made my caribou suit. To my surprise, the routine involved dunking the hide in salt water through a hole in the sea ice! The woman tied a rope around the skin and vigorously swished it up and down and swirled it around. I stood there, crossing my fingers that the rope wouldn't break. I had to admire the simplicity of the method. The hide emerged from the salt water snowy white and beautifully clean. It measured ten and one-half feet.

The Marine Mammal Protection Act of 1972 closed polar-bear hunting in the United States for sport hunters, as my guides had expected would happen. Now visiting sportsmen

Nose blankets and head bolt heaters were needed to keep the engine oil in the planes from freezing.

go after the magnificent white bear in the Canadian Arctic in a more traditional way—spending more time, getting to know native guides and observing their way of life, and moving around with dogsleds or on snow machines.

Reestablished Muskox

I would get my taste of tradition on muskox and walrus hunts later in the 1970s. Change was in the air. Alaskan guides told me about a fellow who had been working with the native people and the game department to open up muskox hunting on Nunivak Island, where a population of Greenland muskox had been reintroduced. The fellow's name was Lynn Castle, and the guides said he was the prime outfitter for some of the less prominent Arctic game species. Lynn was a top-of-the-line master guide, and he was earning recognition as the vanguard of a new generation of hunting guides. He flew a plane, but he also had a wildlife degree and operated a lodge. Lynn was thinking about the long future of hunting and was working toward balancing the needs of Alaskan residents, visiting hunters, and the local native communities.

Nunivak had been chosen for the muskox reintroduction because the island was spacious enough to support the animals and had no large predators. The muskox would be more likely to reestablish themselves there than on the mainland. Lynn and I and another client hunter flew into the island's main town of

Backup pilot Bill Simms joined us on the ice to help skin out my bear as quickly as possible.

Savoonga in 1976 on a commercial plane. Lynn had a twenty-foot boat ready so that we could move around the island easily, nosing into promising inlets and looking for the shaggy muskox.

Much of the time we slept on the boat. Most of the island's coast consisted of soggy terrain that required hip boots for wet stalking, but in places it was dry enough for us to set up a small tent on the shore. For comfort, Lynn had brought caribou hides, which he tossed on the ground in the tent. The thick pile under our sleeping bags kept us warm and comfortable—it was quite luxurious.

We spent the first couple of days fishing for salmon, then got serious about our hunt. The muskox tended to favor the low ridges and often stood facing the wind, using the breeze to help them escape the millions of biting insects. Our challenge lay in finding the larger, older bulls, which seemed to hang together in groups apart from the breeding herds. Because of their tendency to bunch up and stand when threatened, muskox are not difficult to hunt. We took our two bulls in two days.

We still had a few days left, and Lynn suggested I return with him to his base of operation on the mainland at Wood River Lodge to try for a better Dall sheep. My Dall was barely a full-curl ram, and he knew he had some super rams in his area. He arranged things by radio so that guide Tom Kirstein and some horses would be all ready to take me out sheep hunting when we flew into Wood River. I moved my duffel bag right from the plane to a packhorse, and we packed up into higher country. We spent the night in a small outpost cabin. Glassing the next day, we found three or four good rams in a position from which we would be able to stalk them from above. We were back with our sheep at the comfortable main lodge that evening, and I enjoyed some downtime feasting on muskox and sheep.

In 1976 outfitter Lynn Castle and local Inuit guides helped me find a good Greenland muskox bull from the reintroduced population on Nunivak Island.

Wind, Whiteout, and Walrus

My fullest experience with the old ways of the north came during a walrus hunt in 1977. Walrus hunting had been opened for visiting hunters, and members of the Eskimo or Inuit community were involved in the guiding. They were the people who knew how to hunt the great, lumbering beasts; walrus had been a feature of their economy and culture since long before Europeans set foot in North America. Thinking that the availability of these hunts might not last, I decided to go right away.

My guide, Ron Hayes, was waiting for me when I flew into St. Lawrence Island. He told me the villagers couldn't go out after walrus just then. The wind was blowing from the west and pushing too much floating ice up against the shore. We would have to wait until the wind turned and drove some of the ice out to sea. Spring breakup was the time to hunt walrus on St. Lawrence Island, but the conditions had to be right. We needed to have some ice floes around because walrus haul out and lie on them. On the other hand, we needed a fair amount of open water in order to be able to maneuver a boat among the ice floes.

It was several years since I had hunted polar bear, and once again I needed to get a suit of caribou hide made. I had mukluks with sealskin soles and a parka trimmed with wolf fur, which doesn't get frosted up by your breathing. While the wind continued piling the ice up against the shore, I was outfitted with gear that could keep me warm at extremely low temperatures. Caribou-hide clothing is made with the skin on the inside and the hair on the outside. A string ran up the sleeves and behind my neck to keep my mittens attached to me. How does the suit feel when it's on? Awkward, stiff, and bulky. I was already wearing long underwear, wool pants, and a down jacket, and the caribou suit went on top of all that. It took two people to help me into it, and I had to get dressed outside because putting on that suit indoors would be much too hot.

Getting out on a boat can be a chilly business, even in mild conditions. I assure you I needed every inch and every ounce of that gear to stay warm out on the Arctic Ocean. My guide told me over and over again: Whatever you do, don't fall into the water. We would be going out in a traditional skin boat called an umiak to look for a pod of walrus resting on the ice. We'd move closer to them and glass until we found a good bull. Walrus are generally found in small groups in the spring season. When they're hungry, they flop over the side into the water and hunt up some clams or other seafood; later, they haul out onto the ice to sleep.

Finding walrus was not the hard part. The real challenge was that once we had sighted a good bull, we would have to move around to another section of the same ice floe and get out of the boat and onto the ice. If you shoot a two-thousand-pound walrus in the water, it's going to sink, and you'll lose it. You have to take a walrus while it is on the ice. These animals' eyesight is not especially good, and they don't scare easily. If you invade their ice floe, they usually just lean up on their flippers and try to get a better look at you.

Inuit walrus hunters won't go out at all in their open skin boats when the sea is rough—that would be simply asking for trouble. If the swells are rough, the sea is far too dangerous: The rocking and rolling means the ice is moving. The water has to be pretty calm for hunters to maneuver their fragile boats around the floating ice. It's most dangerous when you're getting in and out of the boat to reach your walrus on the ice. Everything but the sea is frozen. Everything is slippery. The water is so cold that anyone who falls in will be dead within minutes.

Even when the weather is calm, the sea still produces great swells. You can't really shoot from a moving boat. You need accuracy to shoot walrus because you shoot them just behind the eye, in the brain. You need the relative stability of the ice floe to achieve that kind of shooting accuracy. I would be using my .375 with steel-jacketed bullets.

Two days went by, and the wind didn't change. Three days. Four days. I'm the first to acknowledge that hunting takes patience, but mine was running out. Finally, I challenged the arrangements. If the wind was piling the ice up on our side of the island, didn't that mean that on the other side of the island the wind would be pushing the ice out to sea? Why didn't we go and hunt over there? Ron said the Inuit were accustomed to hunting walrus from their village, and sooner or later the wind would change. I said well, yes, but I didn't have sooner or later. I only had seven days.

He consulted with our native guides, and they agreed. The next day, they said, if the wind still didn't change, we could try the other side of the island, where they had some rough cabins they used seasonally for whaling.

To get to the other side of the island they hooked big sleds behind two snow machines. One sled hauled our two boats, and the other held plenty of gasoline and food. We set off across the island for our selected whaling cabin. Ron and I followed the sleds in style and relative warmth in a snow machine that had treads and a small covered cab.

On the way over I had my first experience of a Far North whiteout. Whipped up by the wind, the snow began whirling fiercely. It was terrifying. You could barely see your hand in front of your face. If you got one yard off course, it might as well have been a mile. Growing up in Minnesota had never shown me anything like this. A line of skinny poles had been planted in the ground for just such conditions, and our guides pulled out some strange little slit goggles. I had never seen anything like them before, either, but they did help us see a little better through the white nothingness.

It took us several hours to cross the island, and I have to say the whiteout gave me a sinking feeling. There was no way to hunt in those conditions. However, by the time we reached our destination, a plywood shack, the alarming weather had cleared up. It had turned into a perfect bluebird day. The same wind that had blanketed us in a whiteout had blown the ice to the far side of the island. The ice floes were so far offshore that we couldn't

A twenty-foot boat allowed us to move easily around the Nunivak shore for our muskox hunt, and it also served as camp some of the time.

even see them. I wasn't sure whether this was to our benefit or not.

Among the Ice Cubes

We unloaded the umiaks and put them in the water. It was reassuring to have two boats, just as we had had paired planes on the bear hunt. If the single engine of a single boat let us down while we were out on the ocean, we would soon be done for; this way, we could still get back in the other boat. Ron and I rode in one boat, and the men loaded some food, sleeping bags, and extra clothing into the other—just in case.

We motored out until we began to see chunks of ice, and, sure enough, we soon found some walrus. Now we started glassing, and before long we saw a group of about twenty animals hauled out on an ice floe, including a good bull. Ron said we were unlikely to find a better one, so we moved around to the far side of the ice floe. It was hard to believe the hunt was happening just as Ron had described it to me before we left the village. Here we were, way out in the Arctic Ocean, getting out of a tiny boat and climbing up onto a giant ice cube with twenty enormous animals. We were surrounded by nothing but water that would freeze us almost instantly if we were to fall in.

The ice floe was probably not much more than one hundred feet across. Watching us approach, a few of the walrus didn't like the look of us and slipped over the side into the water. Ron showed me a smaller bull, a cow, and

Lynn Castle's Wood River Lodge was our base for sheep hunting once the muskox was in hand.

an animal with a broken tusk. Then the big bull rose up on its flippers to get a look at us. Ron said the bull was going to turn.

"When he turns his head, shoot him on the left side of the head between the eye and the ear, in the brain," he ordered.

I was lying on my belly, and Ron gave me a backpack as a rest. From fifty or sixty feet away, I delivered the brain shot, and the great bull simply dropped.

The sound of the rifle persuaded some more walrus into the water, but others started coming back onto the ice as we walked over to the fallen bull. We started hollering and fired a few discouraging shots. They swam out a little and returned a couple of times before they finally departed. Now we could bring the boats around, closer to where the bull lay.

In that fierce cold, you need to hurry up and get skinning before everything freezes. We took pictures and caped out the head. Our guides collected some blubber for the village—another reason to take a second boat. They took as much blubber as they could safely pack into the boat, and that boat also carried the trophy. We pushed them off into the water.

Now was the time to be really careful. The sides of the boat are open, but the front has a small covered section for stowage. To board, you step up onto the covered bow and then step down into the boat. The boatman climbed aboard and moved carefully to the stern. Then I got on, and Ron got on. The man who was to come aboard last and push us off stepped up onto the nose of our boat, lost his footing, and fell into the ocean.

From Wood River we rode to an outpost cabin, and I collected a Dall ram much better than the one I had gotten before.

I have never seen people move so quickly. The instant he went down, another man was there, and another. They grabbed him up by his parka and dragged him into the boat. In moments his hair was already frozen solid. As he stood there, shaking, his teeth chattering, they ripped all his clothes off, and we each gave him something dry to wear. I gave him a shirt, someone else gave him pants, and we got him into a dry parka. Those people are tough. If I had fallen in, I'd probably have died of shock because I don't know how to swim, but he was just shaking and laughing.

All the excitement of this hunt happened in about three hours, after the days of waiting and struggling through the whiteout. As on my polar-bear hunt, it was the elements that held the greatest danger. Any mistake or mishap could be fatal in those extreme conditions. When Ron had told me in the village how this hunt would proceed, it had sounded OK, but if you use your imagination for a moment, you'll realize that one should think twice before ever climbing into one of those little skin boats. You've got to be crazy.

You can't wear a life jacket over all those heavy clothes, and you'd sink if you swam in that kind of gear. Even with a life jacket, if you fall into the water, you're going to die of cold. Now, on top of that, you're going way out into the ocean, with great chunks of ice floating everywhere. While those chunks are breaking up into smaller pieces with the spring warming, you're turning and twisting in-between ice floes to get close to the walrus. The boat is rising and falling with the swells, and you don't know

My walrus hunt with Inuit guides was off St. Lawrence Island in the Arctic Ocean. Taken with a brain shot, the great walrus bull dropped right where he was on the ice.

what's underneath the water—or when you're going to hit ice you can't even see.

While we were out at sea, I looked around at the blue horizon and wondered aloud: How are we to know where that cabin is? How are we going to find our way back? Was the cabin ahead of us or behind us?

I couldn't see land. All I could see was chunks of ice.

"Oh, these guys know," Ron assured me. "They do it all the time."

I kept my worries to myself. For a while we went on twisting and turning through the ice cubes. Suddenly, we reached open water, and the boatmen opened up the engines wide on both boats. We roared back to the cabin as fast as we could go and got the fire blazing to get our guide warmed up. He was so cold that he was purple.

The cabin where we would spend the night stood up on a high hill from which you could see for miles. It

Using snow machines, we hauled traditional skin boats, called umiaks, on big sleds across the island to waters where the conditions were right for hunting walrus.

was ideal for whale spotting. It was lacking in charm, but whaling parties usually stayed for some time, so it was functional and quite spacious. We fired up the stove with oil we had brought from the village. The fellow who had fallen overboard didn't seem too bothered. We hung his wet gear near the stove to dry while we ate a fish dinner.

The run back across the island to the village went much faster in calm conditions. We fleshed out and salted the walrus cape for a head mount. Beside it today are some artifacts I bought as souvenirs of the Arctic, and several sea ducks I hunted on St. Lawrence Island—an eider, a harlequin, and a black scoter. Hunting polar bear on the blinding white sea ice, muskox on a treeless island, and walrus from a traditional boat had brought me a long way from hunting waterfowl in Minnesota. My undergraduate course in World Cultures for Sportsmen 101 was progressing nicely.

I didn't keep the caribou-hide survival suit. You can't get much use out of such a thing if you live in muggy Houston. But, as a reminder of how quickly you can go from warm and dry to cold and dead, I kept the mukluks.

Chapter 4

Counting the Days for Sheep

Alberta, 1975

The impulse to ski grew stronger as I looked down over a steep and inviting slope. We had panted our way up to this point over a period of hours, wrastling through alders, scrambling over boulders, scrunching in the snow, and slipping on the ice. The views were superb, but the energy cost had been high.

The sheep we were pursuing, however, had figured out that they didn't especially want to meet with us that day, no matter how hard we worked at meeting them on their own turf. We had spotted the group by glassing and planned a cautious approach to catch up with them on a high, snowy ridge. By then, we had already been hunting hard for many days, and we set off driven mostly by hope, not knowing for sure whether there was a legal ram in the bunch.

We weren't going to find out, either. During our climb, on one of those long stretches when you can't see your prey, the wind changed. The sheep winded us and decided the time had come to melt away.

Our horses were far below the ridge where we were perched.

How about taking a nice little shortcut down, I wondered.

Once this idea had struck, the long hike back the way we had come seemed less and less appealing. I glanced again over the tempting slope below me. It looked smooth enough—maybe I could just ski down it in my boots. I decided to go for it.

"Be careful," the guide recommended.

He wasn't planning to try it.

I took a cautious step or two to test the surface, and that's when I lost all control and got the ride of my life. Right off the bat, whooom, my foot slid out from under me. The slope looked snowy, but just under the powder surface was slippery ice. Did I ski down in my boots? No, I flew down that mountainside in a magnificent display of indignity, sliding on every section of my anatomy except my feet.

Miraculously, just before the slope steepened into a dangerous drop-off, the ice gave way to deeper snow that slowed my free fall, and I plowed to a halt at a boulder. I must have been immortal in those days. You'd have to be, to do something so foolish. The fact that I came out of it with just some bashes, bruises, and ripped clothing should not be read as an endorsement for this style of getting around.

My guide was at the top, hollering, "You all right?"

What in the world would we have done if I had broken a leg, or worse? It would have been a mighty long ride out, or I would have had a long and lonesome wait while the guide rode for two days to the base camp, where he could use the radio to round up help or call in a plane. No plane could have landed nearby, anyway. I don't even want to think about what could have happened.

A Boone and Crockett desert bighorn ram taken in Mexico in 1974 left me needing only a Rocky Mountain bighorn to complete my Grand Slam.

Sheep Hunters Are Made, Not Born

How many days does it take to get a sheep? For most people who have taken one, the answer is that it takes longer than you expect. You don't need me to tell you that it's more than a brief assignment to collect a Grand Slam of North American sheep.

When Grancel Fitz coined the phrase in the title of his 1948 hunting article "Grand Slam of Rams," I was not yet ten years old. In the 1960s, when I killed my first sheep, a modest Dall ram, the Grand Slam Club was not yet ten years old. In 1955 Bob Housholder's inquiries about how many hunters had made a Grand Slam brought in an initial list of a couple of dozen names, and the club was founded early in 1956.

I know hunters who love to hunt birds or deer and are satisfied to do so again and again. They seem to have been born to it. Some of this is about familiarity. We love what we know best. Sheep are different. Almost no one grows up closely involved with wild sheep. No sheep ever turned up in a Tarzan movie, and they are hard to find even in the great chronicles of the American West. Loving to hunt sheep is something that just creeps up on you.

The main objectives on my first guided hunts were caribou, moose, and elk. Like many other sportsmen, I was among those who saw sheep as nothing special—until I tried to collect one and began to realize that sheep hunting is tough. The first Dall sheep provided my preliminary training. My second ram was not large, either. By then, I had learned that eyebrows rise over a good elk trophy, but they rise higher for a good sheep. Sheep may be small in stature, but they are big in every other respect.

Once you begin to take them seriously, you are destined to do some growing. You have to make sure you are fit—sheep live in high places, and you'll have to do some climbing. You have to work on your patience—they live in open terrain, and stalking is hardly a straightforward affair. You also have to be confident of your shooting—sheep routinely require long shots at odd angles.

Seeing that I had begun to grasp the challenge of hunting sheep, guides began to talk to me about the possibility of trying for a Grand Slam. I liked the idea, and the timing was right. I was still in my thirties. The obvious time to be sprinting up mountains was before I grew too old and creaky; forty-five might be over the hill. Second, only a small number of hunters had achieved a Grand Slam. If I could pull it off, I'd be joining a rather exclusive fraternity.

I booked with Gary Vince in British Columbia to hunt Stone sheep in the fall of 1973. We flew to his base camp in a Super Cub, and from there we moved into the just-the-two-of-us routine I enjoy so much. I went out with a guide, two horses, and two packhorses carrying our gear and food. We set up a little tent, hobbled the horses, threw on our backpacks, and began to climb and glass for sheep.

We saw plenty of sheep, but we never could find the big rams. For fourteen days we hunted close to fourteen hours a day, moving our camp from time to time. We scoured the slopes, the rock slides, and the small, high meadows. We scanned likely looking resting places. A few times we began an approach, but the sheep always moved on before we got close enough to be sure we were looking at a shootable ram. We certainly couldn't get close enough to shoot one.

Richard Hawkins hunted Stone sheep with me in British Columbia in 1974—he is seen here with guides, packing into camp.

It took two long hunts, outfitted by Gary Vince, to collect my Stone sheep.

It was near the end of this hunt that I succumbed to temptation and tested my skill at downhill skiing without skis. Or perhaps I should say I tested my luck and found that the gods of safe passage were watching over me, despite my stupidity. As the days rolled on without a successful stalk, it became clear that getting a Stone ram was going to require a second hunt. I booked to return to British Columbia and hunt with Gary's outfit again the following fall. This time I planned to go into a different portion of his large hunting area.

As I look back across a long hunting career, it's clear that, although Africa and Asia are exciting, some of the game species most difficult to hunt are right here in North America. Hiking and climbing until you think your chest will burst is not typical of what you have to do in most other countries. Neither is hunting hard every day for two weeks for just one animal. This is exactly what hunters often have to do in order to collect several North American game species, especially sheep. Physically, this is some of the toughest hunting to be found anywhere in the world.

For my 1974 Stone sheep hunt, Richard Hawkins was with us. I was beginning to wise up about all the climbing. One way to make things easier on ourselves was to climb a mountain and then stick to the high ridge tops and progress along them. Instead of endlessly battling up and down and up again, once we got up, we stayed up. At last we spotted three good rams below us. They were feeding, and they were in a position from which we would be able to stalk them. I shot a really good ram around the tenth day of a fourteen-day hunt. Richard collected one from a group of rams that was actually moving toward us as we sat on a high point, glassing.

I took a mountain goat on the same hunt, and it didn't require any difficult climbing or a long shot. We suddenly saw a group of goats in thick brush near a salt lick, and there was a good billy among them. In this case the challenge involved crawling among the rocks on the bottom of the draw to find a spot from which I could get a clear shot.

To Baja for Desert Bighorn

By now, I had taken two Dall sheep on two hunts, and my Stone ram had required twenty-four days on another two hunts. Was it going to take multiple hunts to get a desert bighorn sheep as well? At first it seemed as if I could hardly manage to book even a single hunt. Only about forty permits a year were being issued to hunt desert sheep in Mexico, and it appeared you had to know someone in order to receive one of those permits. You needed some sort of privileged connection.

The Houston Safari Club held its monthly dinner meetings at Sonny Look's restaurant in those days. I went to the dinners and picked the brains of some of the club's prominent hunters—Mike Simpson, Cecil Hopper, Kenneth Campbell—about how I could arrange a desert-sheep hunt. One of them gave me a phone number at the Mexican game department to try.

The man I got on the other end of the line told me he was sorry, there were very few permits available. They were already spoken for, and there was a long waiting list. Click—he hung up. If I wanted this bad enough, I needed to take more creative measures.

I wondered whether I could activate any connections of my own. At the time I was sales manager on a real estate development called April Sound in Conroe, just north of Houston, and one of my clients had a Mexican contact who apparently was a senior man in the game department. I said I was prepared to pay for my sheep permit and was willing to fly down and talk to whomever I needed to talk to in order to make it happen.

Eventually, I did fly down there. Thanks to my developer friend's introduction, I got right in to speak to the game department official. Like the first official, he told me of the pressure for these sheep permits. He said the son of the shah of Iran was on the waiting list. Having notables like that waiting in line seemed to count me out for sure.

Outfitter Mario Luis Cossio's camp for the super-duper Mexican hunt was above the town of Santa Rosalia on the Baja Peninsula.

A modest mount was my desert transportation from the Baja camp to the base of the mountains where we hunted.

I understood that bribes were a common way of getting your show on the road in Mexico, and I fully intended to offer one. But somehow the conversation never seemed to provide the right opening for me to make the offer. Perhaps it was just that if you aren't in the habit of doing this, you don't recognize the right moment when it comes. I was never quite sure whether I had blown my privileged opportunity to negotiate a permit. If I had, I didn't know what to do about it.

A few weeks later, my secretary fielded a phone call from the game department. There had been a cancellation, and a spot on the bid list had opened up. I had a permit for a sheep if I wanted it. Could I go right away? I wasted no energy wondering why the call had come to me instead of someone else on the waiting list.

The game department had told outfitter Mario Luis Cossio about me, and the camp was ready for me. The outfitter said I had a choice between his super hunt at three thousand dollars and his super-duper hunt at four thousand dollars. I chose the super-duper. I flew to Tucson and then to Hermosillo. From there I would head for the coast and take a ferry across to the Baja Peninsula. We would hunt above the town of Santa Rosalia.

Baja is the place where the rain went on vacation and forgot to come back. Our party consisted of my guide, Mario; a cook; drivers and bearers; and a game department biologist whose job was to ensure that I took a mature herd ram. The conservation wisdom of the time was that the older, heavier rams often bred less energetically than younger rams, but the younger males rarely got their

I hunted Rocky Mountain bighorn in Alberta, Canada, outfitted by Ed McKenzie. My Grand Slam ram was the fifth in a single-file line of five rams to emerge from cover.

chance because the big old rams were good at defending ewes. Take out the old man, the theory went, and the sheep population should increase more quickly.

My permit was for twelve days. For the first eight days we could get nowhere near any sheep. We did spot a group of six rams one afternoon, just as we were on the point of returning to camp for the night. They were a long way off, and we thought it might be dark by the time we reached them. Should we go after them? With more hope than good sense, we decided to try, despite the clear possibility that we might wind up spending the night in the mountains.

Sure enough, after three hours of climbing and scrambling through the brush and cactus, we reached the place where we had seen those sheep, but it was too dark for us to hunt. In that season the daytime temperatures reached the high eighties, but at night the mercury plunged into the thirties. We had no sleeping bags and no blankets. Our supplies consisted of one small bottle of water and a single candy bar, hardly ideal for a cold night out. Struggling to stay warm, we burned every dead cactus we could find on that mountain. We did the classic one-side-at-a-time routine, facing our little fire to toast in front while our backs were freezing, then turning around to toast our well-chilled rears. At dawn we peeked over the rise to where the sheep had been, and they were gone.

The failed stalk and cold night turned out to be a prelude to better things. On the ninth day we spotted a group of sheep and stalked them for about five hours. Sometimes we were on our hands and knees, getting all scratched up in that thorny country. The game biologist was satisfied that the ram was an old one and that there were young rams available to replace it. The trophy ram was twelve years old. It had a 17-inch horn base and qualified for the Boone and Crockett book.

Bighorn on the Pass

The year 1974 had provided me with both a Stone sheep and a desert bighorn ram. Now I needed only a Rocky Mountain bighorn to complete my Grand Slam. I booked a horseback hunt out of Rocky Mountain House in Alberta for September 1975. The price was $1,750. I would fly into Calgary and meet my outfitter, Ed McKenzie, at the trailhead to ride into the high country adjoining Canada's Jasper National Park. We would be there for the opening day of the season, 1 September, and would hunt near the Brazeau River.

Traditionally, during sheep season, the cold would drive the sheep down to the lower areas and out of the high country. That year, however, the weather remained unseasonably warm, and most of the sheep were not yet moving down. For fourteen days we rode and glassed, then moved to different country and rode and glassed, but we saw only ewes and young. I departed empty-handed.

After I'd been home for about two weeks, Ed called on 8 October to suggest I get back up there if I could. The season still had a couple of weeks to run, and snow had been falling. The sheep were now moving, and he was seeing lots of sign. He thought we could get a ram.

This time he and his son both accompanied me. Our fly camp did not prove fruitful. The snow had done us a favor by bringing in the sheep, but the hunting was heavy going. Horses and people are not built to function well in the deep snow. Eventually, we tore down our camp to move to a new area for the last couple of days of the season.

The move required negotiating a long pass with seven packhorses. While riding on the pass in snow up to our waists, we suddenly spotted five sheep taking shelter under an overhang that created a kind of cave. We put the scope on them and glassed them carefully, eventually deciding that one of them was indeed a legal ram.

We gauged that if the sheep stayed put, we had just enough time to try a stalk and reach a shooting position before the light faded. If we hadn't struggled so hard to find a ram, and if the season weren't coming to an end, I suppose we might have waited and tried to find that group again the next day. But after so many days of effort, and with so little time left, we were not about to pass up an opportunity to try for a legal ram. We sent Ed up and over the pass with all the packhorses and gear to establish our final camp, and his son and I went after those sheep.

We set about approaching the overhang from above. It was our good fortune that the sheep stayed right where they were, beneath the overhang. As we moved into position above them, the guide told me the sheep were likely to bust out of there in a hurry, one at a time.

"You're not going to have time to get a good look at them," he said. "You just be ready to shoot, and I'll look over them as they come out and tell you which one to shoot."

He was exactly right. The animals suddenly began to come into view in single file: One, no. Two, no. Three, four, five. The fifth was the ram we wanted.

"Shoot, shoot, shoot!" said the guide.

I collected my bighorn ram with scarcely enough light left for photos.

The thrill of completing my Grand Slam was tempered by the fact that we were still many hours away from our camp. Now we faced the slow business of climbing the pass in the dark. Not until about four in the morning did we struggle into camp.

Even then, it was clear to me that I was not finished with sheep hunting. I was now more educated about the quality of sheep horns, so I wanted a better Dall ram. Later, in 1976, Lynn Castle offered me the chance to get one (see chapter 3). What I didn't yet know was how important my introduction to the Old World would prove to be when I started hunting sheep in Europe and Asia.

Changing fly camps for bighorn required packing gear over long passes. First we had too little snow, keeping the sheep up high, and then heavy snows made the hunting hard going.

If I had set myself the goal of getting a Grand Slam within one hundred hunting days—call it twenty-five days per sheep species—then I would have had the satisfaction of meeting my goal. The actual tally was ninety-three days, including thirty-three days on three hunts (if you count the effort to get a really good Dall ram), twenty-four days for Stone sheep, nine for desert bighorn (not counting the negotiating trip), and twenty-seven days of hard work for Rocky Mountain bighorn. If I had actually set such a goal, I probably would have estimated that ten hunting days per species would be more than enough to do the job. I never would have thought it would take an average of more than three weeks of hunting for each sheep trophy.

A few hundred people could have set me straight on that question, had I asked them. They are all sheep hunters, of course.

Chapter 5

Phantom Mountain Caribou

British Columbia, 1981

I've been in fog before, but this stuff was so thick you couldn't see ten yards. Suddenly, we had a young caribou bull sniffing at us. This was not quite what we expected while out hunting caribou in the back of beyond, having trekked for hours into the mountains on horseback. The animal apparently couldn't make sense of the ghostly figures it was seeing, and it trotted all around us. Perhaps the young bull was trying to get our scent and the fog fooled its nose. After an inspection tour of five or ten minutes, it just ambled off, disappearing into the mist.

We knew it was likely the young bull was headed toward the record-book mountain caribou bull for which I had come to British Columbia. We had seen the big bull—in fact, we'd seen six excellent bulls, two or three of them trophy class—in a herd of about sixty-five animals. They were lying in a mountain basin three or four miles

in diameter. It was a beautiful spot, out of the wind, and the sun was shining when we glassed the herd. The caribou could see for miles in any direction.

Now, a couple of hours later, we were in pea-soup fog so thick that we had to follow the tracks of a caribou just yards ahead of us, hoping it would lead us to the herd. The fog had rolled in suddenly, just as we were finishing a difficult climb to get the advantage on the herd. Not only did we no longer know where the herd was; we weren't sure where we were, either.

Fog can be baffling, as any driver who has encountered it knows. The confusing effects of thick fog are equally pronounced whether you're on horseback or on foot. Landmarks disappear. Your depth perception goes south, and you can't trust your eyesight. Familiar places look oddly unfamiliar. Sound is dampened and muffled, making it difficult to sort out where noises are coming from. The young bull's fearless examination of us suggests that even the sharp senses of caribou are scrambled by fog.

We had begun to call the big bull the Phantom Caribou. In retrospect it doesn't seem so strange, but I assure you we felt as if we were inhabiting a world of phantoms.

Snowy Days

When I had booked the hunt with Skipper Bettis, owner and operator of Turnagain River Outfitters in Cassiar, British Columbia, I wasn't thinking about ghosts—just record-book mountain caribou. In 1980 I had hunted with Gene Overton, who sold his area to Skipper in 1981. I'd had great results with Gene and knew he was one of the best caribou guides and hunting partners in Canada.

Leaving Houston on 3 October, I overnighted in Vancouver, stayed the next night in Watson Lake in the Yukon, and finally arrived at Skipper's camp by floatplane. Skipper was

Turnagain River Outfitters of Cassiar, British Columbia, were first-class for great mountain caribou trophies. My guide was Gene Overton (second from right). Bill Casey (right) was guided by Dan Rossman (left).

We reached a small log cabin beside a crystal-clear lake after a six-hour ride, and we were still far from the caribou.

booked, so Gene was going to guide me again. Rounding out our crew were Bill Casey from Kentucky, who was primarily after moose, and his guide, Dan Rossman.

After packing our gear and supplies and gathering up our horses in preparation for our departure the next morning, we set up a spotting scope to look at the mountain range where we would be hunting. We immediately counted more than fifty caribou, with five or six good bulls in the herd. Gene said they were about fifteen miles away, as the crow flies—and we weren't riding crows. I didn't get much sleep that night.

We got an early start into those gorgeous mountains. Six hours into the day, we arrived at a small log cabin on a crystal-clear lake; this would be our "mini-base camp."

"How far now, Gene?" were the first words out of my mouth.

"About another five hours," he said.

It started to snow. This was not the moment to undertake another long ride. It snowed all night, and the next morning it was still snowing. Gene said we would have to wait it out. It snowed all day and all night, and I just knew those caribou would be long gone. When the snow was still coming down on our second morning at the mini-base camp, the guide figured it was not going to let up, and we had better get going after all. We took two days of supplies and seven horses and headed for the high country.

With the wind-chill factor, it must have been fifteen degrees below zero. The snow was three feet deep in places and was getting deeper the higher we went. Around 3 P.M. we approached the basin where we had first spotted the herd. Dan mounted a high point to glass for the caribou while Gene built a fire. We munched on sandwiches and tried to get warm.

Then we saw Dan jumping up and down, waving his arms. The caribou were still there! The three of us ran up after him. That was when we got a really good look at the herd resting in the mountain bowl. The sun was out, and everything was lined up for a perfect stalk. We needed to climb one level higher, work our way around the herd, and then come down on them.

An hour and a half later, we were nearing the top when that thick fog hit us and threw our navigation off. We dropped down again and came out of it. We could see where Gene had built the fire, but we didn't know where the caribou were. There were as many guesses as guessers in our party.

Suddenly, we heard horns banging together. Two bulls were clashing somewhere above us. We slipped back into the mist, practically blind. Without warning, Gene grabbed my arm. We had walked smack into the middle of the herd. One bull was trying to keep a group of cows bunched up, but they seemed intent on checking us out. I put my scope on the bull and found the image was blurred. I took what I thought was a good shot—at very short range—and missed. The bull vanished.

Soon more caribou appeared. I leveled on another bull and missed again! Then I found out why. My variable scope had malfunctioned, rendering every setting useless except 2.5X. Having your senses compromised by fog is one thing, but finding your scope out of action is quite another. I turned the next shot over to Bill.

For a time the ghostly animals all seemed to have vanished. We just sat there in the snow, hoping they would show again. Once more we heard the sound of banging horns, coming from the mist. We eased in that direction and found that the fog had thinned somewhat. At a distance of perhaps one hundred and fifty yards, we made out a bull and about ten cows heading up a slope. The bull was a good one, and Bill dropped it. The antlers scored 331⅞ Boone and Crockett points.

A Presence in the Fog

As Dan was caping out the caribou, I happened to look back down into the basin. There it was—the biggest mountain caribou I had ever seen! The Phantom Caribou had materialized from nowhere and was headed right for us with about fifteen cows.

"Gary, take him!" said Gene. "It's the trophy we want!"

As the little herd veered off to one side, I ran to a rock and used it for a rest. If you've ever tried running down a mountain in snow above your knees, wearing every stitch of clothes you've brought, going after the caribou

Our fly camp was hastily set up near a stream—just a tarp stretched between fir trees.

of a lifetime, you'll understand why I was puffing hard when I reached the rock. My breath fogged the scope. I shot and missed.

"I think you're shooting low," Gene yelled. "Aim high. He's over three hundred yards away."

I held over, shot, and missed again—still too low. I tried again, holding a full foot over the bull's back. When I missed that time, I figured I had completely blown my chance at a record-book caribou. It was now over four hundred yards away. We'd get another chance at it, Gene said, but not today. It was almost 6 P.M., and we hadn't made camp. We left Bill's caribou and got off the mountain as fast as we could. Around 8 P.M. we found a place with a stream and only about a foot of snow. By 10:30 P.M., we had turned in for some much-needed rest.

After breakfast, Bill and Dan set out in search of moose. Gene and I took a packhorse and picked up Bill's

Scoring 334 B&C points, my caribou took second place in the British Columbia awards for the year, and Bill's came third, with a score of 331⅞. Both were taken on the same hunt.

cape, horns, and meat. We went up the mountain and glassed a small group of caribou with one bull in a valley on the far side. That bull looked pretty good, too.

"That's not the herd we're after," Gene said, "but the rest could be near. Let's go."

We found where the herd had passed and followed the tracks around the side of the mountain. We got within three hundred yards and were getting set up to glass them when it happened again—it started to snow, and the fog rolled in. The worsening conditions allowed us to work our way closer to the animals and eventually to determine that the bull wasn't what I wanted, so we returned to camp. Bill had seen two moose, but they were too far away to stalk, and we made an early night of it. In the morning we would head up the mountain for another try.

Picking up the trail again, we followed the caribou to the point where the herd had crossed the broad valley and headed for high ground. You can guess what happened: The fog rolled in once more and drove us back to camp. In low spirits, we went back to our mini-base camp for more supplies. If the weather broke, perhaps we could try again, Gene said.

The next day was a disappointing one for Bill. He missed three shots at a scattering group of moose and had to return to camp empty-handed. But the weather had cleared—it was beautiful.

"If it stays like this, we'll head back and stay on the caribou tracks until we find them, even if we have to go all the way to Alaska," Gene declared.

A Charmed Life

Under the clear morning sky, with two packhorses, two days' food, and a tarp for when the snow came again,

Gene and I headed back up that same old mountain to the basin the caribou favored. We passed up a bull moose of better than fifty inches because we couldn't afford the time. Too many days had gotten away from us in the mist. The caribou were not in their accustomed valley, but when we topped out over the far rim and started glassing, glory be! The herd was resting in a similar valley on the next mountain.

"That's your caribou," Gene said.

There were about forty animals in the herd, including the one with the tremendous set of horns my guide was talking about. It was 2:30 P.M., and they were still three hours away. We worked the horses down the mountain and across the valley. By around 5:30 P.M., nothing but a ridge separated us from the caribou. We crawled one hundred yards on our bellies, got soaking wet, and looked over the edge. There were cows, but no bulls.

All of a sudden, a big bull walked out of a dark patch of shadow on the mountain.

"Gary, that's not the Phantom Caribou," said Gene, binoculars at his eyes.

But this bull suited me fine. It was jousting with a smaller bull around three hundred yards from us. With my faulty scope, I missed.

"Too low," Gene said.

Resting on the guide's back for the second shot, I held a foot and a half over the bull's back, and down it went, hit in the shoulder.

Confused, the other caribou were milling about. Then, up popped my ghostly bull! It was not seventy-five yards from us; it had been lying there all the time.

"That's the Phantom!" Gene said.

We looked at each other and started to laugh. It took off with the rest of the herd. What a lucky mountain caribou.

Nevertheless, the one on the ground was an excellent bull, and it looked more like an elk the closer we got. The antlers were over sixty inches long, with bases 7½ inches around, and the spread was 40 inches. The bull looked more like a Quebec-Labrador than a mountain caribou. It scored 334 Boone and Crockett points, putting it high in the Safari Club record book and giving us hopes for the annual provincial competition.

Around fifty-five hundred feet up we found a nice stand of balsam fir, put up the tarp, and built a roaring fire. We ate delicious caribou steaks and stretched out in the snow under the stars.

The final results of the 1981 British Columbia Best-Caribou-Taken Class exceeded our hopes. The first-place winner scored 341 Boone and Crockett points. My trophy came in second, with 334 points, and Bill Casey's bull was third, at 331⅞—two outstanding caribou taken on the very same hunt. When Skipper bought Gene's Turnagain River Outfitters, he had undoubtedly acquired one of the best hunting areas and operations in Canada. Gene said he had never guided a hunt like this in his twenty years of outfitting. What a way to end a career.

He was right that this 1981 hunt had been a memorable one. By then, I was lucky enough to have hunted all over North America and in Africa, Mongolia, Spain, New Zealand, and Australia, and I was planning a trip to Russia. But it would be difficult to beat this trip in British Columbia. The hardship of the snow and the suspense of the fog were part of the magic. The excellent guide and outstanding hunting companions made a big difference, too. Most of all, what kept that hunt vivid in my mind was knowing there was still a great record-book mountain caribou bull out there in those mountains, waiting for someone.

Chapter 6

The Old Seven and the Twenty-Seven

North American 27, 1980

Seeing all the animals in my trophy room, people often say, "Man, you must have a big gun collection."

They are usually disappointed when I tell hem I shot just about all the trophies with ust two rifles. As big-game hunters go, I have een rather dull in the rifles department—ractically a one-rifle man. The 7mm has ong been my rifle of choice.

I came to it young, when I went moose unting across the border in Canada with a group from Minnesota. A floatplane ferried us over to the lake, where we settled into he cabin that would be our base for a self-guided moose hunt. We each had a .308. It lidn't take long to see that the .308 was too ight for hunting moose.

Looking for a more substantial rifle, found that the 7mm was the hot caliber of the time. I bought a Remington 7mm Magnum bolt action. My friends Tom Rubenstein and Richard Hawkins got sevens as well. The dealer suggested getting some decent optics, and added a Leupold scope. That rifle would serve me well on leer hunts in Minnesota. Then, n the winter, my friends and I would put on our white outfits and walk through the farmers'

fields, hunting foxes. We'd make a line and stage a drive. The seven was good for that, too, and it went with me to Colorado for elk and on my first Alaskan hunts.

When I went after polar bear in 1972, my guide said he thought the seven was a little light. He said I could borrow a .300 Winchester, which I did. He nevertheless fancied my 7mm as a backup rifle for his camp, and I sold it to him after the hunt. Once home, I immediately went to see Bill Carter of Carter's Country and replaced that rifle with a new Remington 7mm mag right off the rack. I used it for nearly all my North American game species, most of my African animals, and just about all my sheep. For thirty years that rifle was my mainstay.

On Bill Carter's recommendation I did pick up a .375 before my first African safari a few years later, but I've never developed a special interest in fine guns or heavier calibers. Armchair gunsmithing is not my thing. Comfort, familiarity, accuracy, and predictability are more important to me. Seeing Alaskan natives shoot caribou in the ear with a .22 because they didn't want to damage the meat affirmed my feeling that you should shoot what feels right for you, and never mind what anyone else favors.

Some of the animals I took with the old seven turned out to be pretty large. At one time I was proud to have fifteen animals at No. 1 in the record books. The tally is now much lower, and my perspective has matured. High-scoring trophies are gratifying, but I've also learned a few things along the way about what it means to get a No. 1 animal.

One conclusion I've reached is that getting an animal that's No. 1 in the book is mostly—and sometimes absolutely—a matter of pure luck. I don't mean to minimize the effort required to collect excellent trophies of any species; it takes effort, no question. We're all trying for the big ones. You have to work to get yourself into the right place at the right time. You do your best and you take your chances. The truth is, on any fair-chase hunt, at the moment you shoot there's no real way of knowing how well an animal is going to score. If it turns out to be No. 1, hey, that's just luck.

On Bears and Cats

My jaguar—No. 1 in the *Safari Club International All-Time Record Book of Trophy Animals* at the time of this writing—is a classic example of a lucky score. The cat was a stock killer. I wasn't heading to Mexico to scout around, look at several jaguar, then try to choose the biggest trophy. I was going specifically to dispatch an individual problem cat that had discovered what an easy living it could make eating livestock. We were after that cat only. It just so happened to be a very big one. I flew into Cancun, hunted in the forested mountains of the interior, and returned to my outfitter's beach house for a few days. I realized only later how big my cat really was.

If you look at Boone and Crockett's *Records of North American Big Game*, you'll see that the No. 1 spot for black bear is occupied by a pickup head. The fellows who entered that enormous black bear skull in the records didn't hunt the bear; they happened across it in Sanpete County, Utah. The interesting thing about it is the date—not the 1920s, 1930s, or 1940s, but 1975. By that stage, black bear had been hunted and measured for so long that the hunting world was astonished when a huge skull scoring 23[10]/16 inches turned up out of the blue in a state not particularly noted for large black bear.

Tom Rubenstein was along when I took this antelope in New Mexico in the fall of 1980, the same month I completed my slam of the North American 27 species.

We were hunting in forested country inland from Cancun when the guides and hounds on my Mexican jaguar hunt took a pause for a drink and a dip.

Two more pickup heads score high in the black bear listings in the 12th (2005) edition of the Boone and Crockett Club record book. One, found in Utah's Sevier County in 1982, scored 22 7/16 inches and ranked No. 20. The other, found in 1992 in Aitkin County, Minnesota, scored 22 3/16 inches and ranked No. 34. A hunter might have killed any of those three bear; it just happened that all three met their end in other ways. What this says about wildlife management in North America is that we must be doing something right. Our woods are still producing very large black bear, big enough to make it high into the modern records.

Once you set specific hunting objectives, work plays a larger role and luck plays a smaller one. At a certain point, after deciding to try for the Grand Slam of wild sheep, I realized I was already well on my way toward getting all the game species then listed as the North American 27. I became more systematic about planning hunts that would bring me closer to that goal.

The North American 27 are the nation's big-game animals, as taken by pioneering sportsman-conservationist Theodore Roosevelt and as recognized by the Boone and Crockett Club after 1971. These animals include four wild sheep species (Dall, Stone,

My Mexican jaguar was a stock killer that turned out to be very large, making him No. 1 in the SCI record book.

bighorn, and desert bighorn); four species of bear (brown, grizzly, black, and polar); four kinds of caribou (barren ground, Quebec-Labrador, mountain, and woodland); four kinds of deer (mule, white-tailed, Coues, and Columbia black-tailed); three kinds of moose (Alaska-Yukon, Canada, and Shiras); plus bison, muskox, cougar, jaguar, pronghorn, American elk, walrus, and Rocky Mountain goat.

Boone and Crockett traditionally recognized both Atlantic and Pacific walrus, and both barren-ground and Greenland muskox, but hunters needed only one kind of walrus and muskox to qualify.

SCI Chairman C. J. McElroy encouraged my suggestion of a formal award to recognize this hunting achievement. The North American 27 was one of SCI's first such major awards, and I was involved in developing it. Changes since the 1970s have altered the math a little by adding the Central Canada barren-ground caribou, Sitka blacktail, and Roosevelt and tule elk. Today, the comparable Safari Club International award is called Trophy Animals of North America and requires more than thirty species.

Had I not been trying to complete the 27, I might have ignored some of the predators altogether, including the jaguar. As a youngster in Minnesota, although I had shot foxes and raccoons, my focus was mainly on birds and deer—game that we could eat. I had taken my share of squirrels, but my mother was not keen on cooking squirrels. She said it was too much work for too little gain. It felt to her like cooking rats. She was happier with game that provided more substance.

I've collected several black bear, all in Alaska. I hunted the bigger bear there as well: polar bear in 1972 (see chapter 3), brown bear on the Alaska Peninsula in 1974, and grizzly out of Kotzebue in 1977. I also took an Alaska hunt that was strictly for wolf, wolverine, and fox. At first, the issue was not so much that I wanted these predator species for the 27; instead, they provided reasons for me to spend more time in Alaska and lent more variety to my hunts.

Mountain lion and bobcat were species for which I took more focused predator hunts. My outfitter for bobcat was an old Minnesota connection: Doug Peterson, from Rochester. He was a fireman who

A Greenland muskox from Alaska's Nunivak Island was among my North American 27 species. Later, in 1987, I also took this barren-ground muskox near Coppermine in Canada's Northwest Territories.

I wore a custom-made parka and pants of caribou hide on my Canadian hunt for barren-ground muskox, which was the best way to cope with extremely low temperatures.

decided to sell everything and move to Alaska. He became a kind of latter-day mountain man and eventually opened a guide service. He guided in Alaska for sheep in the fall and also in Montana, where he built himself a log house near the town of Nixon. He was a fixture at the annual hunting shows, and several of my Minnesota buddies had gone hunting with him.

Doug and I hunted bobcat in Montana's Bob Marshall Wilderness. Even in the early1980s, this was country as wild as anyone would want. That hunt was all about snow. He said he'd let me know when there was a fresh snowfall. When the call came, I flew in from Dallas, where I was working at the time, and drove to his house.

We set off in the morning in the truck, with a snow machine and four dogs in the back. First thing we cut a track, and Doug said it looked like a good bobcat. I asked him how in the world he and his dogs knew it was a bobcat and not a mountain lion? He said he knew because it was a small track, but it was a big small track. He was accustomed to seeing lion tracks much more often than bobcat tracks, so he knew what he was talking about. We were lucky.

He turned the dogs loose, and we followed on the snow machine as far as we could take it. We then switched to snowshoes to head into the thicker stuff after the dogs. A houndsman knows exactly what his dogs are saying by the way they bark when trailing versus how they sound when they've got something treed. I got a nice big bobcat, which I kept as a full mount, with a grouse underneath one forefoot.

Ron Hayes was my guide for wolverine on an Alaskan hunt that also included wolf and fox.

My first mountain lion hunt, in southern Utah in 1973, was similar. We covered a lot of wide-open terrain by truck and saw a lot of mustangs before we found a cat track, turned the dogs loose, and got out on the snow machine. But the mountain lion hunt I really enjoyed, which was also in the 1970s, was with a young guide named Leon Cox, who offered horseback hunting for mountain lion in Arizona. I truly love hunting on horseback. You can move farther and faster than on foot, which lets you enjoy more of the country with a lot less effort. You feel as if you're bringing the pioneer past to life again.

Leon Cox was a great houndsman. He and I and six dogs went out into the red sand desert, northwestern Arizona's rocky canyon and juniper country. Leon had what he called "dry-nose" dogs—elite hounds that can pick up and follow a track even when there's no snow. That's more difficult than following a track when the ground is under a soft white blanket; you need much better dogs.

We rode those canyons looking for a track. Instead of the roar of a snow machine, we listened to the clink of harnesses, the creak of saddle leather, and the clop

Hunting for barren-ground caribou in the Arctic also required special cold-weather gear.

Guide Leon Cox took me hunting for mountain lion in northwestern Arizona on horseback. His mount and one of his packhorses were willing to carry lions.

I took both Quebec-Labrador caribou (pictured, with guide) and woodland caribou in the fall of 1978.

of hoofs. We could hear the wind and the birds. Cats follow trails when they can; why stick to the rocks and brush when you can walk down a trail? So we rode our horses along the canyon trails, the dogs all on leashes, until the strike dog told us we had found what we were looking for. Leon said the track looked promising, and he thought we were onto a good tom. He said he couldn't tell how old the track was, but, from the commotion among the dogs, it seemed likely to be fresh. We slipped the leashes off the hounds.

This is where it becomes really fun to hunt mountain lion using horses. You can go almost everywhere with a horse. Soon the dogs were running, and we were running, too. Cornering the cat took a while because the area didn't have rocky ledges or a lot of large trees suitable for a cat to climb. The tree it finally chose was a small one, and Leon said the lion was not going to hold there for long, once it got its breath back. It was on quite a low branch, and the dogs were jumping up at it.

Sure enough, as we approached with the rifle after tying our horses, the cat jumped out of the tree, sailed clear over the dogs, and dashed right between us, with the dogs barking in wild confusion.

"He's not going far," Leon predicted.

Indeed, the cat soon treed for a second time, and I shot it with my trusty 7mm.

Most horses are scared of carcasses. On that trip we had a packhorse carrying some supplies, just in case we should need to stay out overnight.

"That horse I can put the lion on," Leon said.

The animal that completed my North American 27 was a Shiras moose taken in Utah in 1980; I was guided by Ken Elliott.

He asked me to hold the horse, and he strapped the whole lion right on its back for the trip back to the trailer.

One Moose to Go

My hunting pace accelerated as the 1970s wore on and I got closer to my goal. In 1976 I took a bison in Texas, Coues deer in Arizona out of the Glenn family ranch (which is still in the hunting business), and black-tailed deer in Oregon. In 1977 came Arctic grizzly and Pacific walrus in Alaska. In 1978 I hunted Quebec-Labrador caribou and woodland caribou in September and elk in New Mexico in November. I added a mountain goat in Canada in 1979. In 1980 I took an antelope in New Mexico in September, followed by mountain caribou in Canada and mule deer in Wyoming in October.

I had reached the point where there was just one game animal I still needed to complete my North American 27: the Shiras moose. Learning that a limited number of nonresident permits were to be offered in Utah for the fall of 1980, I applied there as well as in Wyoming. I came up empty in Wyoming, but my name was drawn in Utah. Ernie Sanders and I met up with guide Ken Elliott in Provo, and we set up our camp to be ready as soon as the season opened on 1 November, a Saturday. Like me, Ernie needed only a Shiras moose to complete his 27. He got his trophy on opening day, and on Sunday I collected mine with a nice clean kill.

I had been trying to complete this quest by my fortieth birthday, which would make me the youngest to achieve it. But my 6 September birthday fell just short of the hunting season in Utah, and I was a few weeks beyond the age of forty when I took the moose. Eric Sanderson became the youngest, at thirty-nine. According to the Safari Club International award records, he was the seventh man in the world to shoot all twenty-seven species, and I was the eighth. After all those miles, I was proud to be in that select company. No less than five of the first ten people to receive the North American 27 Award were from Texas. Four were from Houston: Kenneth Campbell, Cecil Hopper, Glenn Slade, and I. Dr. Bob Speegle was from Dallas.

My 7mm would provide steady service for another two decades, becoming quite a globetrotter in the process. By the time the old seven was ready to be retired to the gun cabinet for good—a few years ago—people were laughing at the tired and beat-up state of my rifle. It was definitely showing its age. The bluing had come off. The cheekplate was well worn. After the many hours spent on horseback hunts, the stock had lost its finish from abrasion in a saddle scabbard.

The options for custom rifles had multiplied almost beyond belief while I had been ignoring all the innovations in gunmaking. What would make the most sense? Everyone was talking about lightweight rifles. I decided that, having taken some 330 animals with two 7mms, the answer was to get another 7mm and to take advantage of the miracles of modern gunmaking by moving to a lighter stock.

Lex Webernick of Rifles Inc. was exhibiting at the Houston Safari Club show that year, and he had donated a credit toward the cost of a custom rifle. I bought this in the silent auction. I told him I was embarrassed to show him my aged gun, but he was perfectly happy to get me a factory Remington 7mm mag action, retool it to reduce its weight, and add a lightweight black fiberglass stock.

Like the old one, my new rifle has a Leupold scope. The combo weighs about half what the old one weighed, which makes a big difference on a long hike in the sheep mountains—for example, when I hunted Marco Polo in 2003. I love the new one now. It sits in the gun cabinet in the trophy room, right beside the position of honor occupied by the old seven, surrounded by the North American 27.

Classic Africa

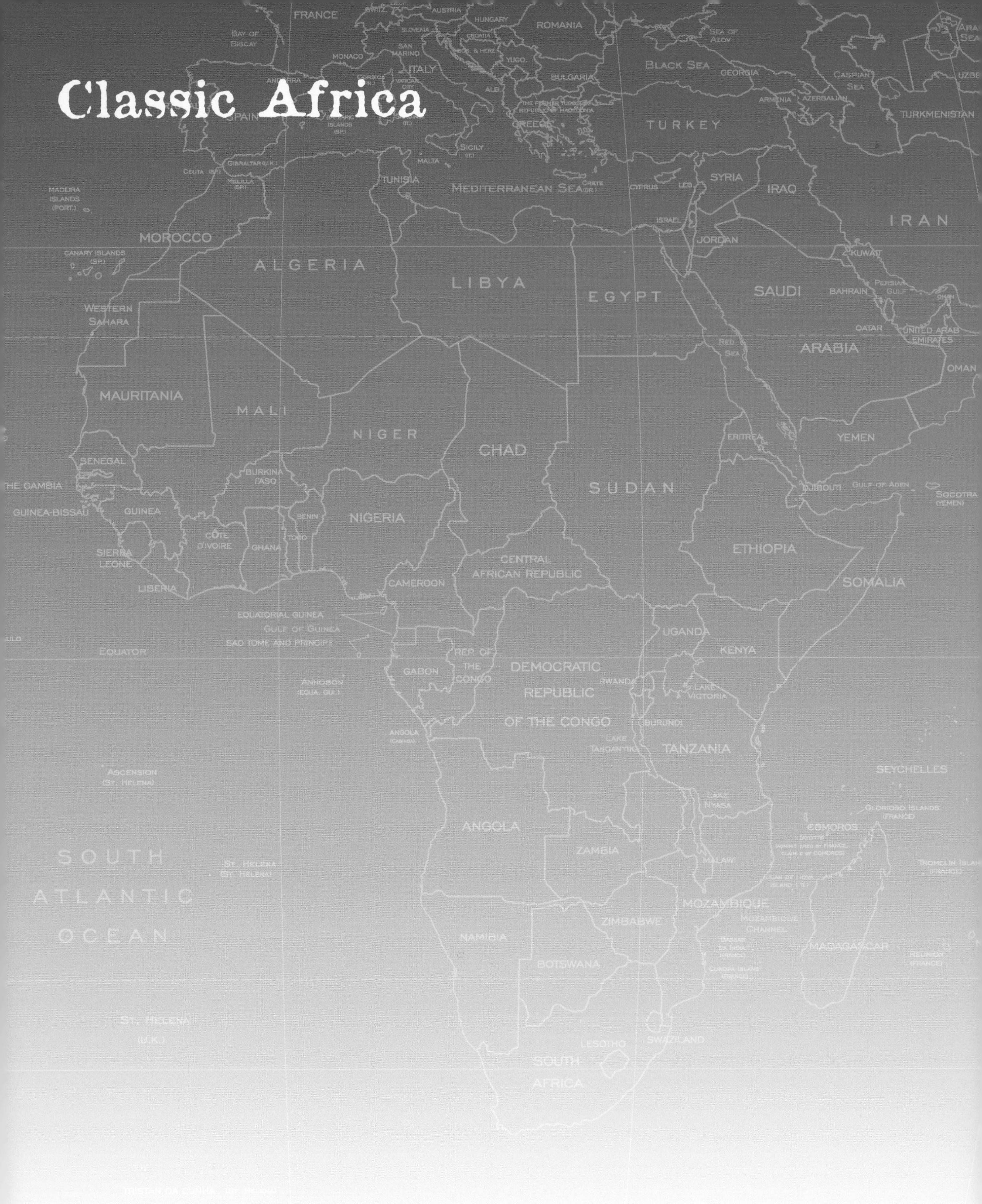

Part 2

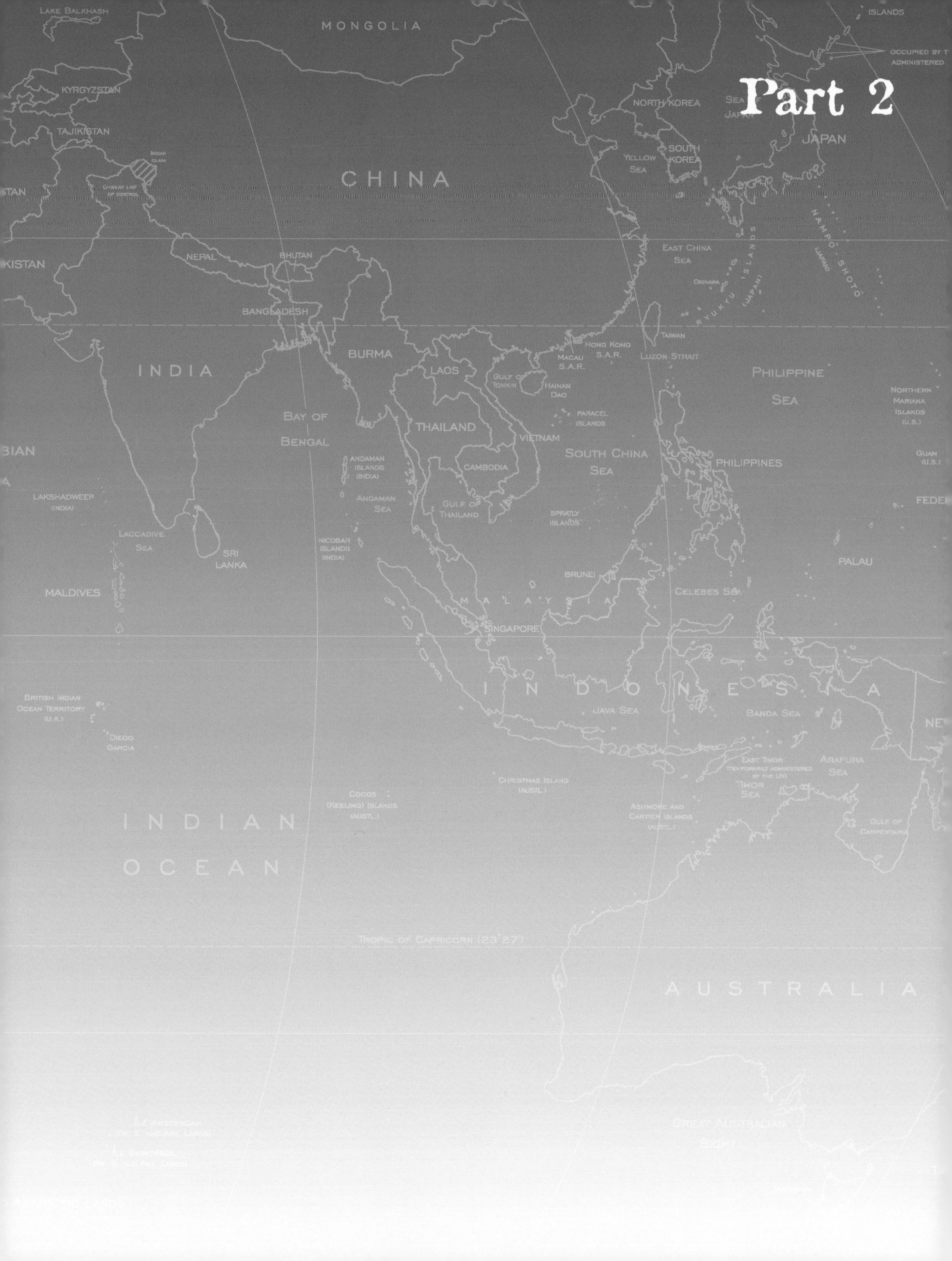

Lake Balkhash
Mongolia
Kyrgyzstan
Tajikistan
China
North Korea
South Korea
Japan
Yellow Sea
Nepal
Bhutan
Bangladesh
India
Burma
Laos
Thailand
Vietnam
Cambodia
Bay of Bengal
Andaman Sea
Andaman Islands (India)
Nicobar Islands (India)
Sri Lanka
Laccadive Sea
Lakshadweep (India)
Maldives
East China Sea
Okinawa
Ryukyu Islands (Japan)
Nampo Shoto (Japan)
Taiwan
Hong Kong S.A.R.
Macau S.A.R.
Luzon Strait
Gulf of Tonkin
Hainan Dao
Paracel Islands
Philippine Sea
Northern Mariana Islands (U.S.)
Guam (U.S.)
South China Sea
Philippines
Gulf of Thailand
Spratly Islands
Palau
Brunei
Malaysia
Singapore
Celebes Sea
Indonesia
Java Sea
Banda Sea
British Indian Ocean Territory (U.K.)
Diego Garcia
East Timor
Arafura Sea
Timor Sea
Christmas Island (Austl.)
Cocos (Keeling) Islands (Austl.)
Ashmore and Cartier Islands (Austl.)
Gulf of Carpentaria
Indian Ocean
Tropic of Capricorn (23°27')
Australia
Great Australian Bight

Kenyan professional hunter Ike Hassan always wore green fatigues and a pith helmet. We moved around with a crew of 17 people. Astride my 40-plus-inch Cape buffalo is my son Jason, then age five.

Chapter 7

Thirty-Five Days Living the Dream

Kenya, 1976

The hunting community was abuzz with rumors that Kenya was going to close all trophy hunting; elephant hunting there had already been closed. The more I thought about it, the clearer it became that the smart thing to do was to book a safari in Kenya as soon as possible. So I was receptive when, through contacts in the Houston Safari Club, I met a Galveston sportsman who invited me to his home to meet his Kenyan professional hunter, Ike Hassan. Ike visited the United States each year to book clients.

I knew Kenya had long been the prime destination for overseas hunters going to Africa. In the 1950s, '60s, and early '70s, most other African countries had few outfitters who catered to clients flying in from Europe or North America. Safari Club International, founded in 1971, was still a modest organization of about three thousand members when I planned my 1976 safari. The Houston Safari Club was founded in 1972 as a chapter of SCI. Ironically, just as U.S. trophy hunters were beginning to get organized and figure out how to provide the hunting outfitters of the world with the perfect marketing pipeline—annual hunting conventions—Kenya was threatening to get out of the safari business altogether.

In 1969 I had booked a safari with Bert Klineburger, but I had to cancel when Hurricane Camille cast a swath of destruction over Mississippi, where I was living. I lost everything, and in 1970 I moved to Houston. By the time I met Ike, I was ready to think about Africa again. I booked my Kenyan safari directly with him for thirty-five days in February and March of 1976.

The rules of the game were different then. Kenya required visiting sportsmen to book a thirty-five-day safari if they wanted to take the Big Five. With elephant hunting closed, it was no longer possible to get the Big Five, but the rule still applied if you wanted to hunt the other four species.

Traditional was the key word for Ike's safari operation. He hunted out of fully mobile tented camps. A crew of seventeen looked after the needs of a single hunting party. With or without the use of vehicles, a safari with Ike bore a resemblance to the famous expeditions of the late nineteenth century and the early twentieth. His trucks were of the basic workhorse variety, not the spanking-new equipment we read about in hunting reports today. Ike had been known to pack tires with dry grass to enable

Traditionally garbed Masai warriors seem to sum up the spirit of Africa.

vehicles to get out of remote places where every tire available had undergone multiple repairs.

Ike had learned his bushcraft hunting elephant for their ivory. He had taken many tusks of one hundred pounds or more. On some of those ivory hunts, he said, he had spent more time dealing with truck trouble than hunting elephant. By the time we met him, he had switched to taking out client hunters in great style, and he knew the importance of having sound vehicles. Luckily, on my safari we didn't have any vehicle problems except some flat tires.

Ike was a distinguished-looking fellow, charming and genteel—a gentleman to the core. He always dressed in green army fatigues and even wore a pith helmet. His wife was a doctor in Mombasa.

This would be the first time I had ever been out of the United States, and it seemed like a good idea to see something of the world's great cities. We booked three or four days in Paris on the way to Kenya and a few days in London on the way home. A friend advised us to try escargots if we went to France. I tasted them for the first time in Paris—quite a change for the meat-and-potatoes

Loading up for the move from southern Kenya to hunt rhino near Mombasa. Ike's safari vehicles were of the reliable workhorse variety.

boy from Minnesota. We were away for a month and a half, more than enough time to move into a very different state of mind from business as usual. There were no satellite phones in 1976, so the trip provided a complete break. There was no calling the office, no pressure, and very little sense of what was going on in the rest of the world.

The plan was to spend two weeks in the savanna in the southern part of Kenya, a week near Mombasa hunting rhino, and two weeks in the north. I took my wife and my five-year-old son, Jason. There were no daily rates for them—they were included in the price of my safari, which offered opportunities for up to twenty trophy animal species. We packed suitcases of books, toys, and medicines for Jason before we realized our overweight charges were likely to cost more than our airline tickets.

I took no camouflage hunting clothes. Hassan advised me to wear old clothing I was ready to part with and to leave them behind as a kind of tip for his staff when the safari was over. This would also lighten our luggage and leave more room for souvenirs. Bill Carter of Carter's Country had recently been hunting in Africa, so I consulted him about rifles. He advised adding a .375 to the 7mm I already had, and I bought a used Sako .375 from him.

This Was Lion Country

Ike met us at the airport in Nairobi and took us to our hotel. We spent a couple of days in the city so that he could show us around and take us to Nairobi National Park, where we would have our first good look at the animal species I would be hunting. The hunting license looked like a restaurant menu, with a list of all the animals you could take. In several cases the price either included multiple animals of the same species or several species at a reduced rate.

The first day of the safari was devoted to hunting for baits. I didn't even have to pay for some of these animals because they provided meat for the considerable camp staff. At that time I scarcely had a clue what the various antelope in Africa were called, let alone what they looked like or what kinds of habitat they favored. Bill Carter had given me an identification wheel with revolving disks that allowed me to turn to a given picture and learn basics like the height and weight of each animal. If I had been better educated about the game animals available, I might have been more discriminating about trophy quality. As it was, I was just thrilled to be there, to be living the dream.

Today, hunters commonly take a kind of reconnaissance trip to Africa as a first safari. They collect an assortment of plains game and generally tune in to African hunting before taking a crack at the dangerous game. This step-by-step approach is a good idea, but our safari was not arranged that way. In the first two weeks, during which Hassan's permit allowed us to hunt in the south, I collected two of the Big Four—lion and buffalo—in addition to wildebeest, zebra, eland, giraffe, lesser kudu, and several other game species.

Hunting lion didn't prove too difficult. This was lion country, with few roads but plenty of wild prey. We also saw hosts of goats and cattle. We were in the part of the country inhabited by the Masai, some of whom dropped by to check us out. When the wildlife left the watering holes, their livestock came in, and when the livestock left, the wildlife came in. There was plenty for lion to eat. We soon had about twenty lion baits out, and the largest chores were cutting tracks to our baiting points and getting around to check what had been visiting our baits. I collected a lion nearby, though not on a bait. We found it as we were approaching one of our baits, where some lionesses were dining. The lion had probably already eaten.

Although we saw plenty of buffalo, they were not easy to approach because of the open terrain. We could rarely get close. There was a drought, and often the buffalo came to the river at night to drink. Three mornings in a row we went to the river before dawn and found them there, but they took off running, and we didn't follow them out into the plains. On the day I connected with buffalo, we had gotten a late start going to the river, but we found a group of seven bulls still heading for the water. Several had horns that probably would go over forty inches, and Ike suggested I take the last one in line, which we gauged to be the largest bull.

My black rhino was among the last few legally taken in Kenya. It required days of hard hunting. Ike was in his fatigues as usual, and again Jason climbed aboard the trophy.

A comfortable tent with a nook for Jason was our home for thirty-five days. The washbasin stood outside, and we had a separate bathroom tent.

By the time we were ready to move closer to the coast to try for rhino, I was feeling much less like a complete novice. The trucks went ahead of us to set up our new temporary camp, and, while Hassan picked up our rhino permit, we detoured for a pleasant meal at a famous restaurant where peacocks strutted on the grounds.

Rhino Called for Sacrifice

The second camp was in a pleasant setting close to a watering point, but the surrounding country was thick and rough, making it difficult to get around. I soon understood why we needed to dedicate a whole week to hunting rhino. They were under tremendous pressure from poachers. A massacre was in progress, and the animals had grown extremely skittish about any human presence. They seemed to move about mostly at night, keeping to the thickets by day.

We hunted hard for six days. Every morning the trackers scoured the riverbanks for rhino tracks. We followed any that looked promising, but our trackers, like the poachers, were unwilling or unable to follow a rhino into the deep, thick, thorny, and impenetrable places where they were hiding. Hassan was a religious person who paused to pray five times each day. I suppose he was praying about other things, but, as time was running out, he decided that special measures were called for to improve our chances of getting a rhino. He said we were

Jason enjoyed sharing maize-meal porridge with the staff, one of whom was assigned to take care of him.

going to sacrifice a goat in supplication to the hunting gods, or the elders, or Allah—I was never quite sure of the doctrinal details.

We went to a village and purchased a suitable goat, which was dispatched in an appropriate manner. I didn't ask too many questions, though I remember thinking that if one goat was going to improve our chances, perhaps we should go ahead and get two. The goat meat went to the local elders, and they may have added their collective good wishes to the project in gratitude for the goat meat or in anticipation of some rhino meat, or both. At any rate, Ike thought our luck would now change. He asked me to use a .460 Weatherby, which he supplied. The rhino were difficult to approach, and he didn't want to take any chances by not using enough gun.

The hunting gods were apparently receptive to the sacrifice. On that last day, we were hunting from the same starting point at the same river as on the preceding days, but this time the rhino we were following didn't go into the thick stuff. It stopped just short of the thickets and began eating under a shade tree near where the really impenetrable bush began. When I shot my rhino in the brain, I had to presume that the goat sacrifice had done the trick. This was among the last three or four black rhino to be legally taken in Kenya. Soon afterward, Hubert Thummler of Mexico tried for rhino in the same area, after I'd encouraged him to go to Kenya, and he, too, got a rhino with Ike.

Then we moved north to focus on a different group of trophy animals. Our northern camp for the final two weeks was beside some very hot mineral hot springs in which we could take a luxurious bath. There was a large tent for the staff, another tent for the skinning and salting, and a big kitchen tent. The staff included two people whose job was to collect firewood and keep the fires going, two or three cooks, three or four skinners and trackers, and two people responsible solely for the laundry.

Jason got a sense of what school was like for Kenyan children when we visited a modest village schoolhouse along the way. We also saw people making charcoal and burning wood in pits. Unlike the open savanna of our first camp, the new terrain was more heavily wooded. Here I took the bizarre long-necked gerenuk, a wildebeest, a waterbuck, a steenbok, and the tiny antelope called the dik-dik.

By now, we had become accustomed to the camp routine. Our sleeping tent had been modified so that the section that normally held the shower served as a nook for Jason, and we had a separate bathroom tent. A tray of tea and toast arrived at our bedside every morning. We usually went out for an early hunt and took a couple of animals, then returned for a big cooked breakfast. In the afternoon we went out for a couple more trophies. We assigned one of the staff to take care of Jason. He spent a good deal of time with the Africans, often sharing maize-meal porridge with them out of a huge pot and sampling the biltong. His mother was convinced he would get sick and come home with worms or worse.

On most days we had a second morning hunt, then a light lunch and a nap. Sometime after 3 P.M. we would go out again for the evening hunt. While we were out, the staff washed our clothes from the day before and ironed them with an old iron filled with hot coals. This routine destroyed some silk underwear, but the rest of our clothes reappeared on our camp beds by evening, neatly ironed and folded. After a shower and a careful inspection under good light for ticks, we sat by the fire, enjoying freshly roasted cashew nuts and homemade potato chips until the bell rang for us to step to the table.

Dinner was a colonial-style affair, usually a delicious roast of whatever had been shot that day, served on a white tablecloth by a waiter wearing a white suit and white gloves. We also had green salads and fruit salads, and cakes would appear for dessert. One night we even had ice cream. Ike's wife was coming out for a visit, and she asked if there was anything special we wanted her to bring with her from Mombasa. I requested ice cream, thinking it impossible, but, lo and behold, she arrived with a big Thermos jug of it, still convincingly frozen. The only awkward note at dinnertime occurred in the savanna camp the day I shot my buffalo. My wife was horrified to realize that our elegant table held an offering of buffalo tongue, which she declined to sample.

Buffalo was the animal Ike considered the most dangerous. His campfire stories included two narrow squeaks during his hunting career, both of them with buffalo. In one case he and a client had been trailing a wounded bull when the animal did exactly what buffalo are reputed to do at times: It circled them and began to approach them from behind. They had just a moment's warning, a noise from behind, as the bull charged. It tripped Ike but did not quite succeed in goring him before he brought it down.

In the other case, Ike said his fatigue jacket saved him. He and a client were following a wounded bull when it charged them. The bull flung Ike in the air, flipping him right out of his jacket. The jacket got caught on the bull's horns and served to deflect its attention. The bull stomped all over the jacket and shredded it, thoroughly killing it dead.

I collected thirty-six animals in Kenya, most of them costing around twenty-five dollars apiece in trophy fees. Jason learned to shoot a .22 on this safari, and he collected an ostrich and an impala. The ostrich prompted a special celebration of his hunting prowess by the camp staff. They elevated him in a chair and sang his praises. Our trophies were salted in camp and then dipped, packed, and shipped to Texas. Taxidermy was big business in Kenya, and the work was top quality. We also got some curio items, all made from the animals I had shot, such as a fly whisk

On this safari Jason learned to shoot a .22 and collected an ostrich. The staff staged a special celebration after his accomplishment.

made of a wildebeest tail, lamps, and humidors. We had our mounts done at Conroe Taxidermy in Houston.

The leopard that would complete my Big Four was to prove something of a cliff-hanger. We didn't find a leopard until day thirty-four out of thirty-five. Ike was beginning to grow distinctly uneasy about our chances for leopard. Plenty of lion had hit our baits in the savanna, but not one leopard. In the north we spent several fruitless evenings in a blind, knowing a leopard had been feeding there, but it only came to the bait after we had left our blind. We took it on the very last night.

It was a fine ending to a first African safari, and the trip would be a fabulous start to a series of safaris. When Kenya closed trophy hunting in 1977, to the lasting dismay of the hunting world, you can imagine how relieved I was that we had already taken this trip. All the professional hunters were forced to switch tracks or move their operations elsewhere. Inevitably, that long and rich safari left me wanting to return to Africa. I was hooked, and now I needed an elephant to complete my Big Five.

We were aware, even then, that we had enjoyed the experience of a lifetime, something not readily repeated today. The total price tag was about ten thousand dollars. (To put that in perspective, the price of our three-bedroom, two-bath house along Houston's Katy Freeway was forty thousand dollars.) My hunting license included four buffalo; I was tickled to death to have taken one, but I could have taken another three. Animals like warthogs, baboons, and jackals were included at no charge. Unexpectedly, the safari package included a handsome photo album, which Ike presented to us as we were leaving. As part of his services he offered to make fine enlargements of the black-and-white photos he had shot of each trophy animal, a wonderful memento.

Some Memorable Moments

As the safari drew to a close, I was preoccupied with other things. Increasing abdominal pain eventually left me unable to walk, and I was rolled into a Nairobi hospital in a wheelchair before we left Kenya. I thought I had appendicitis. To my alarm, the doctors determined that I needed kidney-stone surgery, a procedure that was unfamiliar to me. I was unwilling to go under the knife in a place where you had to take your own soap to the hospital. I told them I was going to London the next day and begged them for something to get me through one more day. I asked my wife to get me out of there. Airlines aren't eager to take on obviously ill passengers, but I persuaded the airline that I had just checked out of a hospital and talked my way into three seats where I could lie down for the flight. By the time we reached London, the pain had receded, and doctors in Houston later said they thought I had indeed had a kidney stone but had apparently passed it.

The other medical incident on this safari didn't turn out so well. One day a woman carried into our camp a little boy about five years old, his hand bundled up in a dirty rag. Local people knew that professional hunters usually had some medical supplies. Four fingers on one of the child's hands had been virtually severed by a machete stroke and were hanging on by the skin. Surely they could not be saved. My heart turned over when I saw this little boy's terrible injury—I had my own five-year-old in the camp with me. Ike said there was little he could do, though he administered some sulfur to disinfect the wound and gave the mother some pain pills for the child to take. The boy didn't even whimper as Ike bandaged up his hand again, and away they went, back into the bush.

Another eye-opening moment, though not quite as somber, occurred when we paused at one of the brush *bomas* where people secured their cattle at night to keep them safe from lion. In the morning the *boma* would be ankle-deep in cattle dung, a handy collection point for dung to be used in hut plastering. We watched a woman enter the *boma* and puncture a cow's neck to collect some blood in a gourd. She was then going to milk the cow into the same gourd, and the mixture would serve as breakfast. It was nourishing enough, I suppose, but it was startling to innocent American eyes. Her hands were bloody, so when the cow relieved itself, the woman rinsed her hands in the splashing urine before proceeding with her milking!

You can never duplicate your first African safari. I still love going to Africa, but I always look back with nostalgia at that first trip to Kenya. I know change is inevitable, but my true African safari—with just my family, Ike, the native people, and their cattle—was the kind of experience that persuades you that change is not always a good thing.

Our Kenyan safari had some interesting fallout once we got home. One day Jason's preschool teacher called me at work, concerned that my son was inventing stories about strange animals in his home.

"We have a problem," she said. "Jason has a big imagination, and he's telling the other children he's been to Africa and at home he has zebras, a giraffe, a lion, and lots of gazelles."

"That's right," I told her. "We do have those things."

After a long pause, she apologized. I asked if she would like to bring her class to see the animals.

For many years after that, we entertained class visits to our trophy room, and we still do from time to time. Thirty years ago the children gawked and gasped at animals that were as unfamiliar to them as many had been to me before I went to Kenya. Today, some of the young visitors have a very clear sense of what they are seeing. I will never forget one little girl waving her hand in excitement when she reached the Australian section of my collection.

"I know what that is! I know exactly what that is!" she announced. "It's a spiny echidna!"

She was perfectly unmoved by the rarity of my Kenyan black rhino mount. Rhinos, after all, turn up on gas bottle logos outside supermarkets, on pillows in discount stores, and even on shower curtains. She was unaware of the challenges of taking dangerous game or the taxing climbs involved in hunting sheep. But the little spiny echidna was something special to her. She knew it from a wildlife program on television. This odd marsupial from a distant land was as real to her as a squirrel or a white-tailed deer, and she was delighted to find an echidna right there in the room with her, where she could inspect it closely. You can never tell which trophies will speak to which visitors.

A bohor reedbuck was among our trophies from Sudan. My PH on this safari was Victor "No Problem" Cabral. Note the casual clothing we all wore—special safari gear was not yet part of the scene.

Chapter 8

Stand By for Rebellion

Sudan, 1977

"Firecrackers," said Richard.

Sure enough, the noise that had woken us in the middle of the night sounded like firecrackers. But then I thought: *Hell, there aren't any firecrackers over here.* Our professional hunter came in and told us to stay low and not look out the windows or go outside.

"They're overthrowing the government," he said.

Sudan's civil strife has been in the news for as long as most of us can remember. The northern part of the country has a largely Muslim population with a strong Arabic influence; it includes the old capital city of Khartoum, whose very name evokes the image of hand-to-hand combat. The south, which is more heavily Christian, is traditionally African.

At the time of my 1977 hunt, civil war in Sudan had been roiling for some seventeen years. No one had taken a guided hunt there in more than a decade. But the fighters had now called a halt to the hostility. During the lull Frank Green, who operated the booking agency Sporting International in Houston, called to tell me that some hunting was opening up in Sudan. It was impossible to tell whether, or for how long, the peace would last. Frank said no one knew exactly what there was in the way of game animals, either; but there were elephant and bongo in the Sudan, and he knew I wanted an elephant. Was I interested in being the first in?

Our party would consist of my good friend Richard Hawkins and my younger brother Don, who would be taking pictures, but I would be the only one hunting. Having been among the last trophy hunters to go into Kenya, I would now be among the first in many years to go into Sudan.

There were some advantages to being among the early hunting parties going into an area newly opened to visiting sportsmen. For instance, the outfitters would probably have to bring in new equipment. There was also not much question that, in contrast with my Kenya safari of the year before, the camp conditions would be primitive. There would be no white-coated waiters at the dinner table. The only thing we could rely on was that there would be plenty of unknowns. There was no way to foresee how terrifying some of those unknowns would be.

My professional hunter was Victor Cabral, an experienced elephant hunter from Mozambique. He had also hunted in Angola. The circumstances in Sudan might be new to him, but elephant hunting certainly was not. We did some sightseeing until the vehicles and equipment were ready, starting out with a boat ride in Khartoum to see the union of the White Nile and the Blue Nile. Then we toured the local historical sites. We took plenty of pictures, but they were not destined to come home with us.

Taken in thick forest, my elephant proved to be carrying ivory of 82 and 84 pounds, and both tusks were more than seven feet long.

People soon gathered at the elephant carcass to get a share of the meat. They cooked and ate some of it right there, and some was smoked for later use.

Safaris in the 1970s required more time than they do today because the camps were strictly temporary. All equipment and provisions had to be hauled overland between hunting areas along exceedingly poor roads, and transfers were slow.

Our first camp was not too far out of Khartoum. Victor was eager to take as many animals there as we could, as quickly as possible, so we would have plenty of time to hunt elephant and other difficult forest species, including bongo and yellow-backed duiker.

In that first area the game was unbelievably bountiful. We didn't know what to expect when we drove out at sunup for the first day's hunting, and we were prepared for the possibility that we wouldn't see many animals. When the safari began, I was astonished to find myself on the high rear seat of the Jeep, looking at a string of different game species, all feeding in the same spacious opening in the bush. From that one spot I shot trophies of seven species, and all of them made the record book. I took twenty-five animals in two and one-half days, including roan and bohor reedbuck. We certainly kept our skinners busy for a while.

When the time came to head south to Juba, our big truck set out ahead of us, and the two Jeeps stayed behind so I could hunt buffalo. The Jeep drivers would then hightail it to Juba while we flew down.

We came upon three buffalo bulls, one standing and two lying down. I shot the standing bull and brought it down. This brought the other two up. I shot a second, but it disappeared into the tall grass. Victor thought the bull was done for and intended to drive into the grass after it. This seemed dangerous to me, but Victor declared, "No problem, no problem," which we soon realized was his eternal refrain. I had two buffalo on

When we came upon the two elderly people living in this house, they were quite sick, apparently from overindulging on elephant meat.

my license, and he wanted me to get both quickly so we could move on to Juba. From there we would go into the forest country to hunt elephant.

Richard, with the video camera, was in the front of the Jeep, and Victor and I occupied the high rear seat with the big rifles. We kept tapping the driver on the shoulder with sticks to guide him because he could barely see beyond the nose of the Jeep in that high grass. I couldn't keep from objecting.

"Victor, this is crazy," I told him.

We had last seen the wounded buffalo near a lone tree, so we headed for the tree. When we arrived, the bull was still there, lying down, but we didn't realize that until it suddenly came up, ready to gore something. The nearest something was the front-seat passenger in the open, doorless Jeep. The bull looked as if it were about to jump right into the Jeep. It probably could have tipped the vehicle clean over.

Richard kept his head and captured on video the buffalo's last dramatic rush, just as Victor let loose with the .460 right over Richard's shoulder. He shot the buffalo in the neck. I shot as well, and the impact of the shots at such close quarters rolled the bull onto its back. By that stage, the video camera was pointing at the sky, its sound recorder capturing Richard's shouts. We were lucky our guns didn't blow out his eardrums.

A Jeep awaited us when we flew into the small town of Juba. The area had been quite prosperous during colonial times, with banana plantations and lumber operations that utilized a steam-powered mill, but the years of civil war following independence had taken their toll. We were a day late arriving at the village of Nzara, our designated meeting point, and our big supply truck was nowhere to be found. Worried, we asked the people at the local mission hospital if they had any news. The truck had been there, they told us, but the staff had been unable to find us, and it had turned back. This meant we had no tents or bedding, and we also had no food or gasoline.

Victor kept declaring, "No problem, no problem," although it was beginning to seem a miracle would be required to rescue the safari. The backup option was to rent a simple "furnished" rest house near the mission. The furniture consisted of wire-spring beds with dirty mattresses, a table, and four chairs—no bedding or utensils. We applied a modicum of DDT to the mattresses and bought all the supplies we could find for sale in the village—a box of crackers, one bowl, two spoons, two forks, a cup or two, and a big pot. The mission also supplied a little food, and we had to go there to fetch water because they had a water purifier. Victor said the truck should arrive in the morning and suggested we get some rest. We ate a few crackers and lay down in the DDT.

When the truck failed to appear the next day, we bought some rice and tea in the village market, Victor hired a local cook, and we went back to our beautiful home for a gourmet meal. All of us ate together out of our single bowl, two using forks, two using spoons. Although we resumed hunting, it turned out we would sleep at the rest house and eat mostly rice and local chickens for almost two weeks. I lost more than twenty pounds.

The drill at the local butchery, we discovered, was to bring in one cow each morning and butcher it. Once the meat was sold, there would be no more until the next day. It became part of our daily program to get in line each morning to buy some meat. Although this safari was supposedly the same kind we had undertaken in Kenya, with mobile tented camps, the contrast between our suddenly makeshift circumstances and the luxury of morning tea trays and daily laundry in Kenya was, shall we say, extreme.

"Look," said Victor. "Did you come here to hunt or to eat?" He told me I was too fat, anyway.

We did have a radio for daily communication at 5 P.M. with Victor's partner in Khartoum. The truck, we learned, had gone most of the way back before Victor's partner had contacted the driver and told him to return to Juba. The staff had encountered other snags, such as robbery and bribery, but we could expect them in a few days.

Less consoling was our discovery that the mission hospital where my brother was fetching our water was among the places coping with an outbreak of the deadly "green monkey fever"—the Ebola virus infection. Several people had died of it while we were in the area. I had spoken with the Centers for Disease Control in Atlanta about this, and they had assured me that the disease occurred only in a small, compact area. They said we would be OK, provided we got our shots and ate no raw food. We were shocked to realize that we were residents in precisely the small, compact area in question. Victor went over to the hospital to confer.

"No problem," he cheerfully told us upon his return. "Everyone who has died so far has eaten monkeys. We aren't eating any monkeys."

We remained uneasy, but we didn't seem to have many choices. It was all very well to adjust to the unexpected new arrangements, but we still needed gas if we were to get out and hunt. Victor improvised by approaching the local Sudanese soldiers and bargaining for five-gallon cans of gas, promising to return two cans for each one borrowed. One day we went out and shot a yellow-backed duiker, which ranked number six in the record book. By the time the truck finally arrived, we decided it would be easier to simply stay in our rented rest house than set up a full-scale camp, and Victor judged that we could begin hunting elephant, which was, after all, the reason we had come to Sudan.

The forest was so thick that tracking was all-important. Elephant tracks, I learned, can tell you something about ivory. An animal carrying heavy tusks makes deeper impressions along the leading edge of the tracks left by its front feet; the toenails dig deeper into the mud because of the weight up front. The trackers had found the promising spoor of a lone bull: average-size imprints with heavy indents, indicating good ivory. We set out at first light and followed the bull in the gathering heat as it meandered along, feeding. At times we went through deep mud. Victor thought the animal was likely to pause for a siesta around early afternoon, and then we would be able to catch up.

The vegetation was growing thicker. Our party included Don, Richard, Victor, three or four trackers, and a government game scout who was required to accompany us on the elephant hunt. A couple of men representing the local chief also came along to watch the proceedings. As we drew closer to the bull, the others hung back. Victor and I went into the final stalk with the head tracker and his small bag of ashes for testing the wind. We spent the last few yards of our approach crawling on our hands and knees because of the dense foliage. We could already hear the bull's stomach growling and its ears swishing.

Victor pointed to the brain. I would be on my knees, shooting up, and the trunk was in the way. In silent but inventive sign language, he conveyed that I should wait until the bull lowered its trunk and then deliver a brain shot. I waited, and then I shot. Victor immediately shot as a backup, and the bull came down onto its knees. The reason Victor shot was that the bull was practically on top of us. Had the animal moved forward at all, it would have been on us.

Then the fun started. The canopy was so thick and dark that it took us well over an hour to clear out enough of the thick vegetation even to shoot photos. The elephant was a good-looking bull with handsomely matched ivory. The bush telegraph quickly drew people to the scene, but it was too late in the day to start butchering. We left the game scout with his rifle and a couple of our trackers to watch over the carcass and guard the ivory while we returned to the village to celebrate.

No, there was no champagne. We had to find the beer peddler or, more accurately, pedaler. People smuggled in beer from the Congo by bicycle, a case of quart bottles at a time, each bearing a big buffalo on the label. It cost about five dollars a bottle. The smuggler collected the empties and pedaled back again for another load.

We returned the next morning to find the elephant bloated, and quite a crowd had gathered, including men, women, children, and dogs, all waiting for us to say, "Go!" First, they popped open the stomach, creating a memorable mess into which people swarmed with knives and hatchets, pushing and slashing to get the meat. The trunk, considered a delicacy, would go to the chief game scout. The heart and lungs, also considered prizes, went to the other men who had guarded the animal. Much of the meat went onto fires and was eaten right there. Then people went back, fighting for more. The dogs were local Basenjis, skinny and starving, and at one point I called a halt to the meat gathering until the dogs had been given some scraps. Everyone thought I was nuts.

The tusks proved to be 7 feet, 6 inches, and 7 feet, 8 inches and weighed 82 and 84 pounds, respectively. Elephant in the forested country typically bear longer, thinner ivory, with dark stains from mud and vegetation, whereas savanna elephant have shorter, thicker, and usually whiter tusks. We were glad to retreat from the fray to our rest house. People remained at the carcass for days, smoking the meat they didn't eat right away. They were delighted to have it to add to their usual diet of manioc.

Next up was bongo, never an easy species to hunt, given the heavy forest, steamy heat, and endless bugs of its jungle habitat. Our M.O. was to visit water holes and salt licks, looking for bongo spoor. Assisted by local trackers, we would follow any promising track we found. At one point, after a long drive, we came upon a hut occupied by two old people and saw a couple of elephant ribs leaning against the outside of the house.

"You don't suppose, so far away, that those are from my elephant, do you?" I asked Victor.

He was sure they were. The occupants were both quite sick, apparently from overindulging on the bonanza of elephant meat.

It was important to trail bongo as fast as possible. If the dew dried off the leaves and complicated the tracking, the secretive animals would be impossible to find in the thick forest. One morning we thought we had our bongo. We had seen a fleeting red shape, and once again we crawled on hands and knees to complete the stalk, only to find ourselves looking a big old forest hog square in the face. Two days later, we did creep up on the correct variety of red shape, and I shot a nice bongo bull. Although they are sturdily built, bongo seem to disappear like ghosts, which makes them really difficult to hunt. Today, hunters in some places use dogs for the tracking. The dogs can hold a bongo for a few minutes while the hunter moves in to shoot. Our hunt was styled the old way. I like to think of all that hard work as real bongo hunting.

By this time we'd definitely had enough adventure for one safari, but we weren't quite done. We were still scheduled to head out into the swamp country in search of species to be had nowhere else: Nile lechwe and white-eared kob. This time we would take just the two Jeeps to the land of the famously tall, naked Dinka and their big-horned Ankole cattle. The cattle graze at the edges of the great swampland, and the Dinka economy relies heavily on fishing and the consumption of dried fish.

As we drove into the village that was our destination, we encountered an amazing sight. Hundreds of people came to greet us, stark naked but also snow-white.

I wondered aloud, "Are they attacking us? Do we run?"

Victor said, "No problem, no problem, they're just coming to get a look at us."

The white body ornamentation was plastered on with grease and ash as protection against the stinging insects of the swamp, which were definitely impressive. So was the

When slogging through miles of swampy terrain to hunt Nile lechwe, it's good to have spear-wielding Dinka guides ahead and in the rear to look out for snakes.

stench. Words like rank and foul don't begin to describe how bad those people smelled.

Some of the Dinka were to go with us. They knew the swamps because they fished there with their barbed fishing spears. They would know where to find the lechwe. This was not a boating holiday. We would be slogging with difficulty through sometimes waist-deep water and mud. There were no crocodiles, but poisonous snakes were a possibility, and bloodsucking leeches were a certainty. Each of us was equipped with a spear for testing the water and for challenging any passing snakes. Some of our Dinka guides went ahead of us; others brought up the rear. I can't swim, so I was relieved to have both the spear and the company.

By the time we spotted lechwe, I was so exhausted from slogging through the swamp that I flat missed a series of shots. It was late afternoon and I was down to three bullets when I finally collected a bull. We saw plenty of white-eared kob, but, for some inexplicable reason, our government game scout told us there was no season on the species and we couldn't shoot one, even though it was on our license. There was no way to call the game department to confirm our right to shoot a kob, and Victor decreed that, under the circumstances, we had better not do it.

Wading back to the vehicles, it was heavy going again. When we struggled out of the water onto terra firma at last, we were all so glad to get out of there that we got down on our knees to kiss the dirt. Our legs were covered with leeches. The accepted remedy was to rub tobacco on them until they let go; if we simply pulled them off, the heads would remain in our skin.

A chartered airplane was to pick us up in the Dinka country, but the plane never arrived, and we couldn't make radio contact to find out why not. How long do you wait for a plane that doesn't appear? We should have realized then that we might be up against a situation more serious than the nonarrival of a supply truck. Victor declared we could make it back to Juba in twenty-four hours if we took turns driving and drove straight through. We had two Jeeps—one bearing us, the ivory, and the bongo and lechwe horns, the other carrying six staff. Did we have enough gas? We emptied all the lamp kerosene into our fuel tanks to beef up our chances of making it. The closer we could get to Juba, Victor said, the better off we would be, even if we ran out of gas. We had no inkling then that Juba itself would present us with a whole new set of hazards.

We drove all afternoon and into the night. The kerosene treatment blew the engine on one of the Jeeps because kerosene burns hot, so we poured all the fuel into the tank of the other Jeep and towed the crippled one. When the second engine began to overheat, still some six hours out of Juba, Victor decided to abandon the crippled Jeep, leave the staff to guard it, and go on in the remaining vehicle. He planned to send out a rescue party once we reached Juba. We limped on all through the next day, pausing often to refill the radiator and nurse the Jeep along. Just before dark, grimy and grubby after being in the bush for two weeks and on the road for two days, we approached a bridge on the outskirts of the town.

Imagine our surprise when, just as we thought we'd made it, the army confronted us at the bridge, pointing loaded machine guns right at us. They might have been forgiven for thinking we were poachers, filthy as we were, in a Jeep festooned with horns and ivory.

Victor and the soldiers hastily held a high-level conference.

"No problem," Victor said when he returned to us. "I told them you are hunters and we have a house in town, and they said there's some trouble—go to your house and stay there."

With considerable relief, we settled in to celebrate our return to the Juba base with a shower, a delicious dinner of roast warthog, and a welcome night in comfortable quarters. But the sense of relief was short-lived. The night proved brief in the rest department. That was the night Richard thought he was hearing firecrackers. Soon enough, we all realized that what we were hearing was the rattle of small arms and machine-gun fire. Peace in Sudan had evidently come to an end yet again. It was becoming clear why no plane had arrived to pick us up after the swamp hunt. We were thrust into a scare much larger than a virus or an approaching band of white-plastered Dinka. This time even no-problem Victor was ready to acknowledge that there was, in fact, a problem.

"They're shooting outside," he said. "Don't be looking out the windows."

The gunfire went on all night. Not knowing what it meant, all we could do was hold tight and figure out how to stave off fear. At first light an army officer, who knew we had guns in the place, came to the house. The rebels had taken down the radio station, he said, and they had shot up the airport, but the army was in the process of dislodging them. The town was in chaos. We were to stay in the house and keep our guns locked up. As the day advanced, we heard drunken soldiers in the market, shooting in the air and shooting up yards. Nobody seemed to be in charge. It was hard to shake the feeling that if either the rebels or the drunken soldiers knew we were there, they would probably come in to take us out.

We learned that some rebels had been killed at the bridge where the army had stopped us before reclaiming it. At that stage there was still fighting at the other bridge entering the town. I think that if we had come in just an hour later, after dark, we probably would have been shot without anyone wasting words on who we were or why we were there.

The officer returned in the evening to tell us that the army had killed twenty or thirty rebels and had taken about fifteen prisoners. In the morning the prisoners would be flown to Khartoum to be executed, in order to show others what would happen if they tried to overthrow the government. That was the plane we had hoped to take to Khartoum.

By morning, things had quieted down somewhat. At the airport we found bullet holes in the walls, windows shot out, and the runways lined with soldiers alongside the wreckage of burned and burning hulks of airplanes. There we were, four white people trying to look inconspicuous among hundreds of Sudanese. When the big jet came in, and out walked the vice president and his entourage, all eyes were on us. Aides inquired what we were doing there, and they quickly assured us that nobody but the prisoners was going anywhere near that plane.

We were obviously destined to spend another night in Juba. We returned to the airport the next day and were the sole passengers on the only flight out. Victor had done a great job of playing Mr. Cool all through our pioneering safari in a country where people knew more about war than about trophy hunting, but a little more cool was still required. Upon arriving in Khartoum, we found ourselves ambushed by cameras and microphones. Reporters asked what we knew about this revolt so far away from the nerve centers of the world. We were the only non-officials who had come out of there. We had to shove our way through the besieging media to reach a taxi. The policy we adopted was: "I didn't see nothin', I don't know nothin', and I ain't sayin' nothin.'"

I told Victor I wanted a flight out of Khartoum as soon as possible, going anywhere at all. By then, word of the new Sudanese upheaval was being broadcast to the world, and we were late getting out. Our families were growing panicky, having received no word from us and having no way to check on our whereabouts. Victor found us a Sudanese Airways flight to Rome. We abandoned our old airline tickets, bought new ones, and fled.

Around that time we really started to get scared and jittery over all the things that could have happened. Machine guns were everywhere. We could have been shot at the bridge. We could have been shot in the house in Juba by the drunks, or at the airport. And who would have cared? Miraculously, the only real casualty we suffered was that, somewhere in the confusion, the briefcase containing most of our film got left behind in a taxi. Before drowning our retrospective fears on the flight, we discovered that Sudanese Airways flight attendants wouldn't accept Sudanese money for cocktails! "Dollars only, please."

Victor had to get out of Sudan shortly afterward, when hunting closed again. And, can you believe it, he even managed to have all my trophies sent to me in Texas.

Kneeling with my lechwe are PH Victor Cabral (left) and Richard Hawkins; the tall Dinkas are a fishing people.

The world of Portuguese professional hunters was a small one. Most of them had killed elephant and buffalo by the hundreds for meat and ivory, and, during the late 1970s, several found their way to the Central African Republic, which became a kind of last frontier for hunting great tuskers. Victor went to work for Bert Klineburger, setting up a primitive hunting camp for clients who wanted to try for big ivory. In 1978 I would succumb to that temptation and hunt the C.A.R.

Victor visited us in Houston a couple of times, and he wound up living and working in Mexico. Years later, Richard Hawkins would be among those who came to California to be in the audience the night I received the Weatherby Award in 1991. I was glad to have him there. He was one of the crew who had shared all our meals out of the same bowl for days in a far corner of Sudan, and he had shared the unnerving business of circumventing the flames and gunfire of insurrection.

Safely on the ground in Rome, we secured a cab driver to take us out on the town. Our cabbie explained to our restaurant host what excitement our last few days had held, and the restaurateur took us on a privileged visit to the kitchen to watch our dinner being prepared. After all those meager meals consisting mainly of rice, we so overdid it on steak and lobster that we all wound up nearly as sick as the elderly couple who had feasted on the elephant ribs. It only goes to show that, despite all appearances to the contrary, and despite the drastic differences among us, in some ways people are pretty much the same everywhere.

I enjoyed both Christmas and New Year in hunting camps with PH Eric Stockenstroom during my C.A.R. elephant safari. My one-tusk elephant was enormous: 8 feet, 6 inches long and 98 pounds.

Chapter 9

Quest for a Hundred-Pounder

Central African Republic, 1978

We had just returned to our boat and were crossing a tributary called the Chinko River to set ourselves up on the opposite bank. There we would have a good view of the comings and goings at a natural salt lick. As we walked along a riverside game trail in single file, one of the trackers up front started shouting and waving his spear. I could not understand one word of his rapid-fire delivery.

"Don't move. Don't move," hissed my professional hunter in the C.A.R., Eric Stockenstroom.

I didn't know whether we had found a lion, a leopard, an elephant, or what. Should I be getting ready to shoot, climb, or run? The crisis turned out to be a puff adder right in the middle of the trail. This is one of Africa's most dangerous snakes, common in wide areas and in many kinds of habitat. The puff adder eats small mammals and ground birds, and a game trail is a great place for an ambush. The species has a reputation for freezing and holding its ground when encountered, instead of departing. I never did see the snake. As we all stood motionless, it wisely moved out of our way.

"That's why we've got you in the middle of the line," said Eric.

Hunters of a certain age remember the excitement surrounding the Central African Republic in the late 1970s, during the bad old days of Emperor Jean-Bédel Bokassa. Most of us had scarcely heard of the C.A.R.

before Bert Klineburger got to work opening up the country for hunting the large tuskers in its equatorial forests. After that, the country entered the limelight for a time.

Landlocked C.A.R. borders Chad, Sudan, Cameroon, the Republic of the Congo, and the Democratic Republic of the Congo. The equatorial forest lies in the south, and most of the country is in the basins of the Ubangi-Shari Rivers. The Shari flows north into Lake Chad, and the Ubangi flows south into the great Congo River. You can read all about Bert's pioneering in the C.A.R. in his *International Hunter: 1945–1999, Hunting's Greatest Era* (1999). He and his wife moved there in 1975, bought out the outfitter Claude Vasselet, and secured several hunting concessions. The roads, as Bert notes in his book, were "anything from bad to terrible." His concessions included the area where the Shari River and the Bahr Aouk River (known simply as the Aouk) meet. There was one on the Chinko River and another where the Chinko and Vovodo Rivers join. Bert's home alongside the Ubangi River was on the edge of the city of Bangui and served as headquarters for his safari company, SACAF.

Bokassa was a very bad dude—your classic dictator. Orphaned as a child in what was then the French colony of Ubangi-Shari, he joined the Free French Forces in World War II and became a sergeant major. In 1964, after the colony had gained independence and was renamed the C.A.R., he joined its new army, rose to the rank of colonel, and soon became chief of staff of the armed forces. Early in 1966 he took over the country in a coup. He would abolish its constitution and rule by decree until 1976, when he declared the C.A.R. a monarchy. Apparently modeling himself after Napoleon, in December 1977 he proclaimed himself Emperor Bokassa I and held an enthronement ceremony costing millions in what remains one of the poorest countries in Africa.

Nothing is too hard to believe about Bokassa. While almost everyone else was starving, he got his water from gold faucets. Despite his apparent insanity and the brutality of his regime, he retained a degree of French support by shipping France the uranium it needed for nuclear energy and weapons of mass destruction. Reportedly, he also took French President Valéry Giscard d'Estaing out hunting and gave him diamonds at strategic intervals.

I arrived in the C.A.R. for a twenty-one-day hunt while Bokassa was still in power, just a year after his big enthronement party; my safari dates were 16 December 1978 to 10 January 1979. Professional hunter Adelino Pires, formerly of Mozambique, had gone to the C.A.R. earlier that year to take over from Bert. Like all the other PHs in Mozambique, Adelino had to fold up his operation in the mid-1970s, when the former Portuguese colony's move toward independence brought civil war, and he went to Sudan. (My guide in Sudan in 1977, Victor "No Problem" Cabral, had left the Portuguese colony of Angola under similar circumstances.) Several other PHs from Mozambique who knew elephant hunting wound up in the C.A.R., where the newly advertised specialty was elephant bearing hundred-pound ivory. If you wanted a big one, that was the place to go.

Arriving in Bangui, the capital of the C.A.R., I was taken to SACAF headquarters. I was to hunt first with Adelino's son, Tim-Tim. The main camp and airstrip were on the Aouk River, which is the border between the C.A.R. and Chad. I knew from the beginning that we would be using truly minimal fly camps, and most of my accommodations would be primitive. Even so, the cost of hunting in the C.A.R. was high because the country's road network was inadequate. Vehicle parts and fuel were wildly expensive, and just about everything had to be flown into hunting camps. At the Aouk main camp, an airstrip had been cut into the forest to serve a series of outlying base camps operated by individual professionals.

The timing of my hunt meant I got there just before the normal safari season opened on the first of the year. Six of the professionals were in and out of the Aouk main camp, busy setting up their individual base camps for the season. Tim-Tim was hunting out of a camp called Vovodo, also on the Aouk River. The river was the border; the opposite bank was in Chad. The day I arrived, Tim-Tim suggested we take an afternoon spin and spend some time out with the camera, just looking over the game. He

When we chanced upon a lion during the first two hours out of camp, I had only my 7mm magnum with me, but my PH recommended that I take the cat.

I shot my great one-tusk elephant bull when it unexpectedly appeared near this natural salt lick on the Chinko River.

did recommend bringing the rifle in case we saw good western kob. My license included two kob. He said game was plentiful because antelope were being pushed into the C.A.R. to avoid the unrest in Chad, and lion were crossing the river to hunt the antelope.

What we saw that day was impressive in both quality and quantity. As we drove up alongside the river, Tim-Tim spotted a good kob and suggested I take it, which I did. We drove a little farther and saw a steenbok, which he also suggested I shoot. After we turned around to go back to camp, we saw a kob that Tim-Tim said was even better than the first—I should take that, too. He was right on all counts. Both those kob made the record book, and the second scored significantly higher than the first.

As you can imagine, I was mighty pleased with the results of what was supposed to have been a little afternoon drive. There was more action to come. As we drove on toward our camp, we came upon a good-looking lion. All I had was my 7mm magnum, but Tim-Tim recommended I take the cat. The lion was hunting a kob when I hit it the first time, and I hit it a second time before it could escape into the bush. This was a pretty astonishing start to my C.A.R. safari. Scarcely two hours after getting into camp, I had four trophies, all of which made the book, and one of them was a lion!

The next day I took a northwestern buffalo. Altogether, out of that first camp I collected Lelwel hartebeest, topi, sing-sing waterbuck, steenbok, bush

The state of my hunting clothes says it all: Getting a giant forest hog is not easy!

duiker, oribi, warthog, and reedbuck, in addition to the lion, kob, and buffalo.

The area had a good population of lion. One day Tim-Tim proposed popping along the river to have lunch at a camp called Njoko. The PH there was guiding an Italian client and his wife. Like the other base camps, this one operated its own vegetable garden, so it had fresh produce. Between freshly caught fish from the river (delicious, big Nile perch), game meat, and garden vegetables, it was possible to cater to clients, staff, and even visitors like us.

We had seen a lion on our way there, and as we drove back to our own camp after lunch, we saw another great-big lion with a beautiful mane, just lazing in the grass. We took pictures and radioed the Italian client to get out there; he had been trying for lion for several days without success. This lion didn't seem inclined to move off and showed no sign of fear. Apparently, it had not encountered vehicles or hunters before. We were still there when the Italian arrived with quite an entourage—his wife, his PH, trackers, and a film cameraman. Everybody got a great look at the lion. Once the Italian began a stalk, the big male stood up and gave a desultory growl. It was just beginning to move off when the rifle boomed.

Salt Lick Bull

Next up was a plan to spend three or four days hunting elephant from a fly camp on the same river. The camp could only be reached by boat. Now I was in the hands of Eric Stockenstroom and three trackers, and I was at the mercy of an unbelievable quantity of biting insects. The camp consisted of only a few boards, hung with a tarp and some netting to protect us from the endless, whining hordes of mosquitoes. We ate inside the lean-to, under the net, to prevent the insects from eating us alive. The shower consisted of a bucket on a rope slung over a branch, with some brush underneath to stand on while someone dumped the water over you. The conditions began to make my stay in Sudan seem like the Ritz-Carlton.

From there we took a boat trip on the Chinko River to a natural salt lick where the bank became an overhang, almost like a cave. We were armed with the 8mm movie camera, to film game coming to the lick, and the .375, in case we needed to discourage any hippo. Hippo were crowding the river near the lick, so we went ashore some distance before the lick and walked in for close-up photos of the scrapings and diggings the animals had made. That was the walk on which we had disturbed the puff adder. Eric said elephant did visit the mineral lick, but they were usually cows and calves.

For a while we enjoyed watching the hippo in the river and some buffalo that visited the lick. All of a sudden, as I was filming, I saw a humongous tusk. An elephant had silently materialized. The grass was so high that I could scarcely see the owner of the tusk until the elephant reached up to get some leaves with its trunk. At that moment the giant tusk filled my view.

"I'm looking at the same thing you're looking at," said Eric. "We never expect to see bulls here."

The animal only had one tusk, but Eric was confident it would go over one hundred pounds. It was time for a conference. Did I want an elephant that was a hundred-pounder, even if it had only one tusk? Or did I want to hold out for matched ivory that might only reach eighty-five pounds? I decided I wanted this bull—I had a spot above a doorway in mind for a beautiful lone tusk, and I already had a fine matched set of ivory from Sudan. Next question: We were armed only with the .375. Could I see the bull well enough amid the grass and branches to shoot it from across the river? I thought I could, if the bull was broadside.

"Shoot him right in the shoulder," Eric instructed, adding that if the tusk didn't go over one hundred pounds, we could carry on with our elephant hunting.

I put in the solids and hit the bull square in the shoulder, then hit it twice more. The elephant disappeared. Soon we heard a great crash as it collapsed.

Now we ran into snags. We knew the elephant was down, but we couldn't get there easily because of the hippo in the river, and it was growing quite late in the day. Eric's decision was to head on back to our mosquito nets and return the next day for the ivory. Maybe the hippo would be gone. More action awaited us, however. En route back to camp a buffalo threatened us from the riverbank, and I collected my northwestern buffalo. The C.A.R. had been bountiful for me a second time. We had not yet spent a night in our fly camp, and I had already collected an elephant and a buffalo!

In the morning we retraced our river route. We stopped where the buffalo had fallen to take pictures and cape it out. It proved to be a very good bull. We had agreed that the bull certainly looked like a hundred-pounder, but after we retrieved the ivory, the scale revealed that magnificent tusk weighed just under one hundred pounds—98, to be exact. It measured 8 feet, 6 inches. We decided we would continue hunting elephant the next day.

Hunting out of the fly camp was a pretty taxing affair. The only easy way to get around was along the river. The forest itself contained no roads and no trails except game trails. We were walking and sweltering, sweltering and walking, and the bugs made every hour a trying one.

Lady Caroline was a giant forest hog piglet rescued during the safari. She flourished as a camp mascot, following us around like a dog.

Taking a Lord Derby eland with 38-inch horns on New Year's Eve was a fine cause for celebration.

Even in forest openings the grass would sometimes be up to our chins. We took off at first light with three trackers. I saw fifteen or twenty more elephant bulls with ivory around eighty-five pounds.

At one point we were mock-charged by a youngish bull, probably a seventy-pounder. It extended its ears forward and threw up its trunk, then kicked up the dirt. Eric said if the bull came any closer, we would have to shoot. We kept backing up as the uneasy bull threw dirt around. Finally, it turned, shook its head, and made off, evidently deciding it had scared us enough.

We were following a game trail through high grass when we more or less ran into two giant forest hog. They were coming directly toward us on the same trail, and they got about as much of a fright as we did when we figured out we were on a collision course. In the ensuing confusion, we didn't understand why one hog came for us while the other departed.

"Shoot!" yelled Eric, and I dropped the charging hog.

Later, we saw that the hog had stepped on a piglet and broken its leg, adding piteous squeals to the melee, and that there was also a second baby. That was why the sow had charged us.

We couldn't leave the intact piglet behind, so we caught it and popped it into a backpack to take it back to camp. We took pictures of the fallen hog but didn't cape it out. Back then, I had no idea how rare it was to encounter a giant forest hog or how difficult it is to collect one.

Lost in Dense Vegetation

Darkness was not far off. We had been wandering all over the area, and I gradually realized that we were definitely lost. When your companions start conducting extended conversations in languages you don't understand, it's a fair guess that you're in trouble. I have never known native guides to get lost before or since, but jungle conditions do qualify as a special case. No landmarks are visible in the thick stuff, and the stars don't do much good, either. We needed to get back to the river and stay near it to reach our boat. Game trails near the river make for easier walking. Then again, when wandering in thick forest in darkness—with buffalo coming down to drink, lion after the buffalo, and hippo coming out of the water to graze—the river is just about the last place you want to be. Our best bet was to make plenty of noise as we went along so we wouldn't surprise a buffalo or hippo.

As we walked, we stopped from time to time to fire off a shot and listen, hoping somebody at our camp was listening and would fire an answering shot to help guide us. We heard nothing, so we walked some more and shot again. For hours we walked, paused, shot, and listened. For some time we walked through bush that had been burned, leaving us blackened with soot. It looked as though we'd have little alternative but to stay out all night, with no matches, no gear, and mosquitoes feasting on all the bits not covered by shorts or tennis shoes. At long last, one of our shots did elicit a response, very faint and distant. It was coming from behind us. We had been walking in precisely the wrong direction. We turned and set off toward where the answering shot had been fired.

It was midnight before we finally reached our boat and crossed the river to our camp, a few yards away. I was never so glad to see a boat in my life. By then, I was so dehydrated and delirious that I couldn't even walk unaided, and my memory of it all is quite vague. I had Africans supporting me at each elbow, practically dragging me along. We had been out in the hundred-degree heat since dawn. Our small canteen of water was gone by noon, and we'd had nothing to eat—we hadn't planned to be out all day. The others drank from the river, but I was not fixing to try that. All I could think was I'd give anything for a cold beer. Two fellows had to hold me up under the so-called shower while a third poured a bucket of water over me to wash off the worst of my coating of ash and soot. They got me inside the little shelter, and I was so exhausted that I slept for twenty-four hours.

The cook was the man who had heard our shots. As the night advanced and we failed to appear, and our shots came from farther and farther away, he realized we were lost. Luckily, there was a rifle in the camp with which he could give us a signal. He had a big, welcoming fire roaring when we struggled in. When I came back to life, Eric had a question. Was I was interested in going back out to hunt some more elephant? I told him I thought the one I had already got was probably quite good enough.

The Aouk main camp seemed downright luxurious after the death march. There were concrete floors and a veggie garden! We dubbed the wild piglet Lady Caroline. Energetic and responsive, she got along fine on mush, and after we returned to the main camp, someone miraculously arranged goat's milk for her as well. She soon doubled in size. She followed us around like a dog.

Several professional hunters were still there, preparing for clients to come in, so we had a sociable time playing cards in the evenings. Christmas must have fallen in there somewhere, though we scarcely noticed it. Lady Caroline stuck right in the mess tent with us, and three incoming German hunters afforded us a little extra entertainment with a .500 Nitro. Their PH wanted to know how well they could shoot their spanking-new big guns before he took them out into the forest, where much of the shooting is inevitably at close range. He painted a black circle on a cardboard box and nailed the box to a tree about fifty feet away. One hunter missed the circle, missed the tree, missed the box—he clean missed the whole rig.

"That's all right," said the PH. "You're just a little nervous. Calm down. Let's try getting you a shooting rest."

They got him a rest, but he missed again. Then they enlarged the black circle, but still the client couldn't hit it, although he claimed to have been shooting wild boar on the run in Europe. The PH encouraged him to try one more shot, and this time he hit a corner of the cardboard, just nicking the box.

"Purrfect," said the gallant PH. "The elephant is a big animal. You'll have no problem."

I suppose the PH figured encouragement might have more positive results than more target practice. He also knew the rest of us couldn't be relied upon to contain ourselves much longer.

The Lord Derby eland was our next project. Though it seems a fairly slow and lumbering beast, this animal can be hard work to hunt. On New Year's Eve we picked up a track right at first light. The company was planning to send a plane for us late that day and fly everyone to Bangui for a celebration in town. We walked our legs off tracking that bull. Several times we lost the track for a while, then found it again and kept going. We jumped some other animals along the way, including what looked like a trophy roan antelope, but I wasn't going to shoot anything else and risk my chances of getting the eland. Around 2 P.M. our moment came. We found the bull lying down for a rest in tall, heavy grass. It jumped up, and we could see that it would score well in the book. I shot twice. The horns proved up at 38 inches.

We rushed back to camp to take a shower and were all set for the jaunt into Bangui when headquarters radioed to tell us that the plane was out of action. Instead, we opened a bottle of champagne and had a fine dinner of eland steaks to welcome in the new year and drink a toast to a great Lord Derby eland. My safari had produced nineteen animals, fourteen of which made the record book, including a gray duiker, a waterbuck that scored 32 inches, and a topi that ranked as the new No. 1. The final days of the safari were mostly an opportunity to kick back and enjoy the wealth of game in the area, and I hunted wild dog and bushbuck.

Ousted later in 1979, Bokassa fled the country and for a few years divided his time between the Ivory Coast and France. He mysteriously returned to the C.A.R. from exile in 1986. He was tried for embezzlement, treason, torture, murdering political opponents, and cannibalism, not necessarily in that order. Although he was sentenced to death, his sentence was later changed to life imprisonment; he wasn't found guilty on the cannibalism charges. In 1993 he emerged from prison when a general amnesty released all prisoners. The C.A.R.'s former emperor would die of a heart attack in 1996.

The C.A.R. continued to roil, suffering bouts of bloodletting and mutiny and additional coups in 1991, 2001, and 2003. The legacy of decades of unrest is a country bristling with corruption, illegal weapons, armed groups, and thousands of people displaced across its borders, especially into Chad. If you want to know more about the place, take a look at *The Winds of Havoc,* coauthored by Adelino Pires and Fiona Capstick (2001).

The period of prime elephant hunting would be short-lived. Organized poaching gangs quickly moved in with machine guns and decimated the elephant. Local people earned hundreds of dollars for ivory, while the merchants who hauled it away on donkeys, pack mules, and even camels resold it for thousands. There were no game scouts to halt the massacre. Elephant hunting was closed. According to Adelino, a hundred-pounder taken in February 1980 by John Shumway of Houston (pictured with it in *Winds of Havoc)* was the last elephant to be legally taken on a hunting license before the closure. The C.A.R. still has its rain forests, and it remains an important hunting country today. The species of interest are Lord Derby eland, bongo, and western greater kudu, in addition to buffalo, lion, leopard, and plains game.

I was struck by the absence of people in the C.A.R. Most of the areas I hunted had no roads, no villages, no people. We saw no one else during our days afield. One wonders what those places are like now, some thirty years later. Emptier? Fuller? Wars and rebellions are usually bad for elephant and other living things, although unrest sometimes drives people away and allows natural habitat to persist. This leaves the potential for game populations to rebound and perhaps even to flourish again in due course. We can hope for that.

PH Russ Broom's instincts proved right on the mark when dealing with a wounded leopard.

Chapter 10

Close Call Leopard

Zambia and Zimbabwe, 1983

As long as I live, I'll never forget the night of the leopard. I couldn't sleep or enjoy the night sounds of the bush. All I could do was lie awake, worrying about the big leopard I had shot out of the bait tree at sundown. Instead of piling up at the base of the tree, as leopard are supposed to do when exposed to the killing end of a .375 H&H Magnum, the cat had disappeared, leaving a marginal blood trail.

"We can't follow him tonight. Not in this tall grass," said my PH and good friend Russ Broom. "We'll let him stiffen up, and we'll get him in the morning."

Russ didn't say it, but I knew what he was thinking: Now we would have a dangerous tracking job on our hands. If the wound was slight, would we find the leopard before it found us? If the wound was substantial, would we find the leopard before the hyenas did?

We were in Zambia's Luangwa Valley, and it was October 1983—the end of the dry season. Game was concentrated along the Luangwa River, not far from our camp. Known for its good leopard population, the area also held buffalo, lion, and some distinctive trophy species not widely available elsewhere, such as Cookson wildebeest and puku.

I had taken a leopard in Kenya in the 1970s, but now, in completing my second Big Five, I wanted a better one. When making safari plans with Russ and his dad, Geoff Broom, I had specified that I wanted a record-book cat, the kind you dream about. Geoff and I had talked at the Houston Safari Club show and then at the Game Coin meeting, and we finalized arrangements at the Safari Club International show in Las Vegas. I chose Geoff because he was willing to construct a safari that began in the Luangwa Valley, took in the Bangweulu Swamp and the Kafue Flats (also in Zambia), and concluded with a few days in the Matetsi area of Zimbabwe.

Soon after I arrived in the Luangwa camp, we began to put out baits. Within a couple of days, leopard had taken apart three of our six baits. I remember Russ and his two trackers squatting in the dry grass beneath the baits, looking for signs that would tell them which leopard we should hunt. The location they picked was being visited by a large, older male. By all appearances, the cat was an aggressive feeder, eating huge chunks of meat each night. We built a blind, a natural-looking construction of grass and shaggy brush, and replenished the bait by hanging a freshly shot warthog. The next evening, after things settled down a bit, we would hunt.

On that first afternoon in the blind, I had great expectations. I was confident, and Russ also seemed confident, that the leopard would come that day, before

Geoff Broom guided me to a world-record tsessebe in the Bangweulu Swamp. Our thirteen days in Zambia produced eighteen animals of fourteen species.

dark. After hours of nervous apprehension, daylight faded to dusk, and the cat never materialized. In the still of the African evening, we heard the truck engine start up. Soon headlights pierced the darkness, headed our way. We boarded and went back to camp.

For the next four days we followed the same program. In the mornings we checked the baits, finding that lion had fed at some and leopard at others. We would replenish the baits as needed. Each afternoon saw us stationed in the blind from about 3 P.M., reading a book, trying to be as quiet as possible. When that leopard visited, I told myself, I would not be the one who scared the old boy off with a careless noise. My view of Africa was a hole in the blind through which I could see a half-eaten warthog buzzing with flies—not a very scenic picture. It got dark around 6 P.M. We would leave the blind around 6:15 P.M., and the next morning the bait would be gone.

As we sat around the campfire after dinner on the fourth night, Russ announced our strategy for the next evening.

"That leopard must know we're near the bait," he said. "He's waiting for the truck to take us away before he comes to feed, and I just thought of the answer to our problem. We'll have the driver start the truck fifteen minutes before the last of the good light and drive away. Then, if what I'm thinking is right, the cat will come."

I confess I didn't believe the plan would work, but I didn't have a better idea. I've also learned that it's usually wiser not to question the hunting strategies of an experienced guide who cut his teeth hunting dangerous game.

The next evening, with daylight to spare, Russ's driver started up the truck and rumbled away. The minutes ticked by and the air cooled as dusk began to settle over the bush. I stowed my book, repositioned myself so I could spring into action, and checked the readiness of the .375. Our eyes ached into the dimming light as we waited. I was still thinking the trick wouldn't work when Russ tapped me on the shoulder.

"There he is," he whispered, "on the branch next to the bait."

How could I have missed the leopard's arrival, and then its leap onto the branch where the bait was wired? The cat had made its approach in absolute silence, like a spotted ghost. I got behind the .375, its forestock nestled in the V of the shooting rest. I found the leopard in the scope. It was getting darker by the second. I found a rosette, or thought I did, in the vicinity of the leopard's vitals. The last thing I heard before squeezing the rifle's light trigger was the leopard tearing meat from the warthog carcass and crunching bone.

The Bangweulu, Kafue, and Zambezi

Our plan was to hunt for sixteen species on a seventeen-day safari. The thirteen days in Zambia would produce eighteen animals of fourteen species, most of which would make it into the SCI records and some of which made Rowland Ward. Among the trophies were reedbuck, hippo, warthog, buffalo, zebra, Lichtenstein hartebeest, sitatunga, black lechwe, puku, Cookson wildebeest, and hyena.

In the Bangweulu Swamp I was fortunate to take a tsessebe that proved to be a new world record, exceeding the best tsessebe taken out of Zambia by 2¼ inches. We then drove for six hours to reach the Kafue Flats, picking up a game warden en route, and I took my Kafue lechwe before flying to Victoria Falls in Zimbabwe to get elephant and sable in the four days left. Geoff had gone ahead to the Victoria Falls camp, and Russ had stayed in Zambia to see to the trophies.

Drought had concentrated the elephant near the Zambezi River, and I saw about forty bulls during my first afternoon in Zimbabwe, all thirty- to forty-pounders. You may wonder why I would go after ivory that size when I already had much larger trophies. I knew some local carvers who specialized in elephant scenes and others who specialized in buffalo scenes, and I had bought some small pieces. Now I wanted to get some carving done on ivory I had collected myself—an elephant herd on one tusk and a buffalo herd on the other.

We hunted for sable for two days without success, then on the third day we switched our attention back to elephant. Selecting a group of three bulls, we set about our stalk. I never could get a head shot at the biggest of the three, which had ivory close to forty pounds a side. Eventually, the bull presented a broadside view, and I shot it in the heart. (It would take the two carvers four months each to complete the scenes I commissioned them to produce on the bull's tusks.)

Two big trucks came in to haul away the meat. This was one of the important differences between hunting savanna elephant in Zimbabwe and the jungle hunts of Sudan and the C.A.R.

In this instance, hunting elephant proved easier than hunting sable. I wanted two matching sable bull mounts to flank the entry to my trophy room. In Zambia we had seen perhaps a hundred sable, but no old, dark trophy bulls. Geoff said not to worry—we'd find our sable in Zimbabwe. On the final day of the safari we proceeded to the Brooms' home. Geoff said he had never been skunked on sable on his own ranch. He had good sable, and plenty of them.

We set out early but simply couldn't find a good sable all day long, let alone two of them. It was after 5:30 P.M. and I had pretty well given up on the quest when a bull jumped up in front of the truck and took off down into a riverbed. I grabbed the 7mm, ran over, and got a rest on a tree. My bullet was deflected by a branch, and the sable departed.

Geoff was shaking his head.

Canoeing through the swamp was a good deal more comfortable than my experience of slogging through Sudan on foot.

"We finally find you a sable, and you shoot a tree," he declared.

Now I really had written off getting this trophy. Apparently I was going to have to come back another time. Within minutes, as we rounded a bend in the track, we came across more sable.

"Jeez, there's another one! Hurry!" Geoff urged.

The big bull was some way off, but we were able to sneak closer as dusk fell. Getting into range behind a bush, with flies buzzing around my nose, eyes, and mouth, I used Geoff's shoulder as a rest.

I hit the selected bull well, but it got up and moved off. I hit it again as it was going away. We had to track the bull briefly. It was just about dark when we found it lying under a bush and dispatched it with a shot in the neck. It was a fine old bull, growing grizzled about the muzzle, with well-worn teeth. The horns were forty-plus inches, with heavy bases. You can't get your fist between those horns at the tips.

Russ Broom was still a youngster learning the trade when I took this safari. Today he runs a large safari operation based out of Zimbabwe. Geoff was among those who had his property expropriated in the Mugabe-era land grabs. He had a beautiful ranch house overlooking a dam he had built. From the veranda you could watch a steady parade of wildlife coming in to drink. Someone

PH Geoff Broom and I pose with my Zimbabwe elephant. I commissioned local artisans to carve game scenes on these tusks. See page 238.

I used Geoff's shoulder as a rest to shoot my fine old sable bull.

in government wanted to enjoy the facilities, but Geoff decided he was going to leave the place just the way he had found it. He bulldozed it all before he climbed into his plane and left.

The Morning After

Geoff's toughness of mind in destroying what he had built was mirrored in his son Russ, as I learned back in Zambia after I shot the big leopard tom. The cat was badly wounded, but it had not conveniently succumbed to my shot. We were going to have to track it. I was awake and dressed when Russ's assistant entered my tent to wake me the morning after the excitement at the leopard bait. We made the drive to the scene in silence. At first light we were looking for sign. Russ had a double-barreled shotgun loaded with 00, I had the .375, and one of the four trackers was armed with my old reliable 7mm Remington Magnum. We wouldn't be doing this, I thought, if I had stuck with the old 7mm magnum, my companion on so many hunts.

The blood trail, though sparse, led through chest-high grass to a dry streambed. We moved slowly, gaining little ground but getting a good idea where the leopard might be hiding. We were all on pins and needles. Tracking any wounded animal is extremely dangerous work, and leopard are specialists in ambush. Any step could have produced a big, angry cat. Professional hunters know they must take charge at moments like this; the client wants to finish off the cat, but the PH is responsible for everyone's safety.

As we proceeded, the tension mounted. The creekbed opened into a ravine with huge boulders, any of which could have hidden the wounded tom. Instead of trying to walk through that rough stuff, Russ opted for us to climb the bank and look for the cat from the edge of the ravine. Looking down from the bank, we tossed a few sticks into the streambed, trying to get the cat to move.

A few hundred yards from the point where we had climbed up the bank, one of those massive southern African termite mounds jutted from the lip of the gully. We climbed the rock-hard mound and searched for the leopard from this vantage point. Not a sign. We descended from the mound and had walked perhaps fifty steps farther when Russ stopped us.

"That leopard is somewhere in there," he said, gesturing back toward the point where the creekbed opened into the ravine. "I know we walked past him. His hideout can't be far from the bait—remember how quickly he made it after the truck started last night?"

We backtracked, with me on one bank of the ravine and the armed tracker on the other. Russ and the remaining trackers moved cautiously along the streambed, looking for any sign on the dry rocks. As we approached the termite mound we had just climbed to scan for the leopard, I suddenly saw a yellow blur streaking away from me, down toward Russ and the trackers.

"Here he comes!" I heard a tracker yell.

Then came the boom of Russ's shotgun. The cat stumbled but kept coming, and Russ hit it again. By the time I made it to the bottom of the ravine, the trackers were already whooping. At Russ's feet was a beautiful leopard he had shot in mid-leap, a seven-footer that made the book. If Russ's instincts had been half a second slower, the outcome of the charge might have been an altogether different story. As it was, I was left with an indelible memory of a wounded leopard's roar and charge and two lightning-fast blasts of Russ's 12-gauge, as the trackers scrambled for their lives.

We now realized that the leopard had been waiting in a hole at the base of the very termite mound we had climbed just a few minutes before. Because the den was on the ravine side of the mound, we didn't see it until after the action was over. Had we moved into the ravine immediately after climbing down from the mound, the cat's charge would probably have connected with one of us. We would not have been expecting a charge from our backs, and the leopard would have been only a few feet away—it would have been on us in a split second, I told Russ. His decision to cover a little more ground before dipping again into the ravine, and his instincts about where we might find that cat, had quite likely saved someone's life.

Russ nodded.

"That's not the kind of thought I like to dwell upon," he said.

My shot from the evening before had severely damaged one of the leopard's front legs. Why was my shot bad? Perhaps in the dim conditions I had shot too low. I don't really know. I just know that sometimes, if you hunt long enough, it happens. But even with only three good legs, a leopard can still move faster than most people can think.

Chapter 11

Ancient Nation, Modern Anguish

Ethiopia, 1985

When I met the American television reporter, he was perched at the bar of the Hilton Hotel in Addis Ababa, nursing a beer. He was from Iowa, and he had already been in the Ethiopian capital for three days. Drought and political upheaval had displaced thousands of starving people into refugee camps. A planeload of food and clothing donations for the refugees had been collected in the reporter's viewing area. He told me he was awaiting a permit from the Ethiopian authorities to accompany the plane and to film the delivery of its contents to the suffering Ethiopians, so that the donors could see their charitable contributions reaching the people so drastically in need.

The history of Ethiopia, Africa's third most populous country, is rather different from that of most other African countries. One of the first countries to adopt Christianity, it is the world's second-oldest official Christian nation, after Armenia. Ethiopia was among the fifty-one original members of the United Nations, and it was the main founder and headquarters for the former Organization of African Unity, now called the African Union. Ethiopia was never colonized, unless you count its brief occupation by the Italians during World War II. Emperor Haile Selassie, reinstated after

The Soemmerring gazelle is among the distinctive species of Ethiopia, where I hunted with PH Tom Mattanovich.

We visited this bleak refugee camp operated by the Red Cross and saw hundreds of people lining up for meager supplies.

the British provided a hand in evicting the Italians, ruled from the 1940s until the mid-1970s.

Ethiopia is nevertheless one of Africa's poorest countries. Some two-thirds of its people are illiterate. The economy is largely agricultural—Ethiopia is one of Africa's major coffee producers. All the people rely upon rainfall. Drought, famine, war, and ill-conceived policies brought millions to the brink of starvation in the 1970s and 1980s. In 1974 a Marxist junta led by Mengistu Haile Mariam toppled Haile Selassie.

Mengistu was a specialist in killing opponents and confiscating property. His regime was an era of purges, uprisings, and enormous refugee problems. He was still in power when I hunted the country in 1985 but would be overthrown in 1991, tried in absentia, and finally convicted of genocide in a trial that lasted until 2006. Since Mengistu was ousted, Ethiopia has achieved several rounds of multiparty elections, but it has also had continuing conflict with neighboring Eritrea. Annexed by Ethiopia in 1962, Eritrea seceded in 1993 after thirty years of war, and border disputes have continued.

For longtime Houston Safari Club members, the memorable thing about Ethiopia is neither conflict nor famine but an enormous elephant collected there in 1986 by Ray Petty, one of our founding members and HSC treasurer for three decades. He took his magnificent bull on a hunt booked with Tom Mattanovich and guided by former Mozambique PH Luis Lopes de Silva. The larger tusk weighed 144½ pounds, measured 9 feet long on its outside curve, and was 22 inches in circumference; the other was 138 pounds; 8 feet, 10 inches long; and 21½ inches in circumference. To save you from doing the arithmetic, that's 282½ pounds of ivory. You can read about the hunt in *Beyond the Horizon,* a collection of HSC members' stories edited by Randy Nichols (1996).

I was in Ethiopia in 1985, slightly ahead of Ray. Beth Levitz booked me to hunt with Tom Mattanovich. My project at the time was to beef up my worldwide count of trophy species and see if I could take a respectable crack at the Weatherby Award. My safari produced twenty-five animals of twenty-three species. People teased me that I'd never be able to win the Weatherby because I didn't shoot a Weatherby. But by this stage I had been hunting for one hundred to one hundred and eighty days a year for several years, and my species count was becoming quite respectable (see hunting chronology at the back of the book).

Ethiopia contained a whole string of game species that would be new for me, among them northern gerenuk, Phillips dik-dik, lesser kudu, Abyssinian greater

The northern gerenuk is readily recognized by its extremely long neck, which is an adaptation for browsing from trees and shrubs.

kudu, Abyssinian bushbuck, Abyssinian bohor reedbuck, Somali Soemmerring gazelle, Menelik bushbuck, and beisa oryx. Ethiopia is also the only place where you can hunt the coveted mountain nyala, and that was my priority. The animal looks more like a kudu than like a southern nyala. You need one if you want a complete collection of all the spiral-horned antelope.

The Solitary Mountain Nyala

It took some time to exchange currency and get hunting licenses, so we overnighted in Addis Ababa. We set out first for the mountains to get the most difficult species. I had told Tom I wanted a good klipspringer, a stubby little antelope that had eluded me during my safari in Kenya. We were on horseback, starting our climb into the high country, when we saw a pair, so I jumped off my horse, pulled out my rifle, and got a good klipspringer.

Hunting mountain nyala was like sheep hunting in some ways. We would be up around ten thousand feet or higher and doing plenty of climbing and glassing. When the sun went down and the wind came up as night fell, we couldn't get enough clothes on. I ate dinner wearing my gloves.

On most days we sent men out to scout in different directions, and they let us know by radio if they saw a nyala. On the day we got the nyala, we were all together. When we stopped on a promontory to pull out our lunch, one of the men said he thought he saw some horns in the brush on the opposite slope. Sure enough,

Mountain nyala is the prime trophy species for which Ethiopia is known. Collecting my gold-medal animal required climbing and glassing at high elevations, plenty of patience, and a long shot.

there were the telltale ivory tips, though the tips were all we could see. We realized the animal had also seen us, a whole bunch of us.

I moved away from the others and hid behind a rock with my rifle ready, but our timing was a bit off. The nyala moved about a little, never presenting me with a clear view, and then settled down for a siesta. Once the bull lay down, it was invisible, but we knew where it was. Tom theorized that the bull probably used the spot regularly as a bed because it gave a wide view of the valley.

"He's going to move just before dark," said Tom. "When he gets up, it'll be a few steps and he could be out of sight again. I don't know if you're going to get a shot. Better stay ready."

How do you stay ready for whenever a mountain nyala gets up after its siesta? I reminded myself of the long journey to this point and all the scouting already invested. This was a difficult animal to find—I knew I'd better not blow my chance. I said to myself, *Patience, Gary.* Sometimes hunting means you have to hustle and expend a lot of physical energy. Sometimes it means you have to maintain concentration, even as furious action unfolds. And sometimes it means you just have to wait. The minutes ticked by, and the half-hours turned into hours. To avoid distraction, we talked little. All of us waited there for most of the afternoon, from perhaps 12:30 or 1 P.M. until 4 P.M. or later. I laid my gloves over the tops of my hands

We had to stay on the move to get the game we wanted. We carried everything with us and made a simple camp wherever we were each night.

as protection against sunburn; high up in the thin mountain air, the sun was fierce.

When at last the nyala did move, we still didn't get a clear view. The bull stood up, took a look around, and lay down once more. It knew we were there, and it wasn't going anywhere. As predicted, it did not get up again until just before dark. All we could really see was the white spot at its throat.

"Can you hit that spot?" asked Tom.

I hit the bull right there, and it dropped. It proved to be a gold-medal mountain nyala, and it was clear from the sign that the old fellow had indeed been using that secluded bedding area, just as Tom had surmised. That was the only mountain nyala we saw on our safari. More than a few people have had to take a second safari to collect a mountain nyala. You could say we were lucky to have seen it over lunch, or you could say Mattanovich knew what he was doing and arranged our lunch stop in a place where it would count.

We proceeded to hunt Menelik bushbuck and other mountain species before returning to Addis to resupply for our southern trip into the open country. My hunt with Tom was not a luxurious affair. We had to stay on the move because I was aiming to get so many animals. We had a big truck and a small Jeep, and we carried everything with us, making a simple camp wherever we ended up each night. We salted the hides and they went right into the truck. Since

Ethiopia has a long history; it is also one of the earliest countries to adopt Christianity. Here we inspect still-standing, Roman-era ruins.

we had been out for five days by the time we started back to Addis, Tom suggested we stop along the way for a shower and a meal at a lake resort to celebrate the mountain nyala.

It looked like the Fourth of July when we pulled into the place. The parking lot was overflowing with boats, trailers, Toyotas, and sleek new Mercedes sedans. While famine ravaged the country, the resort was filled with weekending government officials, including one very senior man and his private pilot. The place was too full for us to get a chalet—we would retreat for the night to our little camp nearby—but an official Tom knew offered us the use of his room to clean up. We hadn't had a shower in a week.

I never was very good at getting my mind around the details of African conflicts, nor am I now. At some level you just have to assume that if a place is falling apart at the seams, the professional hunters will not be trying to get their clients in there. The reverse proposition also holds: If the professionals are trying to get clients in, it means the place contains game populations worth hunting, and the professionals have found a way to work around the current political difficulties. Over dinner at the resort, I learned a little more about the way some governments manage humanitarian disasters.

We ate with the high official and his pilot. After they had inquired about our hunt, the talk turned to current events. Ethiopia was in the grip of a severe drought, the official reminded us. Thousands of people were dying for lack of food.

"We really appreciate all the aid from the world," he said, adding, "You probably don't know much about the African people." He proceeded to explain that in fact they needed one of these droughts every so many years because there were too many people. People had a baby every year. The best thing that had ever happened to the country, he declared, was that now thousands of people were dying, and the government was getting all this aid.

"You people are all from wealthy countries. You need to send us more food and more money," he concluded.

I was disgusted to see a resort full of government officials—of an ostensibly Marxist government—living it up in high style with all their expensive toys, but there was little I could say. Had Tom given me any warning about this? Not a word. He was throwing me stern looks across the table.

"No," the official mused, "we need these droughts. The strong survive."

When we got back to the Hilton Addis after our five days in the mountains, the first guy I ran into at the bar was the Iowa television reporter, still waiting for his permit. The planeload of donated items was still sitting at the airport. After being there for more than a week, he was still telling officials that he couldn't leave the country without filming the delivery of the plane's contents, and he was going to take it all home again if he couldn't get his film made. But a government official had visited him and told him he was not going to be able to do any filming, and they weren't going to let him take the plane's contents home again.

The donations had to go to several different places, the official claimed. They would be unloading the plane the next day, he said, and he recommended that the reporter leave with the empty plane. The fellow was running out of money to pay for the hotel, and he had grasped the situation at last. It made no difference that he had brought in hundreds of thousands of dollars' worth of donated aid—he would not be able to film anything. And he would still have to pay for his hotel stay. I told Tom about it.

"This is Africa," said Tom.

The heat was impressive. A camp bed in the shade was more appealing than a tent.

"Not for Resale"

Next, we would be hunting in the grasslands and desert, where the crisis produced by the drought was the worst. We visited a refugee camp operated by the Red Cross, where we saw hundreds of people lining up for a cup of water and a little rice. Some men were digging sites for the construction of latrines and makeshift quarters. Others were digging graves for the twenty or thirty people who died in that camp every day. I asked someone from the Red Cross where the wood, concrete, and roofing tin were coming from. He told me they could get anything they wanted in Addis Ababa, where the government sold it to the Red Cross.

The Red Cross had come to construct the buildings and run the camp, but they had to pay the government for supplies that had been donated by other countries. It was discouraging, he agreed; but he was face to face with the starving and the dying. What else could he do? By then, we had also seen that food aid was reaching across the country, though not in the way intended. It was for sale in the village markets of almost every little place we passed. The bags of grain were all stamped "Not for Resale."

Guns were everywhere. As we proceeded through the countryside to our hunting area, Tom said one of us should be sitting up high, brandishing a firearm. Tribesmen sometimes waved AK-47s at approaching trucks, and we should be waving our rifles back at them, as if this were the most normal thing in the world. If they could see we had guns, they probably wouldn't bother us. We were in a rural area rich in history. We drove past Roman-era ruins still standing, yet the fabric of the modern nation was so frayed that Tom had to post guards around our camp at night.

Drought and insane heat notwithstanding, we took plenty of game from one of Tom's more permanent

One of Tom's more permanent camps was near a lake, where I collected a Menelik bushbuck when it came down to drink.

camps near a lake. We heard lion roaring all night long, and after some days of trying to find them, Tom suggested tethering a donkey as bait. We bought a donkey and hauled it over to our camp, the astonished animal riding in style in the backseat of the Jeep. For a while we slept through the baking-hot days and hunted at night. We continued to hear the lion roaring, but they did not visit our donkey. I suppose they had a plentiful supply of dead cattle to eat. We never did see a lion, although from this camp I collected a good bushbuck that came down to drink. I also took two small cats that are usually hard to find: a caracal and a serval. Tom paid the villagers to take their donkey back again.

Heading back to Addis, we passed a port city, where we saw boatloads of grain spoiling on the dock and being eaten by rats. Boatloads of grain were awaiting—what? Awaiting some means of sale that would allow several intermediaries to profit from the "Not for Resale" supplies before they were dispensed to anyone who needed food.

Trucking was an issue, too. There were not enough trucks to haul the aid where it was needed. And there was another problem. Armed men were attacking the trucks. Aid trucks that did make it into the hinterlands stood a fair chance of being robbed.

Now it was blindingly clear why that TV reporter never got his permit. The planeload of goods wasn't going to the

The serval is a small predator not commonly seen. This trophy was also taken near the lake camp.

occupants of a refugee camp. He was paying hundreds of dollars to remain at the Hilton until he ran out of patience or his employer got tired of paying his per diem. The plane was, in effect, captive. When he and his TV camera went away, the contents of the plane would be divided up in some creative way to make the most of the windfall and maximize the profits for a series of officials. Anything that wasn't stolen for resale by officials, and anything that hadn't spoiled or been eaten by vermin, was still likely to remain stranded because of the lack of transportation, and any food aid that did make it onto a truck was fair game for plain old highway robbery. It was a miracle that food aid reached any of the camps at all. One can understand why people in other countries wanted to send help, but it was just like throwing the stuff into a hole.

Twenty years later, the montane forests of Ethiopia remain the destination for hunting mountain nyala, and the animal remains a difficult species to hunt. Many Ethiopians continue to depend on food aid from abroad. Since 2004, the government has been attempting to do some social engineering, trying to move large numbers of people out of the arid highlands of the east and seeking a more lasting solution to food shortages. A fragile peace with Eritrea has been negotiated, but it's a touch early to be confident that stability is on the way. In 2006 Ethiopia launched military strikes against Islamist forces in Somalia. . . .

Chapter 12

Three Prime Hunting Countries

Namibia, 1981; South Africa, 1986, 2008; Tanzania, 1990, and the Weatherby Award, 1991

I shot my black-maned lion in Tanzania on a 1990 safari with PH George Angelides. Richard Hawkins and Wally Bohrer accompanied me for twenty-one days in this fabled hunting country.

Who says a family hunt can't be productive? With a wide range of options for non-hunting companions, South Africa is an obvious destination for a family safari. Many of the hunting operations include comfortable places to stay, and you don't have to suffer eight-hour, bone-rattling drives to get into the hunting areas. These days you'll often find an Internet connection at your destination, should you want to stay in touch with the world.

Elizabeth and Jason accompanied me to South Africa in 1986, when Jason was fifteen. By then, I had been to South Africa eight times. Continuing the tradition, we took another family trip to South Africa with Jason and my grandson, JR, in 2008.

I also took Elizabeth and Jason to Namibia. I had been looking for an African hunt on which I could safely take my family. I wanted them to see plenty of wild animals under wild conditions and get a feel for Africa. In 1976 I had taken Jason with me to Kenya for thirty-five days, but he was too young to

A white rhino was not in my plans for my Namibian hunt with PH Jan Oelofse, but it was a great bonus. Ten-year-old Jason took an impala during the trip.

remember much. In 1981, at the ripe old age of ten, I took him on an 18-day trip to Namibia, where he shot his first impala.

An Unexpected Rhino

I had planned a plains-game safari in Namibia, but events caught up with us, and I suddenly found myself on a rhino hunt.

Our outfitter was the energetic Jan Oelofse, one of the major professionals in the early years in Namibia. Jan knew all about big-game capture and handling techniques, having done this kind of work in Tanzania. He had worked with animals, including rhino for the 1962 John Wayne feature film *Hatari*. (If you saw it, you'll also remember Red Buttons shooting a net over a great big tree to catch a bunch of monkeys.) In the 1960s Jan became a game-capture specialist for the Natal Parks

The Eastern Cape is famous for kudu, and my kudu came in at No. 1 in the SCI record book. Next to the kudu are my southern bush duiker (facing left) and grysbok (facing right). We hunted on several ranches with Chappie Scott and Frank Bowker.

Board in South Africa. There, instead of using nets for game capture, he pioneered a switch to funnel animals into an enclosure by using long "walls" of opaque plastic sheeting. This minimized injury and stress to the animals and made it possible to undertake translocations of wildlife on a significantly larger scale. It was also much safer for both the staff and the game.

In 1975 Jan leased some former cattle-ranching land in Namibia that he would later purchase and expand, and he started building up game populations of all kinds. The place would become the Okanjati Wildlife Sanctuary, where hunters today can stay at the Mount Etjo Safari Lodge. The game authorities had begun holding auctions to dispose of excess animals because there was a growing market for them among owners stocking private lands. Other ranchers had begun to realize that they could do at least as well with hunting as with livestock operations, and perhaps much better.

Jan told me he had bought six rhino at a national park auction—two cows, two young bulls, and two older bulls. He planned to have clients hunt the two older bulls fairly soon so that the revenue from those hunts would cover his costs for the six animals. The other four were to become the nucleus of a permanent herd of white rhino on the reserve, which would offer limited hunting from time to time.

While hunting with Garry Kelly, Jason took a fine blesbok with a heart shot.

While I was there, one of the larger bulls caused a slight revision of these plans. It broke out of the sanctuary and set off across a neighboring ranch.

"I can't catch him," said Jan. "You're going to have to shoot him."

Without the full-scale staff and equipment of his years in the wildlife agency, recapture was not a realistic possibility. Jan knew it would make more sense to hunt the bull now, before it got him into any trouble. Did I fancy a white rhino for six thousand dollars? I'd taken a black rhino in Kenya in 1976, and I had no plans to hunt rhino in Namibia, but this was a bargain price. Rhino would soon wind up costing hunters more like thirty thousand dollars. It was just too good an opportunity to pass up. Even in the 1980s, rhino hunting had already become extremely limited.

By the time we got after it, the bull had already crossed three ranches, so we found ourselves following a trail of broken fences. Perhaps it was heading instinctively toward the park from which it had come. An ordinary ranch fence is no impediment to an animal the size of a rhino. Jan would have some damages to settle with his neighbors.

This tiny blue duiker, also taken with Garry Kelly, earned me another No. 1 spot in the SCI record book.

It turned out to be a hell of a hunt—a satisfying if untraditional stalk that got me an unexpected and unplanned-for rhino.

South Africa Yields Sixteen for the Book

Our 1986 family trip to South Africa, arranged for us by Beth Jones Levitz of Trophy Hunter Safaris, accomplished all it was intended to do and then some. Besides the great hunting, we soon discovered three things about the big ranches of South Africa. First, hunting African species on ranches was not easy. The animals were wild and usually ran at the first sign of people or a vehicle. Second, the country's political difficulties didn't get in our way in the least, although the U.S. media was making it seem as if the whole nation of South Africa were in a state of political upheaval. Our hunt took place during the uncertain years before the majority-rule election that brought Nelson Mandela to the presidency in 1994, but we never felt threatened while moving around among various ranches. Third, the food and wines offered to ranch guests were excellent. We left South Africa with a special appreciation for its fine wines.

We departed in June for the southern tip of the southernmost country in Africa. June meant it was winter in the southern hemisphere. Our trip consisted of two seven-day hunts in different parts of the country. We spent the first week in the cold, mountainous region of the Eastern Cape, hunting with Chappie Scott and Frank Bowker. Later, we would hunt in the northern part of Natal, near the Mozambique border, with Garry Kelly and professional hunter Peter Holbrow. In both areas our hospitable hosts and seasoned guides arranged hunts on neighboring ranches as well as on the ranches where we stayed.

Upon arriving at Chappie Scott's ten-thousand-acre ranch, we enjoyed a cookout, locally called a braai. South African wines complemented the barbecued steaks wonderfully well. Cool weather had arrived, and the ranch house, like most dwellings in South Africa, had no heating. We followed the local tradition of sleeping with hot-water bottles.

A day of ranch hunting began at 7:30 A.M., when tea was served. Soon after that, hunters went off to the big-game areas. Anyone not interested in big game (is there anyone like that?) could sleep in or get in a little bird shooting near the ranch house. Francolin and pigeon were plentiful. Hunting a series of ranches, I took springbok, black springbok, white springbok, mountain reedbuck, vaal rhebok, Cape eland, bontebok, Cape bushbuck, grysbok, and southern bush duiker, all of which made the record book. Ten species in the book within days was certainly gratifying. Jason took a mountain reedbuck that made the book.

One morning, hunting the ranch of Arthur Rudman, we spotted from the hunting truck a fine pair of Eastern Cape greater kudu. The Eastern Cape is famous for its kudu, and certainly these are the animals the professional hunters of the region find most absorbing. The PHs do much of the hunting from trucks with high shooting and spotting towers, similar to the rigs in use in the South Texas brush country.

Jason tried a shot on the larger of the two kudu bulls but missed. The bull was getting away, so I took a shot. I was shooting my tried-and-true 7mm Remington Magnum, which broke the bull's back. Down it went. I had awfully good luck that whole trip, surprising the guides and trackers as well as myself. Perhaps we can attribute this to the encouraging effect of having the family along. At any rate, if I hadn't been shooting as well as I was, I would probably have taken only about half as many animals.

The kudu bull had perfectly matched 54-inch spirals. It was the best ever taken from that ranch, and it made No. 1 in the SCI record book. Before leaving the Cape, we also took two bushpig and a large male ostrich.

On 16 June we arrived at Garry Kelly's ranch in Natal (now called KwaZulu-Natal). It is difficult to describe just how beautiful the base camp was. We had big thatched huts with concrete floors and hot running water, in a setting that looked rather like the Texas Hill Country. There were open expanses of grassland punctuated by rocky hills and patches of shade trees. It was idyllic.

Hunting the Kelly property and surrounding ranches, I took trophy red duiker, suni (antelope), blue wildebeest, and southern impala. Jason collected a fine blesbok with a great shot through the heart. One hunt produced quite a rare trophy—the No. 1 blue duiker in the SCI record book. I was hunting a brushy ravine between fields of sugarcane and had taken a stand with a shotgun as beaters pushed game toward me. First I saw two female bushbuck; then some vervet monkeys scampered past me. A split second later, a fine male blue duiker ran by, and I let it have a load of buckshot.

There was no quarreling with my bag of seventeen species, of which sixteen made the record book; fifteen were new species for me, and two proved up at No. 1. Numbers like that are difficult to achieve in any other country. Both Arthur Rudman and Garry Kelly were already established outfitters by the time we hunted with them, and, two decades later, they were both still routinely exhibiting at the Houston Safari Club Convention. The great trophy quality was by no means a one-time proposition. We were in very good hands. Besides his mountain reedbuck and blesbok, Jason took impala, springhare, and rock rabbit (hyrax).

We topped off our hunting with a few days in Durban with Peter Holbrow and his girlfriend, staying in a twenty-second-floor room at the Maharani Hotel and enjoying the culinary delights of that coastal city. There we realized that South Africa's white wines go just as well with shrimp and lobster as the red wines go with game and beef.

I have to say I've been on easier hunts. If anyone tells you South African ranch hunting amounts to a sad business of hunting animals inside fences, either they don't know what they're talking about or they were hunting the wrong areas. Our experience was completely different and fully satisfying for fair-chase hunters. South Africa had offered us a wide range of game species, some of which are available nowhere else.

I hope to make several more three-generation family hunts. At the time of this writing, Jason still needs a leopard. Two decades after his hunt in South Africa as a high-school student, he is thinking about a leopard hunt in Botswana with dogs and Bushmen guides. Such a hunt was not an option when I was after leopard, and it promises to be an experience entirely new to us all.

Five Is the Perfect Age

You'll recall that Jason was five when I took him on my first African safari in Kenya in 1976. As soon as my grandson JR was born, we decided he would also make his first trip to Africa when he turned five. He was at that impressionable age when we took him on our April 2008 safari to South Africa. Alas, we could not include the entire third generation of Ingersoll men. In January of that year, twin grandsons, Kyle and Reed, joined the family, but at the time of our trip they were only three months old.

We booked the family hunt with Tam Safaris in the Eastern Cape. Irvin Tam has several large ranches on which he has fenced only the perimeters, and he has refined South Africa's ranch hunting in some very twenty-first-century ways. We were not in tents. No one was using an old iron full of hot coals on our laundry, and there was no need to shower under a water bag hung from the branch of a tree, as on my 1976 Kenyan safari. Instead, we had hot and cold running water in a two-bedroom suite with all manner of modern amenities, right down to the hair dryers. Most people these days prefer not to rough it too much, especially when taking the family. It's pleasant to be able to take a real shower and sleep in a comfortable bed after a day's hunting.

George Angelides took a leaf out of the honey gatherers' book, hanging a hollowed-out log to create a new hive from which honey could be gathered.

Ironically, this hunt strongly reminded me of our Kenyan safari in some respects. You'll recall that when I left Kenya, my PH, Ike Hassan, presented me with a gift album of black-and-white photos of my trophy animals. Every night Irvin graced the dinner table with a big digital photo of the prime trophy taken that day. The custom treatment began before anyone in our party had collected a trophy. When we arrived, hunting hats embroidered with our names awaited each of us.

Some people pay a good deal to have safaris professionally filmed, but Tam Safaris includes this service in its package. After you get home, an edited DVD with music turns up in the mail, showing the highlights of your hunt. You don't have to bring a video camera and wrestle with battery packs. Irvin's philosophy is that it doesn't take much more effort on the part of his staff to go first class.

My only trophy on this hunt was something I had never seen before—the unusual copper springbok. Both Jason and Elizabeth darted white rhino, and Jason also decided to hunt lion. The Tams offer lion in a twelve-thousand-acre area, where the lion hunt their own prey and big-cat hunting is not over bait. Jason and Elizabeth were glad to know these Big Five hunts would follow us home on DVD. Elizabeth was also captivated when our host presented her with some bottles of wine bearing custom labels that featured a photo of her with her prize rhino trophy. Ike Hassan wasn't quite in that league!

Besides the high-tech components, the Tams have also revived some age-old safari traditions, such as a special celebration when someone brings in one of the Big Five. A sedan-chair procession honors the successful hunter, and tribal drummers and dancers add to the festive air. I was glad my grandson was able to ride in his father's lap during Jason's chair procession and get an idea of the way things used to be.

Honey and Hippo in Tanzania

There are advantages to the good roads and comfortable ranch-homestead quarters that hunting clients typically enjoy in South Africa and Namibia. Tanzania also has many trophy species and is now considered a premium hunting country. There, clients occupy classic safari-style tented camps. The outfitters don't own their properties and must pay concession fees. They also must cover the cost of all logistics where roads are poor and supplies have to be hauled or flown long distances. As a result, hunting Tanzania is expensive, and I would not advise taking the family. The reward for the client is vast expanses of hunting country with no fences, few roads, and game that is very wild indeed.

We had a gorgeous view of Mount Kilimanjaro on the flight in. Richard Hawkins and his friend Wally Bohrer accompanied me on this safari. We had booked a twenty-one-day hunt with outfitter George Angelides for September-October 1990, aiming to collect a full range of species and planning to hunt in several different areas. Elephant was not on the agenda, but I wanted good lion and buffalo, plus roan, puku, Grant and Thomson gazelle, Coke hartebeest, Nyasaland wildebeest, bushpig, and some of the antelope in the higher forested country: mountain reedbuck, red duiker, and the tiny suni. The latter three animals cost me plenty of effort, but all three scored high in the book.

We spent most of our safari based out of a tented camp, and we went up to Mount Meru Game Lodge near Arusha for a day to hunt the duiker and suni. I took a topi with 18-inch horns that scored well, and my bohor reedbuck made the book also. We tried hard for leopard, but the cat that presented me with a shot was a small one, and I decided against taking it.

Richard and I both took hartebeest early on; they would become our lion bait. Richard also took hyena and a spurwing goose on the first day. For me, a highlight of the safari was the beautiful black-maned lion I collected the next day, some distance away from our bait. We were out driving and scouting when the men suddenly saw a good lion and began pounding on the roof of the truck cab. With the lion were three lionesses and two or three cubs. They had made a kill and were lying near the edge of some burned grass. My chance for lion came up much sooner than I could have hoped.

It was in Tanzania that I learned of the honey gatherers. In places where people have little cash and there are few stores where they can buy sugar or sweet foods, wild honey is a coveted commodity. For generations unknown, honey hunters have made a living by running a circuit of beehives. In some ways it resembles the way a trapper runs a trapline.

Honey is a renewable resource. As a trapper, you kill the fox in your trap, assuming that the surrounding population will yield another fox for another day. As a honey hunter, you don't destroy a beehive or cut down its host tree to get at it. Instead, aiming to conserve a flourishing hive, you merely make a hole in it with a special long-bladed ax designed for that purpose, and you harvest some of the honey, leaving the queen alone. You leave the colony intact to make more honey for collection next time.

Queen bees and beehives do not live forever. Eventually, the hive fails, and you need to find new hives along your established gathering circuit. One way to do that is through a bit of interspecies collaboration with a bird called the honey guide. Honey gatherers learned long ago that the honey guide also likes to eat honey, so, when they see the bird, they simply follow it. Sooner or later, it will show them the location of a hive, just as its name implies.

The collaboration goes quite a bit farther than this. Honey guides also follow people, having learned that, besides wielding axes, people are good at smoking bees out of hives so they can get the honey without the risk of being stung by angry bees. Tradition requires the human honey hunter to provide some honey for the bird. Waiting for a man with an ax and a box of matches to do his work is much easier for the bird than running the gauntlet of bee stings while breaking into a hive using its beak.

The human honey gatherers also create hives. They hang gourds or hollowed-out pieces of wood from trees to encourage bees to set up housekeeping. In this way both the honey gatherer and the honey guide can regularly collect some of the spoils. As long as they don't take too much honey or compromise the hive, they can both keep coming back for more.

Among the memorable moments on my Tanzanian safari with George was an episode involving local customs and beliefs. I wanted a hippo and had tried for a good trophy bull several times from our first camp. So it was that after a long drive to change camps and a lot of stops to fix flat tires, we learned that in our new area a large hippo bull had been terrorizing the locals. It had already killed and injured several people on the riverside trails at night.

From this camp I had taken a good roan antelope, a bushbuck, and a buffalo, and I was still trying for a bushpig. Each evening, after our day's hunting, we would go out again to see if we could find the troublesome hippo bull. For six days in a row we tried without seeing it. One day, when we got back to camp, some men arrived to tell us where we could find the bull. It's best to take a hippo on shore or up on a sandbar, or in shallow water, so that it won't simply sink and be taken by the crocodiles. We ran down in the truck, and, sure enough, the hippo bull was lying in shallow water on a sandbar in the middle of the river.

I shot it in the brain with the .375. The good news was that we had found the problem hippo, and now it was dead. The bad news was that our men refused to go into the bloody water because of the crocs. They were scared to death, unwilling even to go close to the shore. How were we going to retrieve the hippo?

George suggested the solution. We had to go and find a fisherman, he said, because the fishermen were blessed. They went into the water all the time, and the crocs did not eat them. I stared at him in disbelief.

"You're out of your mind," I told him.

"No," he said. "That's the way they believe."

We sent the truck, and our men came back with a fisherman, a little rubber raft, and a cable.

There were crocs swimming everywhere, but the fisherman got to work. He set the small craft in the water, climbed aboard, and paddled that little boat right out through the crocs to where the hippo lay. He got out of the boat and stood in the shallow water, fastening a heavy winching cable around the hippo's neck. We would use the winch on the front of our truck to haul the hippo to the bank.

To our collective astonishment, the fisherman climbed up on top of the hippo carcass and sat there,

My hippo was a large bull that had killed and injured several people on riverside trails. Local people told us where to find it, and then helped retrieve the carcass from the crocodile-infested water.

holding the bow line of the raft. We winched him back through the water, the blood, and the crocs. He just sat there, looking around, as if this were nothing special at all. We winched the bizarre arrangement right up onto the bank. By then, all the crocs were stirring because of the commotion and the blood in the water, but the whole procedure was accomplished without incident.

"I told you. The crocs don't bother the fishermen—that's how they believe," George said again.

I was still having trouble processing what I had just seen with my own eyes. This time I said nothing, but I thought: *You sure made a believer out of me, pal.*

I took the hippo's head, and the rest went to the villagers, who used the windfall of meat to throw a big celebration.

The Weatherby Award

I was in for a celebration of my own at the end of that Tanzanian safari. When I got home, I learned that Dr. Bob Speegle of Dallas had called my family to let them know I was on the 1990 short list of nominees for the Weatherby Award—a thrill indeed. As a past winner of the award, Bob was on the nominating committee and in the know about current nominees. I was not selected that year, but in 1991 the honor would come my way. The ten-man selection committee consisted of famed World War II Marine Corps aviator Joe Foss, former Secretary of Commerce Maurice Stans, and seven past Weatherby Award winners: Dan Madddox, His Imperial Highness Abdorreza Pahlavi of Iran, Valentin de Madariaga of Spain, Watson Yoshimoto of Hawaii, Mahlon T. White, Dr. Jim Conklin, and Bob Speegle.

I was the fifth Texan to win the Weatherby. Created in 1956, the award went to Herb Klein of Dallas in its first year, presented by General Nathan F. Twining. George Landreth of Midland earned it in 1970, with presentation by astronaut Captain Jim Lovell. The next two Texans were Bob Speegle in 1979 (presentation by Gene Autry) and Glenn Slade of Houston in 1982 (Lorne Green), before I received mine in 1991 (Jameson Parker). More Houstonians would follow—Irvin Barnhart in 1993 (General Norman Schwarzkopf), Dan Duncan in 1998 (Ray Arnett), and Mike Simpson in 2003 (Oliver North).

Attending the 1991 gala award dinner with my family and me were three of my trusty Minnesota hunting buddies: Richard Hawkins, Tom Rubenstein, and Bob DeWitz, who had been my companions on some of my earliest big-game hunts nearly thirty years before. Each has accompanied me on later hunts as well. I thanked them all, and I thanked all the booking agents, outfitters, and professional hunters who had contributed to my success. By then, I had collected more than two hundred game species and had collected Africa's Big Five twice—but there was still so much to do!

Return to Africa

In January 1982 I had gone back to Sudan with Mike Simpson and Irvin Barnhart, but it was not for elephant or buffalo, as on my original 1977 safari. Our 1982 quest was for Nubian ibex in the sparse and rocky Red Sea Hills of eastern Sudan, where the Eritrean gazelle was the other unusual trophy. Far from fending off legions of biting insects in heavy forest, we would be sleeping on the ground out in the open with the Fuzzy-Wuzzy people. British soldiers applied the term to the fearsome warriors of the Beja tribes, who for forty centuries have worn their hair in a distinctive, unkempt style guaranteed to terrify enemies. Rudyard Kipling immortalized the name in his poem "Fuzzy-Wuzzy."

There would be other kinds of returns to Africa, a mix of something old and something new. There is always something old in Africa, and there is always something new in hunting. I was back in South Africa in June 1988, hunting again with Chappie Scott. We covered a series of different areas in order to collect the southern African species I was still missing—eland, Chobe bushbuck, waterbuck, red lechwe, and the diminutive and difficult-to-hunt grysbok.

One ranch we hunted on belonged to Tim Otto, where Richard Hawkins and Bob DeWitz had been hunting in 1987. On the 1988 trip my gun case underwent a dreadful airline assault of some kind. The case looked as if it had been run over by a vehicle, and I was amazed that the rifle inside escaped unharmed. A connection of Chappie's named "Opa" Blackwood, a fiercely independent and highly entertaining old fellow, was one of our hunting ranch hosts. He offered to take care of that little problem for me. The magic he performed on my gun case was unbelievable. It looked virtually new when he passed it back to me. Where does a rancher in the deep interior of South Africa learn how to do that?

In 2008 Jason and his son JR and I were back in South Africa (see chapter 22), and I hope to make several more three-generation family hunts. At the time of this writing Jason still needs a leopard. Two decades after his hunt in South Africa as a high-school student, he is thinking about a leopard hunt in Botswana with dogs and Bushmen guides. Such a hunt was not an option when I was after leopard, and it promises to be an experience entirely new to us all.

Asian Sheep Beckon

Part 3

ARCTIC OCEAN
NEW SIBERIAN ISLANDS
EAST SIBERIAN SEA
WRANGEL ISLAND
CHUKCHI SEA
ARCTIC CIRCLE (66°33')
BERING SEA
LAKE BAIKAL
SEA OF OKHOTSK
SAKHALIN
ALEUTIAN ISLANDS (U.S.)
KURIL ISLANDS
OCCUPIED BY THE SOVIET UNION IN 1945, ADMINISTERED BY RUSSIA, CLAIMED BY JAPAN
NGOLIA
NORTH PACIFIC OCEAN
NORTH KOREA
SEA OF JAPAN
JAPAN
SOUTH KOREA
YELLOW SEA
CHINA
NAMPO SHOTO (JAPAN)
RYUKYU ISLANDS (JAPAN)
EAST CHINA SEA
OKINAWA
MARCUS ISLAND (JAPAN)
TROPIC OF CAN
TAIWAN
BURMA
HONG KONG S.A.R.
MACAU S.A.R.
LUZON STRAIT
LAOS
GULF OF TONKIN
HAINAN DAO
PHILIPPINE SEA
NORTHERN MARIANA ISLANDS (U.S.)
PARACEL ISLANDS
THAILAND
VIETNAM
SOUTH CHINA SEA
PHILIPPINES
GUAM (U.S.)
ANDAMAN ISLANDS (INDIA)
CAMBODIA
ANDAMAN SEA
GULF OF THAILAND
SPRATLY ISLANDS
FEDERATED STATES OF MICRONESIA
PALAU
BRUNEI
CELEBES SEA
SINGAPORE
EQUATOR

Chapter 13

Afghan Urial with James Bond

Tajikistan, 1985

Riding in the back seat of a Jeep, I wasn't expecting to have to drop to the floor and huddle every time we drove through a place where it would be better if no one realized I was in the car. But, hey, you do what you have to do. I hadn't expected to be going out hunting with a kind of Soviet clandestine operative, either. As it turned out, he was a masterful escort, and we could not have fared nearly as well without him.

The Cold War was still very much with us in 1985. Although I already knew from earlier visits to Russia and Mongolia that living conditions in the USSR were on the thin side, I still had the typical American standpoint on the geopolitics of the situation—we had to make sure our military capability more than matched whatever the Soviets could muster. By the early 1980s, the Soviet Union had the largest military-industrial complex in the world in terms of scale, troop numbers, and types of weapons.

My hunt for urial sheep along the Afghan border suggested to me that we seemed to be fearing the wrong things. On the face of it, the Soviets held a significant military advantage in their confrontation with the Afghans. Yet, to anyone looking at the situation on the ground, it was readily apparent that we should be careful not to overestimate Russian power. It was mostly smoke and mirrors. Equipment was old and tired, in poor condition, and often hopelessly inadequate. The soldiers of the Eastern bloc may have been numerous, but many of them were youngsters who were in the army because they had to be, and the rest seemed to be there just for the reliable government paycheck.

Mikhail Gorbachev came to power in 1985. At that time the Soviets had an economic growth rate right around zero percent, as far as I could see. Petroleum exports made up most of the USSR's export earnings, and, as world oil prices dropped during the 1980s, matters got worse and worse for the Russians. The military, I would later read, was consuming up to twenty five percent of the gross national product, a punishing situation.

The Gorbachev era of rapid reforms—glasnost, perestroika, and the opening up of all that had been closed—was largely a last-ditch attempt to achieve more profitable private and civilian use of the country's resources than the costly, unproductive, and draining Cold War military commitments. Gorbachev offered the United States major concessions on nuclear weapons, conventional forces, and policy in Eastern Europe in an effort to stay the Soviet Union's downward slide.

That was the backdrop for my venture to Tajikistan, on the northwestern edge of Afghanistan. Officially,

This view into a valley in Afghanistan from a mountain in Tajikistan gives an idea of the stark terrain. Soldiers charged with securing the border kept watch with binoculars.

I got along fine with the Russian two-star general who accompanied us. Besides his more traditional pistol, his special equipment included a .22-caliber fountain pen and a knife that doubled as a .32-caliber handgun.

the Soviet-Afghan War ran from 1979 to 1989, though, as we now know, more complications were to follow in Afghanistan. In 1985 the Russians were exhausted and depleted, but they were still trying to contain the determined effort by Afghan mujahideen to throw out Soviet invaders.

I flew into the capital, Dushanbe, for a hunt guided by Alexander Lisitsin of Russian Expeditions. Our party included, of all things, a genuine Russian two-star general, whose job was to stay with me at all times and see to it that I made it safely to my hunting area in the contested border mountains and back again. When I arrived, Alexander said this guy, a friend of his, was going to accompany us.

"Super," I said.

Perhaps he was also supposed to watch over me to make sure I was not a spy and that I committed no unauthorized photography or dope-dealing in the war zone. Those were matters of no concern to me. I knew I wasn't an outlaw, and, soon enough, he knew it, too. We got along fine from the start. In light of the Cold War, I formed the habit of not using the man's name. To avoid any repercussions that might still come his way, I'll simply call him the General.

On the front of our Jeep were two stars denoting the presence of the General. Those two stars made our progress a good deal easier than it would otherwise have been. The men at the numerous military checkpoints of the border zone would simply take one look at the car, salute, and wave us through.

We drove south for about six hours and trundled into the valley nearest our hunting area just before darkness descended over those inhospitable mountains. This was not the moment to attempt the climb on rugged gravel roads draped in inky blackness. We couldn't stay in town, either, because there was no town—just a little village of modest houses. It was the last village before the road really started to climb. Where were we going to stay?

The General said he knew the local military commander, and the local army base would be our best bet for a safe and reasonably comfortable night. My eyes widened. I had not anticipated joining the Russian army. The base was not on our official itinerary. Nobody there was expecting us. A little creative work on his part was required, and I would have to adopt the policy of being flexible.

Leaving us in the second Jeep on the road nearby, the General went off to the post in his two-star Jeep to confer with his connection, the commander. Soon he came back and told me we would stay the night there, but he said it was important that no one there see me. He instructed me to disappear by crouching on the floorboards and keeping my head down. There are times when darkness can be your friend.

Overnighting with the Russian Army

I wondered if any other Americans had had the dubious privilege of spending a night in a Russian army base in farthest Tajikistan. Even the local Tajik civilians were not allowed on the place, but here I was, being invited in, provided I stayed out of sight as we entered and remained out of sight while there. It didn't seem like the best idea I had ever heard. On the other hand, I didn't have a lot of options. I could hardly knock on the door of a local home and ask politely to spend the night. No one would have had the least idea what I was saying. They would probably have turned me over to the army, anyway. I slid to the floor of the Jeep.

The engine ground to life, and we rolled to the gates of the post, where we were quickly waved in. We drove around to the area where the officers were quartered. The Jeep stopped, but I did not move until I was summoned. Someone announced the coast was clear.

"Quick," said the General. "Go on inside and up the stairs." I jumped out of the Jeep and bolted indoors.

By now, I had begun to feel like an outlaw, and I suppose you could say I had become one. Once I recovered my wits, I looked around the place. It was the worst, saddest military facility imaginable—and these were the officers' quarters. The Russian commander who was letting us stay there had given us his own room. Frankly, the building was so old and decrepit that I'd rather have slept outside. And the toilet—I can't even begin to tell you how bad it was. Our crew cooked up a few eggs on a little stove, and everybody sat around smoking. Everything about the place was tired and worn, from the structure to the furniture to the smoky air. I lay down on my sleeping bag and went to sleep.

Staying out of sight did not mean I had to remain unseen by the commander of the camp. In the morning he dropped in to check on us, visit the General, and inquire how everything was—had we slept well? Pleasantries out of the way, he was eager for us to be gone as soon as possible. But he said we should wait for another hour or so, until all the soldiers had gone off to their duty stations for the day. This would reduce the likelihood that anyone would see anything the commander would rather they did not see.

We breakfasted on eggs, the great standby of poorly provisioned places, and then we reversed the proceedings of the evening before. Once more, we made sure the coast was clear.

"Let's get you out of here. Run, quick," said the General.

We set off downstairs, and I dashed for the Jeep, getting only the swiftest glance at what the rest of the base looked like. Military barracks are never an architect's dream, but this place looked even sadder in the light of day than at night. I settled down on the floor of the Jeep. As a concession to daylight, this time I was covered up with a blanket. We drove to the gate, where the soldier on duty saluted our Jeeps as we sailed on out of there, ending my night in a Russian army camp.

Meeting the Soldiers

The purpose of the camp was to secure the border. The soldiers were supposed to be helping the local people fend off Afghans who came across periodically on lethal raids. I can't say the operation was very effective, based on what I saw from our hunting camp. The camp was right on the border, near the town of Pyandzh. Nearby was a

The driver's home where we had a party.

military outpost I was able to visit without pretending I wasn't there, and the main thing that struck me was the almost complete absence of military equipment. The soldiers manning the border had almost nothing except their machine guns. They had an old army tank, with its barrel pointed ominously toward Afghanistan. It may have looked dangerous to Afghans peering at it through binoculars, but the tank had broken down, and there was no ammunition for its guns. One wonders what harm anyone thought the Russians might do to guerrilla fighters with a single tank. With no shells, all those soldiers could really do was to keep watch.

This they did from trenches on the slopes overlooking the valley, where the Pyandzh River formed the international boundary. These poor Russian kids, eighteen years old, had to go and do two years' service in this barren landscape of the Kara Tau mountains. All day long, they would sit in the trenches with their machine guns and look at Afghanistan across the valley with binoculars. Then they would come back down to their camp.

When I was perched on nearby mountain slopes, glassing for sheep, I could see some of the Afghans, but they were no more alarming as a military force than the Russian boys trapped in the trenches, dying of boredom. The Afghans were busy with their primitive plowing, using a cow to pull along a wooden contraption and create modest furrows for planting seeds. I could see them walking down to the river and entering the shallow water at the edge to collect mud, which they would pat onto the walls of the mud houses they lived in. These people did not look like rebels, insurgents, or mujahideen. They were just peasant farmers, going about their hardscrabble subsistence farming.

Then, as the sun went down, the helicopters would come, flying noisily along the valley that separated the two countries. At first I thought these were military helicopters patrolling the border. It's possible some of them were. But gradually I understood that the helicopters flying so dangerously low were the choppers of dope dealers exporting heroin. Opium poppies were Afghanistan's biggest cash crop. Every night, as darkness came on, we could hear the smugglers flying along the river in choppers loaded to the gills with drugs. To my knowledge, no one challenged them while I was there. The Soviet military presence had no way of doing so.

One day I climbed into one of the trenches with the Russian guys. Noticing my curiosity about the soldiers, the General had arranged for me to meet them. These Russian kids and I had something in common. We were occupying these mountains far from home, but up to that point we had only peered at one another through our respective binoculars while they glassed for Afghans and I glassed for sheep. We'd had no chance to talk face to face. Perhaps the General had gauged that, after I had come through the night in the army camp without complaint or incident, there couldn't be any harm in my chatting to a few of the soldiers. They took me to their training facility and let me shoot one of their machine guns, asking me to be cautious because they didn't have enough bullets as it was. They had to be careful not to wind up with none at all.

I learned that Saturday was a big night for them. They got to bathe only on Saturday evenings, when coal was supplied and the water was heated. For the rest of the week they had no coal. I assure you it was cold out in those mountains, and a hot bath felt like the utmost luxury. When Saturday came, they invited me to come to their mess hall and graciously offered me the first hot shower. All the soldiers took their showers after me.

Again, I was stunned at the primitive conditions. It was 1985, but it looked like 1895. These poor kids weren't on short-term postings for a week or two, either. These soldiers were at the border for months on end, and they were expected to function without showers for a week at a stretch, every week. Given their meager equipment and the conditions of service, it was ridiculous to suppose they could actively defend anybody. They went out on patrol using two skinny old horses. There was no other way to get around because they had no fuel. The horses were their only reliable transportation. The mighty Soviet army had a Jeep, but there wasn't enough gas to use it on patrols.

Spy Toys

Just as unlikely as the drastic shortages that marked the lives of the soldiers were the interesting toys in the possession of the General. Once we had established a comfortable trust, he showed me his special equipment. It was regular James Bond stuff.

His elegant fountain pen was not merely a refillable ink pen. It was also a cute little .22-caliber shooter. You cocked it in the middle to insert the bullet, and this also exposed the trigger. If you were up close and personal to someone giving you problems, you could nonchalantly pull out your pen and shoot your problem in the heart. Very handy. It didn't seem especially appropriate for use on a mountain-sheep hunt—it was more suitable for downtown-hotel types of applications—but when we stopped by the roadside one day, he invited me to shoot his killer pen.

The general also had a heavy, Rambo-style knife that he kept in a holster on his lower leg. It was big enough to suggest it was meant for going hand-to-snout with a wild boar or for use as a throwing knife. It was not the kind of thing you might use to skin out a sheep. The knife was a firearm as well. If you opened up the handle and put a bullet inside, you had a .32-caliber handgun, as long as you didn't mind holding the knife by the blade. Twenty years later, now that we have entered the era of computer hackers, cyber-crime, and digital eavesdropping, the spy-thriller quality of the General's gear sounds downright quaint, but, at the time, I assure you it was great fun for me to play with his secret firearms.

Fresh bread cooking for the party. Look how it sticks to the side of the oven.

The General also had a more traditional weapon, a 9mm pistol. He had been a special forces paratrooper. I told him I'd been in the army, too, which helped cement the bond between us. We got along famously. I got to shoot the knife and the pistol, as well as the pen—he was happy to have me try them all out. I think I can safely claim to have shot more kinds of firearms on that hunt than on any other. The General also gave me several of his paratrooper pins.

Beyond the soldiers of the regular army, the passing drug smugglers in their noisy choppers, the invisible Tajik villagers on our side of the border, and the Afghan farmers at work on the other side, there were two other categories of the local population. The night we were getting ready to leave, we saw some Russian mercenaries who were helping in the fight. They and some Tajiks in their party reportedly had their own freelance checkpoints spaced along the border-zone roads, though we saw very little of them.

I was glad the mercenaries didn't turn up in the army camp where I was staying, or at the local army post, because these Russians were evidently a particular target for the Afghan forces. Every so often, I was told, half a dozen Afghan fighters would sneak across the river and attack a mercenaries' camp. I suppose they knew full well that the regular army was a toothless affair, hardly worth fighting. The Afghans came into one camp fairly near us and killed four Russian mercenaries by slitting their throats. They killed only the Russians because, after the invasion of Afghanistan, they hated Russians; they did not touch any of the Tajiks. I presume the assassination party then slunk back over the border.

Talk about security! All posts went on high alert after that. On our way back to Dushanbe the army seemed to be looking furiously for the perpetrators, and some broader crisis seemed to have developed as well. Now even the good offices of the General didn't save us from long checkpoint delays.

When we drove into Dushanbe at last, the city was virtually locked down. There were men with machine guns on every street corner. No one could leave. The

General took me to a safe house, where I had to remain for two days. He didn't even permit me to look outside. As you can imagine, I was mystified by it all. Ironically, I had felt safer out in the remote borderlands. My lodging was a unit in an apartment building where the people were kind and attentive. I was not about to raise any issues with anyone.

There was only one problem. By the time I was sequestered in the safe house, I hadn't taken a bath in three or four days of hunting and hard travel. I was in no condition to be occupying anyone's apartment. The place did not have a bath; there was only a community bathhouse downtown. I told the General I really did need to take a bath, so he promised to call and make arrangements. The next day I was taken downtown to the public bath in broad daylight.

I had never been to a public bath before—this would be a whole new adventure. The bathhouse turned out to be bigger than my house. It had been temporarily closed to others and was all blocked off. I went in gratefully and got cleaned up enough to face the world again. I was then shepherded back to the safe house. During the outing, I saw just enough to convince me that the apartment was the right place for me. Machine guns were still everywhere on the streets, and I was told there had been some shooting. I suppose the civil unrest was part of the general breakdown as the Soviet Union approached its inevitable implosion. I never fully understood what was going on.

Planes were leaving only once or twice a week, the General said. They flew out at night, and I would soon be riding one of them. He said I should stand by and be ready to leave. When word came that a plane was coming in and I would be going out on it, that was my cue for one more round of traveling on the floor of a car. I hunkered down, hoping this final leg of secret travel would be as hassle-free as the others had been.

The General was still with me when they got me out of Dushanbe. He took me to an airport VIP lounge, and he stayed with me as they shook me down. He walked out to the plane with me, my gun, and my sheep, and said: "You're safe now."

Yes, I did collect a respectable Afghan urial with a guide named Yurij. But the more lasting impressions of the trip had to do with the military setting and the lessons in how to function in places like that. Alexander Lisitsin had the formula. Another outfitter might equip visiting clients with an interpreter to overcome the language barrier, but an interpreter was simply not enough. I'd had experiences with interpreters who were not interested in hunting. They thought their job was done once they had brought me to a hunting camp and would laze around, drinking, while I went hunting. An interpreter typically is not very effective at resolving delays or other logistical hang-ups, either.

In contrast, Alexander knew that sportsmen visiting the far corners of the Russian empire needed a full-time troubleshooter/guide who had good connections in the area and who could be relied upon to keep the show on the road. He cultivated people like that for his hunting operation. We would have been unable to function in Tajikistan without the General. He knew how everything worked, and nobody messed with him. If we needed something, we got it. If a safe bed for the night meant becoming the only U.S. citizen who ever stayed in a Russian army camp in Tajikistan, sleeping beside James Bond, that was a bonus.

Pays Off for Blanford Urial

Pakistan, 1986

Most of us prefer not to settle for second best. Obviously, we all want to try for the best. It's equally obvious, though, that we are constantly forced to make compromises of one kind or another, often without even realizing it. It would be nice to watch every baseball game your kid ever plays, but real life inevitably requires you to miss some of the games. You have to go for second best, and you do it without a second thought.

Some second thoughts were in order, though, as I looked at my options in early 1986. I had been scheduled for Asian hunting at its finest for almost two full months at the end of 1985. From 9 November to 8 December, I was to hunt nilgai or blue bull, sloth bear, barking deer, spotted (axis) deer, and sambar in Nepal, a country noted for its jungled valleys, tremendously high mountains, and humble villages. From there I was to fly to Pakistan to hunt markhor, one of the world's most sought-after trophies. I was pleased to have arranged a markhor permit through princely connections, which seemed a feat in itself.

I knew my chief local guide in Pakistan only as "the Old Man." My No. 1 Blanford urial measured 32 inches, while the No. 2 animal scored 30 inches.

Things looked promising when I touched down in the magical city of Katmandu. Though the setting was beautiful, the hunting turned out to be less than what I had expected—a lot less. I consider myself a lucky hunter, even a notoriously lucky hunter, but nothing went right in Nepal. Villagers had the run of the place, and the elephant that were to be used on our hunt were not properly trained. Believe me, I can think of much better shooting platforms than untrained elephant. Out of more than fifty drives, I collected one nilgai, an axis deer, and a rather small sloth bear. The whole time, I was reminding myself: Don't sweat this. You'll get your markhor in Pakistan, and things will be wonderful.

Then, just days before the Nepal hunt was over, my guide handed me a telex from the United States. It read: "Mr. Ingersoll stop Pakistan government cancelled permit stop return home stop."

Dejected, I returned home, trying to remind myself that politics had probably messed things up for me, as sometimes happens in emerging countries. I did get a refund of my deposit on the trip, so it wasn't a total loss. Then, before the end of December, I got a call from Beth Jones Levitz of Trophy Hunter Safaris, the booking agent who had helped set up the Pakistan hunt. She put me in touch with people who had been working with Pakistani wildlife officials in developing game-conservation programs.

These people told me that my markhor permit had indeed been cancelled because of politics. They asked whether I'd be interested in a sheep permit in Pakistan, should something shake loose. I knew that a number of urial inhabit parts of Pakistan, but the situation seemed questionable. Should I settle for second best? What the hell, I decided. This was not really a choice between best and second best. It seemed to be a choice between second best and nothing.

"Fine," I said.

In January someone contacted me and asked if I could leave for Karachi, Pakistan, a few days later, on 1 February. Beth was still making the final arrangements for my hunt as I was packing my bags. She told me Dr. M. Saleem Khan headed up Pakistan's hunting program, and the tribal chief in charge of the area of my hunt would be Naseer A. Tareen.

I arrived in Karachi at 5 A.M. on 3 February. After I was escorted through customs and my visa was issued, my guide and interpreter, Zeb Jogezi, met me. Zeb had spent four years at Georgetown University in Washington, D.C., and he was full of questions about all things American: McDonald's hamburgers, Ronald Reagan, the latest rock music, and so on. We spent that day sightseeing in Karachi, a hot city on the Arabian Sea near the mouth of the Indus River.

This was my first visit to Pakistan, and I was curious about life there. I asked Zeb how he usually spent his days. Come to find out, he was not really a hunting guide at all. His father ran a large company, and his brother was chief of police. While Zeb was away studying, his family sensed he was becoming too Americanized. They forced him to come home and took away his passport to make sure he stayed put. His main job was to have dinner with his father every night. All the brothers and their wives and children lived in the same household. The women were consigned to their own quarters and did the cooking, but they did not eat with the men. When his father had retired for the night, Zeb would go to his own quarters and watch movies. In the daytime he went out and met friends at tea shops.

All marriages were arranged, Zeb told me. He had never even seen his bride without her veil until the first night of his honeymoon. The girl was his cousin. I asked how well that worked, and he said that was just the way it was. They had a daughter, and once a year they would take a vacation, going somewhere by train. The rest of the time he saw his wife and daughter very little. Was he happy? He told me airily that, according to local custom, if a marriage was unsuitable or your wife was giving you trouble and you wanted a divorce, all you had to do was clap your hands three times, and the marriage was over.

I could see that, in fact, it was not that simple. Although Zeb was at ease with Western ways as a result of his time overseas, he was trapped within the web of a traditional family. He told me that if you found a woman you wanted to be with, it was almost impossible to do anything about it. In the world of arranged marriages, being caught misbehaving could lead to a harsh penalty, even death. It was when we pulled up in his car at a coffee shop that I realized he carried a pistol underneath his robe. He explained that the wealthy faced the risk of being kidnapped. He loved the United States, but he had come home to Pakistan and was planning to do his duty and prepare to take over the company from his father in due course.

As we headed out the next day for Dureji in Pakistan's province of Baluchistan, the country reminded me of Mexico, with mud huts and dry, brushy terrain. I could almost have sworn I was setting out to hunt desert bighorn in Baja California. We arrived at our camp at dark. Our lodging was a mud hut with a mud floor and no windows. A welcoming committee met us with a delicious feast of goat roasted over an open fire, vegetables, and tea. Zeb told me the village's head tracker and two of his assistants would take me out the next morning for my first day's hunting. That was the good news. The bad news was that they didn't speak English, and he wasn't coming with us.

I equipped myself with a quart of water, a quart of Tang, four oranges, and a banana, and we set out at 8 A.M. The Jeep took us as far as the mountains would allow, and we climbed and glassed the slopes for two hours. The head tracker spotted several sheep more than a mile away. Upon closer observation, one of them turned out to be a pretty good ram. The rest were ewes.

We closed within four hundred yards of them, but they noticed us and hotfooted it out of there. I never got a shot. I was trying to tell the trackers to stay down, but they didn't understand me, and I couldn't understand them. At their insistence we spent the rest of the day trying to catch up with that ram. Age was no impediment, even to the most senior of the guides. He walked ahead of the rest of us, glassing as we caught up and setting off again as soon as we reached him. My journal records his tirelessness, concluding: "Boy, can he walk!" But I knew that once a ram gets a good look at you, it's likely to be gone. The same holds true for all sheep.

Weary after eleven hours of solid walking and climbing in ninety-degree heat, we made it back to the Jeep around 7 P.M. I was so tired I could barely move, and I told Zeb we couldn't walk like that all day—the trackers would have to slow down. I cooked a freeze-dried Salisbury steak and ate it, consoled my blisters, and went to bed.

The second day of hunting was even more disappointing, although I did have the luxury of a horse, which I rode part of the way into the mountains. Near the top of a high ridge, I sat under a meager shade tree with one of the guides while the others went out glassing. When they came back to collect us around 4 P.M., they had seen no sheep. If you can imagine me, a salesman, going twelve hours without a single word, you can imagine what kind of day I had, although I did get a chance to rest.

That night our dinner of Pakistani chicken was excellent, though the chicken was on the skinny side. We had a big powwow with the trackers and a brother of the local chief. The decision that emerged was to hunt a mountain that was two and one-half hours' drive away, a place so secluded that it had probably never been hunted.

When we arrived there after the long drive, the situation did not seem promising. The villager who was to bring a horse for me failed to show. I had just about decided that the third hunting day would be worse than the first two when the fellow did appear, half an hour late. I have never been so glad to see a horse.

As we began to climb, we saw four ewes—an encouraging sign. To make the most of the glassing, we split up when we reached the crest of the mountain. Around midafternoon the guide I knew only as "the Old Man" spotted two urial rams halfway down the slope, five or six hundred yards away. We decided to get closer, thinking—hoping—they were good rams.

At this point I tried to take charge of the hunt. The sheep began to act nervous, so the Old Man and I started a crawling approach that allowed us to get within three hundred yards of the animals. My grip tightened on my trusty, beat-up 7mm. The rams were looking right at us when I got up to shoot, but I missed. They both shot like arrows straight down the mountain, and they didn't slow

While on a sightseeing tour, we came across a local tire shop.

down until they were seven or eight hundred yards away. I had no rangefinder in those days.

Now what? Could I shoot a ram at that kind of distance? Not likely. My guide wanted to try to get closer. We worked our way down the mountain until we were within three or four hundred yards, at which point he suggested that trying a shot might be our best option. All I could see of the sheep in my scope was their horns. They are strange-looking animals, with fifty- to seventy-pound bodies and disproportionately large, curled horns. This was not going to be the kind of shot I could undertake with any confidence.

Aiming way over the back of what I gauged to be the larger animal, I shot, hitting the ram in the back leg. As it limped down the mountain, we started after it. We were within two hundred yards of it when we suddenly saw two more rams—big rams! They ran down the slope a little and then stopped. A third ram appeared, as if by magic. One of these three new arrivals was an outstanding trophy, and I decided to shoot again. This time I dropped the selected ram.

To our considerable surprise, just as we needed to begin thinking about the ram I had wounded, it emerged from behind a rock where it had been resting. I finished it off, and it turned out to be the better of the two I had taken, with horns measuring 32 inches, compared to the 30 inches on the other animal. The trackers were dancing. I couldn't have been happier, though I didn't fully understand their excitement at the time. Only later did I learn that the biggest ram to have come out of the area before these two had measured 28 inches.

After taking measurements, the guides couldn't cape the sheep because I wasn't going to let them cut anything. The men's religious convictions and the local customs of Halal slaughter complicated their handling of dead animals, meaning they were unfamiliar with the details of the caping process. For such unusual trophies as these, I wanted full mounts, so I fully intended to do that critical work myself. This meant carrying both animals down, which presented some awkwardness because the horses had left.

I started to cape out the smaller animal, and we found some straight cactus ribs to produce a makeshift carrying pole for the other. We used my belt to tie on the sheep so that the men did not need to touch it. As we set off down the mountain, I was carrying one trophy and helping to carry the other on the pole. Soon I found I couldn't carry both, so I put down the smaller one. Halfway down, I changed my mind. How could I leave that sheep behind? I went back up the mountain and got it. Using the cactus ribs, we started a fire to attract the truck to our new position. It was around 10 P.M. by the time the people with the truck could see us, and they came to retrieve us.

It would be 3 A.M. before my head hit the pillow that night, after driving back to camp and caping out the trophies. It had been a wonderful day of sheep hunting—maybe my best ever. The long journey back to Karachi would begin the next morning, with Zeb driving.

Now we had to verify whether the animals belonged to the Blanford, Afghan, or Ladakh subspecies of urial. They would turn out to be Blanford urial, and they scored No. 1 and No. 2 in the trophy records, no less. Between the terrain, the climate, and the language barrier, this hunt certainly had entailed difficulties, but it was also one of my most enjoyable and satisfying because it was unusual and the trophies proved so special. Do I still hanker to hunt markhor? Occasionally. But if my plans hadn't collapsed, would I ever have booked to hunt this urial species? Probably not. At the time, I thought I was settling for second best, but you never can tell until you get there.

Chapter 15

Super Slam Blue Sheep

Nepal, 1984, 1985; China, 1991

In a moment of madness some years ago, I thought I might take myself on a grand "Around the World" tour. I wanted to see whether it would agree with me to cut back on my working hours and concentrate instead on traveling and hunting in new lands. Strategically including plenty of hunting, I booked to spend several weeks in late 1984 visiting places I had never seen—Nepal, India, Greece, Turkey, Austria, Germany, and Holland.

The flight to Katmandu, Nepal, was full of people of a species new to me: mountain hikers, known as trekkers. Just about everything else in Nepal was an eye-opener to me as well. I was astonished to see ritual bathing in the river flowing through the city—nobody does anything like that in Houston! The streets were full of unfamiliar sights: beggars, hawkers, cows, and even monkeys. Nepal is an old country with dignified historic temples and monasteries, but the living conditions I saw were grimmer than anything I had seen in Mexico, which was then my standard for comparison.

An Introduction to the Mountains of Asia

My objective was the Himalayan blue sheep, or bharal, an animal of the high mountains of Nepal, Tibet, and western China. Bluish gray with dark leg markings and pale underparts, it is a creature of

elevations starting around ten thousand feet. Blue sheep may be solitary or may occur in bands of a dozen or so. They eat grasses, lichens, and other hardy mountain plants, and the young are prey to leopard, snow leopard, fox, and tawny eagles. The distinctive blue sheep more closely resemble ibex and tur than they do other wild sheep. Just as the Rocky Mountain goat is the only species in the genus *Oreamnos,* the blue sheep is the only species in the genus *Pseudois.* Some authorities consider a small population of dwarf blue sheep to be a separate species; others challenge that.

My hunting outfitter was T. J. Thapa, and my hunting companion was Ed Aremia. A helicopter flew us to ten thousand feet. Then it stopped on a mountain to set down the extra gas and part of its load before ferrying us into our high mountain camp at an elevation of 11,200 feet. The helicopter would return for the rest of the load. Peering down as we flew toward our area in the Dhorpatan Hunting Reserve in western Nepal, we saw that every mountainside was cultivated to the absolute limits of steepness, crisscrossed with trails, and punctuated with homesteads. The pleasant camp was manned by thirty-seven people because that was how many porters it took to carry everything in. They had spent five to seven days carrying in our gear and supplies on their backs. They carried the bags of rice on their heads. A water buffalo and some wandering chickens were part of the larder. There was one chicken fewer as soon as we arrived because we had it for dinner.

The nights were extremely cold at that altitude. On the first night I was sleeping in a little pup tent when I woke up, gasping for air. I got up and went outside, telling myself, Calm down, Gary, you're not going to die.

The next morning, when I told Thapa about it, he said, "You had the flap open on the tent, didn't you?"

We took a look, and the air vent was still zipped up tight. The camp attendant had forgotten to open it. With ice forming on the tent, I had simply used up all the oxygen inside. No wonder I was gasping.

We saw good numbers of blue sheep in bands ranging from half a dozen to about eighty animals, but they all seemed to be smaller than I wanted. Porters accompanied us on each day's scouting to carry our gear, and it was a relief not to have to carry anything while climbing to even higher elevations in that thin mountain air. Oxygen aside, the abundance of trails made for fairly easy walking most of the time. We spike camped at sixteen thousand feet for two days, with Sherpas carrying our

I collected this sloth bear, an unusual trophy, on a 1985 hunt in a forested region of eastern Nepal, near Rajbiraj.

On my 1984 Nepal hunt with outfitter T. J. Thapa, a helicopter ferried us in. It stopped at 10,000 feet to set down extra gas before delivering us to our camp at 11,200 feet in the Dhorpatan Hunting Reserve in western Nepal.

gear in, and on the third day we returned to our base camp. I was amazed at how my guides managed to sleep just curled up in a blanket. After I took a modest ram, there was no way to escape the freezing nights by leaving early. I had to wait until the chopper brought in the next hunting client.

A year later, in November 1985, I saw a completely different side of wild Nepal. Once again my incoming flight contained numerous excited trekkers, and once again I would be hunting with Ed, this time guided by a fellow named Mahesh. We flew on to the town of Bhairwa and proceeded into forested country near Rajbiraj in eastern Nepal. Styled more like an African hunting camp, our tented camp there was comfortable.

I collected a fine nilgai, or blue bull, after much patient searching. The nilgai's short horns make trophy quality difficult to judge in the field. I took one, then took a much better one, and was surprised and delighted when the larger bull turned out to be No. 1 in the SCI records. It's not likely to be topped because nilgai hunting in Nepal was later closed. We hunted several unusual species, collecting sloth bear and barking deer as well as axis. We also saw sambar deer and wild peacocks and other exotic birds. We hunted leopard, though unsuccessfully, and I was struck by how the bait-and-blind style of leopard hunting differs from the method in Africa. On an African safari you hang your bait in a tree and build a blind on the ground. In Nepal our blind was in a tree, and the bait was on the ground in the form of a goat tied to a tree.

At the time I had no plans to try again for blue sheep, but I later learned that these animals were a good deal more numerous in China, and the country was beginning to open up to visiting sportsmen. I was curious. Here was a chance to experience some wild country that scarcely anyone I knew had ever visited, and to learn something of a culture totally new to me. And, although I know very well that the formula for a great hunting trip does not rely on bringing home a record head, it did sound as if China might well present an opportunity for a ram better than the blue sheep I had. My theory was that the experience should come first, and the trophies would follow. It was time to book a hunt to China.

Bands of One Hundred Rams

My 1991 visit to China's high, lonely Qinghai province was rich confirmation of that theory. It offered unparalleled hunting for blue sheep, which exist in the tens of thousands in some hunting sectors. Other game species included Tibetan gazelle, also abundant, and red deer. The hunts were inexpensive, as sheep hunts go, and everyone—tourist officials, hosts, and guides—treated visiting American hunters like gentry.

Our group left San Francisco on 12 September. In Houston it was still hot and humid, and we looked forward to cool fall days in Qinghai. Russell Selle of Houston-based Hunt Masters expertly arranged the expedition from start to finish. After clearing immigration in Beijing, we spent five days touring one of the world's most interesting cities. One thing I had always wanted to do—don't we all?—was to stand on China's Great Wall. On 17 September this old country boy from Minnesota got to do just that. Other highlights included the Summer Palace, the Forbidden City, and the Beijing Zoo, which houses some of the world's rarest animals. I brought Jason along for the sightseeing portion of the trip, thinking this would be a once-in-a-lifetime opportunity for him to visit China. Little did

Russell Selle arranged my later hunt in China's Qinghai province, where we hunted for blue sheep at elevations between 12,000 and 16,000 feet.

I took this modest blue sheep in Nepal in 1984, with a guide I knew as Hawkeye. The species is far more numerous in China.

we know that twelve years later, Jason would be working and living in Beijing.

I was really looking forward to a traditional Beijing duck dinner. My mouth was watering as the chef stood by our table, carving our duck for us. My hunger soon turned to shock as I watched him throw away the "good parts" of meat and serve us the skin and fat! That same night, on our way to the bathroom, we spotted eels thrashing around on the floor of a mop closet. Soon some cooks came and gathered them up in baskets and took them to the kitchen, but not before we were able to snap pictures of them.

It turns out the hunting world is quite small. On the last day of sightseeing, we were in the hotel lobby when we ran into Don Cox and Dr. Jim Conklin. They were returning from their hunt just as we were about to begin ours.

On 19 September Jason and the wives left Beijing for the United States, and the hunters flew west-southwest to Lanzhou and Xining, the capital of Qinghai province. Xining sits at seventy-two hundred feet, and an overnight stay there helped acclimate us to the even higher elevations of our hunt area, where the base camp was at twelve thousand feet. The trip there took twelve hours by Jeep through countryside that ranged from cultivated cropland to expansive pasture to a sparse, high-altitude desert. About sixty miles outside Xining is Qinghai Lake, a cobalt-blue lake as salty as Utah's Great Salt Lake. Our trip happened to coincide with the fall migration of waterfowl and shorebirds, and vast flights of them used the beautiful lake as a stopover.

The big, tawny mountains that backdropped our base camp rose to 16,000 feet. The skies were almost as blue as Qinghai Lake. Temperatures climbed to comfortable levels during the day and dipped near freezing during the autumn nights. No trees or brush existed, only calf-high grasses that supported good populations of gazelle and red deer—and more of the majestic, stone-colored blue sheep than I could imagine. While the possibility of a good ram was the impulse for flying halfway around the world, I chose to concentrate first on gazelle and save the best for last. I scored on a nice twelve-inch gazelle the first day out.

The sheep stories shared around the campfire that evening were amazing. Bob DeWitz told of seeing a new band of one hundred rams, seven of which he swore were world records. The problem was that the sharp-eyed rams bolted before Bob and his native guide could get close enough. I talked the matter over with my guide. For the next several days we would concentrate on blue sheep in another area he knew.

At the end of the third full day of hunting, Bob came in with the blue sheep of all blue sheep. The monster ram would later hold the No. 1 position in the Safari Club International record book. Bob's advice to me: "There are six more world records in the herd. It's just a matter of getting close enough to let that 7mm magnum of yours do its magic."

Each morning's hunt was much the same. On surefooted ponies that appeared too small to carry western riders, we scurried to peaks and ridges to glass the distant slopes. It was a good thing, too, because we never could have covered as much ground without those horses. At elevations between twelve thousand and sixteen thousand feet, climbing a few hundred yards can leave a fit man wheezing for air. By this time, Bob and Ruby had come down with altitude sickness—in fact, they were in such trouble that I had the camp foreman take them below ten thousand feet. The foreman didn't want to take them down because it would use up too much gas. Bob and Ruby were both spitting up blood, and I told the foreman he'd better get them down before they died. Once they got below ten thousand feet, they were both fine. The horses, on the other hand, could cover miles without difficulty. The good news was that I saw plenty of sheep; the bad news was that they saw us at basically the same time and hightailed it for the next province.

During this hunt, we joined in on the local villagers' fall festival with a big party held right in our camp. Like our Thanksgiving, the festival celebrates an ample harvest, and I can say I've never seen such a huge sampling of delicious food and drink in my life. We were treated like royalty. Richard Hawkins, Bob DeWitz, Tom Rubenstein, our interpreter, and I were seated at the head table, and each of us received a special hat to wear. A good deal of vodka flowed. Villagers

In Nepal, Sherpa porters carried our gear to a spike camp at 16,000 feet. Porters also accompanied us on scouting forays, and it was a relief not to have to carry anything at such elevations.

Flanked by Tom Rubenstein and our Chinese interpreter, I was seated at the head table for a wonderful dinner organized right in our camp by local villagers.

Guide Mahesh and I were thrilled when my nilgai, or blue bull, turned out to be No. 1 in the SCI record book. Nilgai hunting has since been closed in Nepal.

brought us dish after dish of food, an all-vegetarian feast of everything they grew on their farms. Much of it was unfamiliar, though we recognized the watermelon and some varieties of squash grown in the area.

There were also two long wing tables for our large camp staff. We cranked up our country-and-western music to add to the celebration and had a downright unbelievable party out there in the mountains of China. In the morning, when I was to go out and try for a sheep in the area where Bob had taken his, my guide was sporting such a hangover that there was no way in the world he could go with me. I went out with just a small crew of local guides while my main guide nursed his delicate condition.

We rode up a valley Bob had hunted and found the herd, just as he had said we would. For a sheep hunter, or any other hunter, to see a band of one hundred rams is mind-boggling. They were one thousand yards away, tiny even through the lens of a powerful spotting scope, and I had to get closer. We sent one of my guides around to flank the sheep and try to spook them our way. They spooked, but the wrong way.

We rode on up the mountain to the point where the herd had disappeared. Then we saw them—ten big rams leaving the main herd, traveling almost parallel to the ridge where we were concealed. They didn't see us, but they knew something was up. I got off my horse and ran just below the ridgeline to keep up with them on the other side, hoping they would drop down the mountain on my side, closer to my level. Finally, they did so, in single file, fifty yards in front of me!

My Chinese blue sheep was the animal that completed my Super Slam of wild sheep, one more trophy downed with the old 7mm that has served me so well.

The hard part was keeping my composure while I tried to pick out the best ram of the bunch. From my rocky position I could never see more than two or three rams at a given moment, but when one old ram with exceptional horns walked past, I put the cross hairs just behind its blue shoulders, flicked off the safety, and tightened the trigger. The ram that would round out my Super Slam of the world's wild sheep species dropped at the shot from the 7mm magnum, one more kill for the rifle that had served me well all over the world. My sheep wasn't as large as Bob's, but it was a fine record-book animal, a trophy that will hold a special place with the eleven other rams that contributed to my Super Slam.

Would I recommend a hunt for Chinese blue sheep in the high mountains of Qinghai province? You bet I would. When I left, there were at least six more potential world records up there.

Chapter 16

From Gobi Argali to Snow Sheep

Mongolia, 1981, 1984, 1985; Kamchatka, 1993–2004

Asia is a vast continent, mostly invisible to us in North America—a land of confusing names, impenetrable languages, and mysterious customs. Chances are I might never have thought much about going there had it not been for my interest in wild sheep. Even then, I might have had second thoughts if I had known I would wind up attempting to process my own trophy in a hotel bathroom.

Hunting opportunities for visiting sportsmen in Asia began to open up during the 1980s. Ten years before the palisades came down and the Soviet Union dissolved, I got my first look at Russia and Mongolia. In 1981 Houston Safari Club past president Cecil Hopper and I took a hunt for white-tailed gazelle, Siberian ibex, and argali sheep in the Gobi Desert. In those days most of us knew little about the game animals occurring in the far republics of Central Asia, but here is a brief primer to help you make sense of the geography and the sheep.

In a nutshell, Mongolia is central to the international hunting landscape. The northwestern part of the country is largely mountainous and includes the Altai Mountains. The mountains yield to the Gobi Desert in the southeast, and the capital of Ulaanbaator lies where the two regions meet. Mongolia is flanked by China to the south and southeast and by Yakutia and Siberia (part of the Russian Federation) to the north and northeast. The long finger of the Kamchatka Peninsula reaches southward from eastern Siberia, just across the Bering Sea from Alaska.

To the west of Mongolia lies the wide expanse of Kazakhstan, and stringing out in a southwesterly direction are Kyrgyzstan, Tajikistan, and Afghanistan. The largest and southernmost of the three is Afghanistan, bordered by Iran and Pakistan. Got all that? Picture high desert plains and wide valleys punctuated by stunning mountains, and you have a good sense of most of the region, although parts of it also have wooded valleys, grassy steppes, and boreal forest.

Trying to summarize the region's sheep species is a little harder because the Grand Slam Club/Ovis recognizes numerous Asian species and subspecies. Among the easiest to understand are six regional kinds of snow sheep belonging to *Ovis nivicola*—Kamchatka, Yakutia, Kolyma, Koryak, Okhotsk, and Putorana snow sheep. They all look rather like the North American bighorn.

Grand Slam/Ovis recognizes five kinds of urial belonging to *Ovis vignei:* Trans-Caspian, Afghan, Blanford, Punjab, and Ladakh—and no less than fifteen categories of the much larger and more dramatic argali sheep that share the species name *Ovis ammon.* I will save you from a full listing of their names. You can get a good look at pictures of all these sheep and various others at www.wildsheep.org.

Mongolia is the core habitat of argali. Heaviest in both body and horn is the Altai argali *(Ovis ammon ammon),* occurring in the Altai Mountains of Mongolia. The smaller Gobi argali, *Ovis ammon darwini,* is found in both Mongolia and China, and the Hangai argali *(O. a. ssp. Hangaii)* occurs only in Mongolia's Hangai Mountains. Typically, the Hangai argali is intermediate in size between the Gobi and the Altai argali (formerly known as the mid-Altai argali), and Safari Club International now recognizes it as a separate trophy category. When I first hunted argali, the Gobi

Alan and Barb Sachman and I got around in Kamchatka on an ATV we called the tank.

My Mongolian guide Bajra pulled up at a herders' yurt, where he negotiated some help from the elderly occupant, the man's son, and the grandson. They helped us ambush my mid-Altai argali ram.

argali, expected to carry horns in the forty-inch range, was priced at sixty-five hundred dollars; the mid-Altai argali, carrying around fifty inches, was ten thousand dollars; and the Altai argali, with horns in the high fifties and sixties, was fifteen thousand dollars.

The longest horns are borne by the magnificent Marco Polo argali sheep *(Ovis ammon polii)*, a creature of the high mountains of Tajikistan and Kyrgyzstan, China and Afghanistan. These animals live at altitudes of seventy-five hundred to sixteen thousand feet. The usual jump-off points for hunting them are the towns of Bishkek and Osh in Kyrgyzstan.

Argali in Kyrgyzstan to the south of the Naryn River are considered Marco Polo argali sheep "proper." Those found north of the Naryn River are considered to belong to a subspecies of Marco Polo known as the Hume argali *(Ovis ammon humei)* or to be Tian Shan argali *(O. a. karelini)*. Much of the hunting in Kyrgyzstan at present is in the area that Grand Slam/Ovis defines for the Hume argali.

An Ovis World Slam requires twelve sheep species or subspecies from a list of forty-five sheep of the world, with some restrictions on which ones can be entered together. For example, only two subspecies of the eastern Siberian snow sheep can count toward your twelve.

Things are not quite so intricate in the ibex department. Grand Slam/Ovis lists four kinds of Asian ibex *(Capra sibirica)*. The widespread mid-Asian ibex is the largest and grows the longest horns. It is commonly a rich brown and occurs in the high mountains of Afghanistan, Tajikistan, Kyrgyzstan, and China, including the Pamir and Tian Shan mountains. The Himalayan ibex, also brown, is an animal of Pakistan and northern India. Mongolia has two species, the Altai ibex and the smaller

The excellent mid-Altai argali ram I took in 1984 measured 54 inches—and caused me some consternation in a Moscow hotel. It would become a full mount in my trophy room.

Gobi ibex, both usually somewhat paler animals than the other Asian ibex, with dark legs and a dorsal stripe. Both of these are found in China as well.

Texans in Russia

When going into Russia to reach Mongolia in 1981, what we saw was drabness. A bright, utopian series of republics this was not. Everyone was dressed in dark and muted colors. Almost everything around us looked old—not old in the sense of being elegant and richly worked, but just old and tired. Dominant among our impressions of Russia were tight government control, military presence, and a population still living in a bygone era.

Moving around with the irrepressible Cecil Hopper was fun. In his western boots and hat, he was instantly identifiable to everyone as a Texan, and the Cold War receded from people's minds in direct proportion to his Texan-ness. He brought a smile to every face, just as he does at home.

I hunted the Gobi in 1981, collecting a nice ram and an ibex, and I formed a bond with my Mongolian guide, whom I knew only as Bajra. He worked for the official government hunting/tourism agency Zhuulchin, and he hunted the way I like to hunt. In 1984, when I went back for mid-Altai argali and mid-Asian ibex, I wanted the same guide, but I had no idea how to go about arranging this. Imagine my delight in finding the very same fellow standing on the front steps of the hotel in Ulaanbaator when I arrived. This was a good sign. Bajra did not know I was the incoming hunter until he laid eyes on me, and we hugged each other in the street at this discovery. Our party consisted of a Russian Jeep, a driver, and the two of us. We rounded up a case of vodka and some food and were on our way.

One reason I favored this guide was that he had no commitment to a base camp. He believed in driving and stopping to glass, then walking or climbing and stopping to glass, then driving some more, and stopping for the night wherever we were. We simply lay down on the ground next to the Jeep. He had a gunnysack, and he would send the driver off with that sack to collect enough livestock dung to use like charcoal briquets for fuel. Once they had boiled some water, I ate my freeze-dried food, and the guide and the driver made tea and cooked what they wanted over the fire.

Bajra's English was very good, sufficient for us to conduct substantial conversations at night as we lay in our sleeping bags, looking up at the stars. The first thing he wanted to know was this: If America was the most powerful nation in the world, how could we elect a president like Jimmy Carter, a peanut farmer? He wanted to know about my work, and I wound up holding an informal workshop on real estate equity. I told him about the economics of buying a home.

"Why would you want to do that?" he asked.

It was still the communist era, when nobody owned homes, and electricity cost five dollars a month.

I suggested to Bajra that someday a home would be worth more money than when one bought it. Perhaps he could be earning money both as an English teacher and as a hunting guide—two jobs, two incomes. No, he said, he did both jobs because that was what he was told to do. I suggested that, with his command of English, he had an important skill, like a doctor or a lawyer, and he really should be earning more than others did. No, he told me, the place to earn the really big money was working in the coal mines because your life was a lot shorter. Teachers and lawyers and doctors did not earn that much because they worked in safe jobs. The idea that education might result in a higher income was quite novel to him.

When you drive through that country, it smells as if you're in an onion patch, and your eyes burn because of all the wild onion plants. On the third day out we saw two exceptional rams, but they were several hundred yards away and were looking right at us. There was no way to get close to them in the exposed terrain. I was going to have to try a long shot.

My shot broke a front leg on the better ram. We tracked it all day, up and down, jumping it twice. The ram was not going to die from the wound itself, pronounced my guide, but the wolves would get it. He reckoned he knew where the ram was going and thought we could get it the next day. He suggested we stop in at a sheepherders' camp not far from where he thought the sheep would wind up. Coming from anyone else, I might have assumed such speculation was merely fiction designed to snow the visiting hunter, but I was inclined to believe this guide. He evidently had a plan in mind.

We drove the Jeep for a distance and pulled up beside the herders' yurt. A grandfather emerged, followed by a younger man, evidently his son, and a child. My guide proposed a chat with the old man over some vodka. Out came the fine china, the three best cups in the yurt. We drank a toast to sheep hunting, and I gave the grandson a Snickers. It turned out that Bajra wanted to hire these three and their horse and dog as helpers. What he had in mind for the morning was that we would set up an ambush before first light and ask the herders to try to push the sheep toward our position. I couldn't imagine they would be able to push the wounded sheep to us, so I told them, "If you can do it, I'll give you a five-hundred-dollar tip."

Before dawn, we set out on our long drive to the ambush point. As the sun rose, we saw the three herders heading toward us, tracking the wounded sheep. They were on the far distant mountain—the old man on horseback, the son and grandson walking with their dog on a leash. They had disassembled an old pair of

Bajra had no commitment to a base camp—he was happy to keep moving and stop wherever we wound up. The yellow tent was mine.

binoculars, and each had his own "scope" tied to his wrist with a handkerchief. They were determined to help me get my ram. Pretty soon, peering through our own binoculars, we also saw the sheep in the distance, approaching us. The ram kept glancing back, concerned about the three behind it.

When the guide thought the ram was in range, he nudged me to ease over the low ridge for a shot. Sure enough, the sheep was less than fifty yards away. One clean shot and I had my ram. Its horns measured 54 inches, with bases over 16 inches—an excellent mid-Altai argali. I have rarely seen people as excited as our three herder-drivers were when they arrived on the scene. We photographed them with the ram and gave them all the meat. As promised, they received their five-hundred-dollar bonus, which surely helped out during the harsh Mongolian winter. As impromptu guides, they had earned it.

Getting the mid-Altai argali home presented an interesting hiccup. The guides had processed the trophy horns as best they could and had salted the hide, but, after I flew out of Ulaanbaator on my homebound run, I found I had a problem. In my room at the National Hotel near Red Square in Moscow, I realized that some ugly seepage and a horrendous smell were emanating from the canvas bag containing the trophy. The head had not been properly boiled, and the weather was warm. The area around the horns and skull was infested with maggots. I had a day before the next flight to do something about it.

First I tried washing it and washing it and washing it some more, using the bathroom shower head. Managing a 54-inch set of horns in a bathtub is not a very straightforward affair. I put the skull out on my little balcony, hoping the sun would do it some good, and I draped the dripping hide over the balcony railing. I also

Tough little Russian horses saved us from slogging through wet brush while hunting bear and snow sheep in Kamchatka.

washed out the stinking bag. Then it occurred to me that I might be able to get some bleach from the floor attendant. Each floor of the hotel had a big Russian woman in charge, and I thought perhaps the one on our floor could supply me with some disinfectant to kill the worms.

As I approached her, I noticed she had the same hairstyle as many of the other Russian women—black hair with a bleached white spot. I'm guessing this was their attempt to become Americanized. I pointed at the spot on her hair and said, "Peroxide." Unfortunately, she thought I was telling her how pretty her hair looked. Thinking she was returning the compliment, she pointed to my gray hair, smiled, and began talking to me in Russian. Knowing I wasn't getting anywhere, I went down to the front desk and asked where I could get some peroxide. They advised me to check at the pharmacy across the street.

The Russian pharmacist seemed to think I was out of my mind. My hair was already graying—why on earth would I need to bleach it? I bought a large bottle of peroxide, a jar of salt, and a big bottle of strong perfume. Back in my room, I peroxided the hell out of that skull and horns and put the head back out on the balcony overnight. I salted the hide again and washed the bag again. In the morning I gave the head another dose of peroxide, offering up a prayer of thanks to the floor

A helicopter flew us to our snow sheep base camp in the soggy, foggy mountains, and afterward flew us out in heavy weather to the town of Chumikan. Our outfitter was Alex Rybalski.

attendant for this idea. I then repacked the head and splashed perfume liberally all over the bag. The bundle no longer stank when I flew out of Moscow. Instead, my luggage and I now both smelled like a cheap whore. I'm not sure whether I fooled the sniffer dogs or there were simply none on the job the day I flew home.

I arranged to hunt with Bajra again in 1985, this time for a big maral stag. We planned to use ponies and hunt from fly camps, but the weather was not on our side. Rain and fog rolled in. We were soaked from morning until night, every day. I borrowed some rubber boots so that at least my feet would be dry. Stags were everywhere, but each time we tried to get a shot, the animals disappeared into the fog. Our fallback plan was to retreat to a base-camp yurt and hunt roe deer. We were sitting on a rock bluff not far from the camp, glassing for deer, when we saw a good wolf, which turned out to be a No. 1 animal. On the last day I also took a roebuck that made the book.

The mid-Altai ibex I took on the 1984 hunt earned me a silver award in the Houston Safari Club's annual trophy competition. The majestic mid-Altai argali, with its great, sweeping horns, became a full mount in my trophy room—a reminder of good hunts in Mongolia, of the wide expanses where argali sheep live, and of my adventures with peroxide. I didn't realize then that the sheep was part of a project with no end yet in sight. My 1980s argali hunts were merely a prelude to a whole lot more sheep, ibex, tur, and chamois hunting in the mountains of Europe and Asia. Not until 2005 did I finally collect the magnificent Marco Polo ram I consider the pinnacle of this endeavor (see chapter 18).

Snow Sheep Are Elusive

Getting my snow sheep took several hunts. I hunted Russian species three years in a row: in Kazakhstan in 1993 and, in 1994 and 1995, north of Vladivostok along the eastern mainland coast of the Russian Federation. I was back to hunt snow sheep on the remote Kamchatka Peninsula in 2003 and 2004.

Our October–November 1993 party was a group of fourteen, including Richard Hawkins, Tom Rubenstein, and Bob DeWitz from Minnesota, plus Houston Safari Club members Irvin Barnhart, Mike and Barret Simpson, and Jerry Rubenstein. Three inches of snow greeted us in Moscow, and we first headed for the Smolensky Reserve for a series of driven hunts for moose and wild boar. A lot of the pig we saw were young, and a lot of the moose we saw were cows, but Richard did get a good stag, and I shot a large boar on the last day. Even with dogs, we could not find the boar before we had to leave, but the guides later found it and sent it along with the rest of the trophies.

Next, we went sheep hunting in Aktau, in Kazakhstan. I was lucky to take a Transcaspian urial ram on the first day. I dropped it with one shot from above at two hundred and fifty to three hundred yards. Rich and Tom both got good sheep, and, after quite a search, I took a gazelle that went 14½ inches, the best taken from that area.

I first went out after snow sheep and bear with Bob and Tom for two weeks in August 1994. This time we flew from Alaska into Khabarovsk, then flew on to Iru in a twin-engine plane that carried about fifteen people. One passenger was a woman with a box containing two live rabbits! We landed in a field to gas up, which required that we disembark just long enough to get eaten up by mosquitoes. A big chopper awaited us at Iru. Loaded with camp gear, a boat, two dogs, and nine people, it flew us for another half-hour and landed beside the ocean, where we set up camp and enjoyed a king crab dinner.

Tom and Bob hunted first from the boat, while I went inland. I can't remember when I climbed any harder. On the first day I got back to camp at 10:30 P.M., so dead tired that I hit the sack without dinner. In the morning, going out to meet another group, the chopper dropped Bob and me on top of a mountain, where we saw about twenty-six sheep but no rams. Heading back to camp, we encountered a dangerously steep thousand-foot drop and faced a truly hair-raising climb down. I struggled in at 11:30 P.M., utterly exhausted.

It seemed prudent to ride the boat the next day and try for a bear. I was not destined to get either a bear or a sheep on that trip, however. Heavy weather and high winds skunked us, though we moved our camp to try another area near Ayan. We eventually did see a band of five rams, but they escaped us in difficult wind. The outfitter offered us the opportunity to return at no cost the following year.

Jason Brings Me Luck

My sense of a time warp began even before leaving the United States on my Kamchatka hunt of 13–26 August 1995. This time Jason accompanied me. Again, we set out from Anchorage. The little diner where we had supper strongly evoked an eatery I'd known when I was a kid in Minnesota—it was just like the restaurant in Pine Island. The little woman who ran it said she'd been in Alaska since 1959.

Our flights took us to Anadyr on the Arctic coast and then south to Khabarovsk, where we stayed in a pleasant hotel built by Russians and South Koreans. Then we flew on to Polina Osipenko and the village of Nelkan. Bad weather in the mountains trapped us in Nelkan; this meant we had to stay at the home of our outfitter and guide, Alex Rybalski.

We explored the 150-year-old village and photographed its quaint church. The population was only a little over one hundred people, and the most impressive facilities were at a nearby camp for gold

In 1995 I took a 39-inch Russian bighorn or snow sheep north of Vladivostok along the eastern mainland coast of the Russian Federation. The ram was thirteen years old and made the SCI record book.

miners. They had a large sauna and invited us to try it. Who would have thought we would start out a Russian sheep hunt with a sauna? It must have been two hundred degrees or better inside. After our first stint in the hot room, we took a cold shower, then submitted to the local tradition of being flayed with branches of an aromatic shrub. When we returned to the sauna chamber, attendants poured water over hot rocks to ratchet up the steam.

At dinner we discovered a kind of melon new to us both. It looked like watermelon but was yellow. There was another interesting aspect of food on this trip. At Alex's home there was no store food. We went out into the hills on the first afternoon to pick mushrooms, which appeared on the breakfast table accompanied by eggs from the henhouse out back.

Awaiting our plane in the morning, Jason and I played cards. He thought he could beat me at gin rummy but wound up owing me sixty dollars before noon. The fog and rainy weather did not lift. We could not fly into our hunting camp that day, and it continued to rain all night. Sasha, the cook from my previous year's visit, stopped in during the evening to pay us a call, armed with a bottle of red wine.

The helicopter arrived, and I saw that it was the same one we had flown in the year before. When we arrived at camp, it was cold, windy, and raining. The camp consisted of three big tents: one for the guides, one for Jason and me, and the kitchen tent. We could see snow on the tops of the surrounding mountains. Alex did not come with us. My guide, Ivan, was the same man as the year before, and Jason's guide was Yuri.

After a breakfast of tea, pancakes, and a hot bowl of rice cereal, we split up to hunt in different directions. The mountains were still fogged in, but I was in for a lucky hunting day. Ivan spotted two nice rams around 10 A.M. They were below us, hunkering down out of the wind. Training the scope on them, we could see that one was very good—in the range of thirty-eight to forty inches. It was an old ram with horns heavily broomed off. The other was good but not as heavy.

We kept our altitude and circled to another point for a better approach as we came down toward the sheep. As we drew nearer, they got up and began to feed. We were still too far away to shoot, and they were progressing across the valley and up the far side. We tried another approach, again failing to get close enough for a shot. When the animals went over a ridge, we stopped for some lunch and tea. It was now noon, and it was snowing so hard that we could barely see. The snow eased off as we finished our lunch, and we started after the rams again.

As we topped the ridge where they had disappeared, lo and behold, they were close-by and coming toward us.

"Take the one on the left," Ivan instructed me.

The distance was only fifty or sixty yards. With one shot, the sheep was down. The second ram hung around for several minutes, unsure what to do. My ram was a handsome trophy with horns of 38 and 39 inches and heavy bases 14 inches in circumference.

It was around 2:30 P.M. when we started back up the mountain with the skin and half the meat, leaving the rest to be picked up the next day. The hike along the upper slopes and then down to our camp took about four hours, getting us back at the civilized hour of 6:30 P.M. We were tired, but Ivan was one happy guide, and we celebrated with vodka. Lying in a tent at nine thousand feet, listening to some country-and-western music, and enjoying the heat of our little shepherd's stove, I thought, *Hey, it doesn't get any better than this.*

Jason spent several more days walking himself to exhaustion without getting a sheep. We changed camps twice. Ivan took over as his guide, and I went with them some of the time. The weather remained taxing, and we were grateful for the little stove at our first camp and for a trapper's cabin at another. But all Jason got were wet boots, sore leg muscles, and blisters on both feet. He gave it up when one knee began giving him trouble as well.

"He gave it a hell of a try," I noted in my journal.

We were rather impressed with our cook, Sergei, who went out hunting around ten o'clock one morning and reappeared in the late afternoon with a sheep that measured about thirty inches. He had shot it in the heart at one hundred yards with a .22 from which the stock had been cut, so that he shot it like a pistol.

Our way out was not exactly straightforward. The helicopter could not get in to pick us up because of bad weather. Plan B was that Ivan would walk down to the village and ask the gold miners to fetch us in their all-terrain vehicle, a strange critter with a tube-shaped cab riding on large treads. We thought the helicopter was likely to be able to reach the gold mine. It was, but the continuing heavy weather meant we had to practically skim the surface of the river in order to get out of the mountains and down to the coast.

The pilot delivered us to the dirt runway of a town called Chumikan, where the streets were also dirt. From there we were supposed to take a commercial flight back to Nelkan and Khabarovsk. I inquired when that might be. No plane was coming in that day, said the woman who seemed to be in charge. Maybe tomorrow. Other planes were present, but they were being loaded with fifty-gallon barrels of caviar, of all things, and were not available for unexpected passenger traffic.

Our pilot, a military man, was the only person there who spoke some English. He graciously invited us all to his house, and it seemed most of the town's population turned up to take a look at us. One of them sent for a woman named Tanya, who also spoke English. Someone produced a delicious meal of salmon for us, and we pulled out the vodka and country-and-western music. Would you believe we all wound up dancing? The bad weather provoked a fine impromptu party. Along about the second bottle of vodka, Tanya said she wanted to go to the United States—could I get her a visa? I brought out some chocolates to conclude the evening, and our hosts gave us a large fruit jar of caviar to take home with us.

We made our peace with the fact that we would just have to get home whenever we got home. There was no way to call to explain. Our hosts laid sleeping pallets on the floor for us, and we were all sound asleep when the rapping at the door started, sometime around midnight. The woman from the airport had arrived to tell us a plane was coming in. We packed up and struggled back there in time to see a little twin-engine plane arrive, and we watched its passengers disembark. We loaded and took off around 2 A.M. in weather that still seemed decidedly questionable for flying.

Arriving in Khabarovsk at 4:30 A.M., we checked into a brand-new hotel built by the Chinese. At first we were excited about the prospect of taking a bath, but we found that the place still had neither running nor warm water. It only had buckets of cold water standing forlornly beside the commodes for flushing. Our stay in this establishment was destined to be brief. We were awakened at 7 A.M. for a 10:30 A.M. flight out. It was here that Jason's six-minute phone call home set him back one hundred and eight dollars!

More Punishment

You'd think I would have had enough of all the bad weather Russian destinations had to offer, but in August 2003 I went back to Kamchatka for more. I hunted bighorn and bear, accompanied by Alan and Barbara Sachman. A new and creative Russian airline rip-off greeted us this time: a charge of two hundred and ten dollars for taking a gun case. We flew out of Anchorage to Petropavlovsk, close to the tip of Kamchatka. Guides Alex and Yuri were waiting for us, and we had a three-hour bus ride to a regional center called Esso, which looked much like Alaskan bush villages.

You won't be surprised to learn that weather caught up with us right away. Rain meant planes could not fly. We passed the time playing gin rummy until Alan owed me twelve dollars. We were stuck all that day and all of the second day. And then a third. By that time, I was down one hundred dollars at rummy. Alex told me that because of rain, Jerry Rubenstein had sat in the camp we were trying to reach for eight days of a ten-day hunt and had gone home with no sheep or bear.

At last, on the fourth day, we flew the one-hour hop by helicopter to our first camp, which stood by a river. The banks were flooded from all the rain, and one tent was already awash. Alan tried fishing, but no fish were biting in that roiling river. The chief guide told us he had seen sheep farther up the valley and we would try for them, but I saw no sheep. Alan, Barb, and their guide set out on horseback for an area where three rams and a bear had been seen ten days before, but they saw no sheep, either. The guides suggested moving to a lower base camp—perhaps the sheep had moved down. During the night, the wind came up; it blew stronger and stronger until it must have been blowing fifty to sixty miles per hour. Our big tent blew down, others partially collapsed, and the wind broke the zipper on my tent so that the flap was wide open. I spent most of the night holding up the tent post.

The wind was victorious. With all our tents down, we needed a change of plan. Alan, Barb, and I now argued for hunting bear instead—we were running out of time. We packed up the camp in howling wind so fierce that it almost blew us over. The crew had an ATV we called "the tank" because it looked much like a tank with no gun. You could ride either on top or inside. We agreed that Alan, Barb, and their guide would proceed downriver in the tank and see if they could find a bear, while the other two Russians and I would take the packhorses and meet up with the Sachmans at the alternate base camp. I had understood that camp was about six hours away, so I was mystified when we still

My Kamchatka snow sheep was a 2004 trophy. For once it did not rain or snow during the hunt, and the decent weather made a world of difference.

had no camp in view after a long day's ride. It began to rain, and the Russians stopped and began setting up a tent for the night. Neither of them knew enough English to give me a clear explanation of what was going on.

In the morning we packed up and rode out, and again we rode and hunted all day long with no sign of either a bear or a hunting camp. We did come upon a little outpost, a wooden cabin with smoking racks used during the salmon run, and we slept in the cabin. In late afternoon on the third day out, our little caravan finally reached the camp where Alan and Barb were waiting, bored to tears and wondering what in the world had happened to me. Local people with their reindeer used this camp in winter, and bear reputedly came to the area to fish.

It rained all night and most of the next morning. We finally caught a glimpse of a big bear and went after it, but hard rain resumed as we stalked, and we never saw the bear again. We overnighted in a trapper's cabin with a resident dog that was mighty glad to see us because we fed it. Later, a second dog showed up. We left them all our food when we departed for the long ride back to our base camp to fly home.

In a replay of our 1990s experience, Alex's partner, Anatoly, suggested we come back the following year and try a different area, at no charge. I had to hand it to these people—they were as disappointed as we were, and once again they intended to set things right. Thus it was that on 19 August 2004 I returned to Kamchatka for one more try for the Russian bighorn, the snow sheep, an animal that in my opinion should probably be called the rain-wind-and-snow sheep.

Two Florida hunters were in this party. Arriving in camp, guides told us they had spotted four rams, and the plan was for all three of us to go after them together. It did not rain. It did not snow. It did not blow. Kamchatka is a perfectly respectable hunting area when it's not raining, snowing, or blowing. I was to move into position above the sheep while the other hunters stayed below them, in an attempt to cover all possible escape routes.

One of the Florida hunters shot first, hitting but not downing one of the rams. All four animals headed up toward me. Halfway up, they stopped on a ridge. I had a good rest, and I also now had a new Leupold scope with a rangefinder calibrated for two hundred and fifty, three hundred and fifty, and four hundred and fifty yards. The ram I chose was at three hundred and forty yards. I dropped it. My guide then told me to shoot the other ram that had already been hit. It was at four hundred and twenty yards; I hit that ram, and it went down, too. The biggest of the four rams was farther away, at five hundred and fifty yards. The guide now instructed me to shoot that ram. I shot twice, but, from the way the big ram took off, I didn't think I'd hit it.

After taking photos of the two downed rams, the guides advised us to start for camp. They would follow with the trophies. I pondered matters on the way down. Having shot two sheep so early in the hunt, and knowing about the many ways weather can scramble sheep hunts, would I at last be able to quit this? Could I refrain from going back to the Russian Federation for more punishment, or was it written in the great scheme of sheep hunting that I would return? Surely two snow sheep in two minutes was about as good as things were ever going to get.

We got into camp just before dark. When the guides arrived, well after nightfall, imagine our surprise to see them bringing in all three rams! They had gone looking for the third one and had found it. I took the biggest ram, the others took the other two, and we all went home happy. My question was answered—I think.

Chapter 17

A Gracious Reception

Iran, 2002

Two-thirty in the morning is not exactly the perfect time to arrive anywhere, especially in a country you know mainly from bad news on television. Mighty few of us are at our peak at that ungodly hour of the morning. If I could have arranged it differently, I would have. I would be flying out of Erzurum, Turkey, at night and reaching Tehran, Iran, in the early hours of 6 November 2002. The United States was clearly getting ready to invade Iraq. Many Iraqis were already crossing the border into Iran to escape the troubles they knew were coming. I would be arriving alone, and I was bringing in my rifle and ammunition. I wondered how this was going to work.

When I got in, my passport was stamped without incident at the first checkpoint. I picked up my big red duffel bag and gun case and, with some trepidation, headed for customs to see about my gun and bullets. Gravely, the officials started their proceedings. When they reached the point of counting out the bullets, they told me I had too many. I would not need that many bullets, an inspector declared.

"Well, just give me what I'm supposed to have," I suggested.

I was coming in for a week as a guest of my friend Kaan Karakaya of Shikar Safaris in Turkey, directly after my chamois hunts in Bulgaria (successful) and Turkey (unsuccessful). Kaan had suggested going to Iran to hunt two Iranian reserves. I had started out with forty bullets and, after the earlier hunts, was down to thirty-two. The chief customs man told me I could only take in twenty. That would be ten bullets for each of the two reserves where I would hunt, he said.

Then he corrected himself.

"You're only going to shoot two sheep—you only need two bullets!" he declared.

The Esfahan mouflon is a sheep that can only be hunted in Iran. On my 2002 hunt, the regional game warden joined us for a barbecue as I was the first American to have hunted in the area since 1979.

I stared at him in disbelief at the changing rules before it dawned on me that my customs man was cracking a joke.

I told him I wasn't quite that good. He laughed and said I could have twenty bullets, but I would have to relinquish the extra twelve until I was leaving the country. I invited him to keep them, but he insisted "No, no, we'll give them back to you when you leave—you just can't take them into the reserves."

We packed the permitted bullets and the rifle in the metal gun case and snapped it shut. Now another official strode up. He had a more commanding look—handsome, sophisticated. He was dressed in black leather. This was a more senior man. had learned something about the pecking order in Eastern European countries—when you reach the senior KGB type, he's usually the good-looking one wearing the black leather. I had made it through with the underlings, but now, as I was installing the bolt on the gun case and locking the padlock, this fellow said, "Just excuse me a minute. Obviously that's your rifle."

I said, "Yes, sir."

"And what are all those stickers?" he asked.

I said, "Oh, those are from all the places I've taken the rifle, all the different countries."

"What's this one?" he asked.

I told him it was Russian.

He said, "What's this one?"

I said that was from Africa—Tanzania.

"This one?" Spain. South Africa. We wen through a dozen of them.

Then he stood back, surveyed my gun case again, gave me a piercing look, and said, "CIA?"

"No!" I told him. "I'm just a hunter."

It could have been a moment for high alarm, but he was already beginning to smile He laughed and shook my hand and said "Welcome to Iran."

Another little Iranian joke. He mus have known that, with all those brigh

My hotel overlooked the crowded capital city of Tehran, where I was received by Siamak Khonsari, known as "Mac," of the hunting company Persian Shikar.

Guide Mahmoud Sakhtbaz picked me up for the nine-hour drive to the Ghamishloo hunting area. En route we bought some delicious fruit and pistachios at well-stocked roadside markets.

stickers festooning my gear, loudly drawing attention to myself and what I was carrying, the last thing in the world I could possibly be was an agent of the CIA.

It was the happiest day of my life when I emerged from customs and saw a small man holding up over his head a sign with my name on it.

A Little Background

I had gone hunting in Turkey in 1984 (see chapter 21) during a trip to several Old World countries. When ibex hunting opened in Turkey, we were one of the first to go in with Pamfilya Tourism Incorporated. Kaan's dad was my guide. Over the years our friendship grew, and I sent several of my friends to hunt ibex with him.

As Kaan became more established, he started his own hunting organization. One day, while sitting in his booth at the SCI convention, he asked me if I had ever considered hunting sheep in Iran. I was under the impression Americans could not go there, but he countered that there was no law against *visiting* Iran; it was just that one could not do business there. Eventually, he proposed coming along with me himself. Kaan had a business partner in Iran who would smooth the way. As we arranged it, I would hunt in Turkey and then meet up with him, and our flights to Iran would start and end in Turkey.

I felt the need to consult with my lawyer and Elizabeth. The lawyer initially said I was crazy to even contemplate this, but he said he would check it out. When he called back, he confirmed what Kaan had told

I was spoiled with special meals throughout Iran. Our cook (right), guide Mahmoud, and a college student who spoke good English (left) made up our party.

me: It was not illegal to visit Iran, only to do business there. The lawyer nevertheless discouraged me from going. Elizaeth was opposed to the venture as well, but she was too wise to challenge it.

"Just get your will up-to-date," she suggested.

I called the embassy and sent along my passport, and I got a visa without any trouble. So far, so good.

Then Kaan got hung up. When I completed my hunt in Turkey, he was stuck somewhere in the Russian world on a Marco Polo hunt. I was to fly to Iran at midnight, and he was not going to be able to join me. His staff suggested I simply go ahead without him. I had been jittery enough about a joint trip, and now I had to embark alone. I didn't dare call and tell my wife.

During the flight, out came the scarfs. Women began to cover their heads in preparation for arrival in Iran, underscoring the sense of leaving Europe and the modern era to enter another land and another time. I was scared, and, once on that plane, I was trapped. That's why I was so relieved to see the man with the sign. My tension at last began to ease as he hustled me out of the airport.

Feasting in the Hinterlands

The joshing from airport officials had set the tone; we need not have worried. Although almost everything I had heard about Iran up to that point had been negative—revolution, fundamentalist rule, high-handed government, nuclear disobedience—my experience was that the people were welcoming, curious, gracious, and friendly. It's quite difficult to merge the image of Iran in the U.S. media with what happened to me on the ground.

Receiving me was Siamak Khonsari, known as "Mac," who ran the hunting company Persian Shikar. He would attend to me on Kaan's behalf. Having spent some time in Washington, D.C., Mac was fluent in English and familiar with life in the United States. He took me to my hotel and set me at ease. Tehran is like Mexico City—full to overflowing, with twelve million people and fourteen million cars, or something like that. Many of the younger people were wearing American clothes, some even bearing the Stars and Stripes.

Mac had a family funeral the next day and did not appear. Guide Mahmoud Sakhtbaz, accompanied by a cook and a college student who spoke good English, picked me up for the drive to the Ghamishloo reserve and hunting area near the old city of Esfahan. I would be hunting Esfahan mouflon, a sheep that can be hunted only in Iran. Mahmoud had been a paratrooper in the Iran-Iraq war of the 1980s. He was a great fan of American basketball—Michael Jordan was his man. The nine-hour drive was mostly along smooth, wide highways.

Along the way we stopped at roadside markets well stocked with wonderful fresh produce and picked up some delicious fruits, vegetables, and nuts—especially pistachios. We broke our journey with a fine chicken dinner in a small town. It rained on us, and we arrived at the reserve manager's comfortable home to find him delighted about the much-needed rain. I would be staying at his house.

A fine spread of fresh fruit and nuts greeted me, and that was before anyone had given any thought to dinner. I wasn't very hungry after our sizable lunch, and I also had a cold coming on. Later, our hosts laid the dinner out on a large cloth on the floor—tomatoes, cucumbers, bread, eggs, fries, and a supply of Iranian cold medicine. I viewed the pills with suspicion but took some anyway.

The reserve was one of a network of twenty-seven around the country. We drove out in the morning and soon spotted a herd of thirty to forty sheep, mostly ewes and young rams. Glassing farther up in the mountains, we found a herd of seventeen more sheep, twelve of them rams. One was large and heavy, and our guides judged it to be seven or eight years old. Mahmoud asked whether I wanted to try for the ram or keep looking.

We decided to try. It was a great stalk, and we were able to get close enough for a shot at one hundred and twenty-five yards. One shot and the ram was down. It never even moved. Mahmoud was so happy that he hugged and kissed me. Over and over he said, "Great shot! Great shot!" and I said, "Great guide! Great stalk!" He repeated, "Great shot!"

My Esfahan mouflon ram's horns were heavy and broomed on one side, measuring twenty-four inches. This was certainly a good sheep, and we carried it down the mountain to a spot more suitable for photos. We were going to have a barbecue and eat the liver that evening, the crew told me. I was the first American to have hunted in the area since the overthrow of the shah in 1979, so they had invited the regional head game warden to join us.

At dinner, the regional warden wanted to know exactly what I thought about everything I had seen in Iran so far, and he wanted to show me another reserve in the morning.

Mahmoud cooked me some chicken that night, in addition to the liver.

"Special meal," I told him.

"Special hunter," he said.

He was spoiling me.

The reserve the senior warden wanted me to see was an area with ibex and other species. The game department was preparing to open it to hunters in a couple of years. They were building a large tank to hold water from a local spring so that they could supply watering points for wildlife, and they were also putting in some food plots for the animals. On the way in we saw a bunch of about forty rams, some of them real wall hangers. The game department had bought the land from livestock operators, and now it had only wild animals.

The hospitality never lagged on this reserve visit. Taking a nap after lunch was a straightforward affair. We were already eating on the floor, so all we had to

The game department had built a new guesthouse and was preparing to open the reserve to hunters. Food plots were going in, and wildlife watering points were planned.

do was stretch out full-length right there. Back at my quarters, dinner was a new culinary adventure. The main course was apparently a typical Iranian dish, featuring several kinds of vegetables baked with nuts on top and served over rice.

After Armenian Sheep

The second reserve I was to hunt was near the town of Arak, about five hours' drive from Esfahan. We stopped en route for a fine lunch. The food was getting better all the time. Each day we had a hearty breakfast consisting of fried eggs with fried potato or pancakes—all quite familiar to the American palate, and easy on your mind first thing in the morning.

At Arak I would again stay with the game warden, though in more modest quarters. The countryside was similar, but I think we were at a lower elevation. Kaan called to check on my progress. Was everything OK? Was I enjoying Iran? Mahmoud remained attentive, drawing up a list of all the sheep of Iran for me. Because the first sheep hunt had gone so well, we turned up a day earlier than expected, and we found that our new hosts were not quite ready for us. We did not hunt the first day. Instead, we took a game drive through the 83,000-hectare reserve. In effect, we had the luxury of a scouting trip. Here the water supply system involved a 1,600-year-old network of furrows that brought water down from mountain springs to the lower elevations, where it was piped to storage tanks.

We saw two groups of Armenian mouflon. Most were females, and we avoided going too close to them—we wanted them to be around the next day.

Lunch was yet another new, delectable dish—meatballs, potatoes, onions, and corn. In the evening, trying to do my bit to thank these hospitable people, I offered to cook up some of my freeze-dried food so they could taste it. Clearly, I would not be needing it for backup.

Getting serious about hunting the Armenian mouflon involved setting out around 5:15 A.M. in order to be on the mountain by 6 A.M. We climbed on foot, reaching the top of the mountain just as dawn was breaking. Very soon we saw a group of seven ibex, all youngish animals. As the morning advanced, we began to see sheep: five rams and thirteen ewes with young. They were below us, in a good spot for a stalk, and it was still only around 9 A.M. We decided to wait until they lay down for their siesta before attempting a stalk.

That was a mistake. As we watched, a wolf came loping along and scared the sheep away.

We followed the rams for three or four mountains before we found them again. This time we saw that the biggest ram was starting to knock the younger rams about. The rut was beginning. The five rams started heading toward our position, and one of them looked pretty good. As they proceeded along the valley, we sneaked behind a ridge to try to get closer to the animals without being seen. We peeked and retreated behind the ridge, repeating this maneuver a couple of times, and then realized the wind was not in our favor. When we eventually decided to try a stalk, the rams we had been following were suddenly no longer below us. In fact, they were nowhere to be found. They had probably got our wind and disappeared up the opposite slope, heading for the high country.

We climbed high enough for some glassing and stopped for lunch at a small winter holding camp for domesticated sheep. As I explored the area, I discovered a small house, a hay barn, a small corral, and a large underground cave. I came upon a chimney as I walked along the roof of the cave and then found a gated ramp leading down into the cave.

I asked the interpreter, "What is this?"

He replied, "Sheep down there."

I said, "What do you mean, 'sheep down there'?"

Again, he told me, "Sheep down there."

I went to Mahmoud to see if I could find out the whole story, and he explained that, in winter, two men stayed at the mountain camp with their herd of sheep. In the evenings, after they had rounded up the sheep, they put them in the cave for two reasons: one, so the wolves couldn't get them; two, it kept them warm.

After lunch, we moved to a different area, and a band of sheep immediately caught our attention. They were resting, and we couldn't get a good look at them until they started moving around again. When they did get up, all the rams proved to be on the small side. I said I would pass on shooting. We nevertheless stalked them within four hundred yards, getting a great opportunity for a shot that I didn't need.

Now the wind intensified and made it difficult to move about on the open slopes, so we went down into the more sheltered valley—only to see a band of sheep on a ridgeline. We went back up after them. Breaking the ridgeline, we scared up a big group of sheep, but they disappeared in a hurry, and we were back to fighting the wind. We had dispatched some of our party to tell the truck where to meet us, and when we all met up, we learned the driver had also seen plenty of sheep where he had been waiting. There was definitely no shortage of mouflon on this reserve. I was exhausted after all the up-and-down hiking; I would sleep well that night.

We had another day of climbing, during which we saw three groups of ibex and a large band of fifty to sixty sheep in a valley where the mountains began to peter out. We set up our scope and studied them during our lunch stop. We determined that the males in the group were all younger animals, not what I was after. Time was running out. I had just one more day.

A misty rain greeted us as we returned to the same area we had hunted the first day. We repeated our initial climb and around 10 A.M. were rewarded with a large herd of sheep, very close to where they had been when

While hunting Armenian sheep, we stopped at a winter holding camp for domestic sheep. A gated ramp led down to a cave where sheep were kept at night for warmth and to protect them from wolves.

the wolf scared them off. They were too far away for us to judge trophy quality. We needed to get closer. It was slow going. By noon, we had gained on them enough to see that two of the rams were possible candidates, but they were still a long way off. We continued our careful stalk.

By 3:30 P.M., we were within four hundred yards of them, and the two best rams were looking better and better. Mahmoud and I crawled on our bellies toward a little rock outcropping at three hundred and sixty yards and could not get any closer. There were eleven rams and six ewes. I regret to tell you that I blew the shot. The sheep ran, and that was that. It was a long walk down the mountain.

When I got back to Tehran, Kaan's man Mac met me again to organize taxidermy and take me sightseeing. Like the others helping with my visit, he was all hospitality. We dined at a pleasant restaurant on the top floor of the hotel, and he invited me back to his home, where I could see that he was quite well-to-do. I was surprised to find that the signs in the hotel were in English. Older women in the streets were dressed in black and well covered up, but the young people I saw belonged to the computer age and looked like citizens of any European capital.

It was just a matter of weeks before the United States invaded Iraq. When we stopped at checkpoints, officials were repeatedly taken aback when they saw my passport, and I was amazed at their proficiency in English.

"American?" they asked.

"Yes, sir," I always replied.

"What are you doing here?" they would ask.

When I said I was hunting wild sheep and showed my license, they said, "Ah! Well, have a good time in Iran," or words to that effect, and waved us on. They never asked to see a gun permit. Even though they had not seen American hunters on their reserves since the 1970s, I'm not sure I have ever been treated as well in any other country as I was in Iran. I'd go back in a heartbeat.

My 50-inch-plus ram from Kyrgyzstan was eleven years old. The tight curl of the horns is typical of the Marco Polo subspecies known as the Hume argali.

Chapter 18

Three Tries for Marco Polo

Kyrgyzstan, 1995; Tajikistan, 2003, 2005

Call it a one-two-three hunt. My trip to the former Soviet republic of Tajikistan in late November 2005 resulted in one sixty-plus-inch Marco Polo argali ram, taken right at the boundary of two countries, along with three wolves my guides and I encountered while stalking the magnificent sheep of the High Pamirs. Sounds like a snap, doesn't it?

Not quite.

This hunt with Alexander Lisitsin of Russian Expeditions surely ranks as one of the high points of my four-decade trophy-hunting career, and it went ever so smoothly. Two arduous attempts had preceded it, however. It took me two hunts to get really good trophies of each of the North American wild sheep species, and for the Marco Polo it was going to take three.

First, Kyrgyzstan

Bob DeWitz, Tom Rubenstein, and I planned a joint hunt for ibex and Marco Polo for September 1995. We met up in Frankfurt and flew to Russia, then on to Almaty, a city of about 1.2 million people and the major commercial center of Kazakhstan. Alexander met us there and squired us through customs. Now we began the long drive to the Kyrgyz Republic, also known as Kyrgyzstan or Khirgizia. About five hours on the road got us to the capital city of Bishkek, where we stopped to get visas and visit the game department. Another five hours of driving got us to Naryn, where we were to stay at a hotel. The place looked so unpromising that Alexander scouted up a local game department official and arranged for us to spend the night at his home.

After breakfasting at the only eatery in town, we had another long day's drive. After eight hours on the blacktop, we took a gravel road better described as a trail. About eight inches of snow had fallen, and our three trucks got stuck three times before we reached our camp at 9:30 P.M.

The camp was at twelve thousand feet. I was conscious of the difficulty of breathing at that altitude, even when just rolling over at night, but we adjusted to it. Bear in mind that on that first night we were still recovering from the journey. People groan about the long flights required for African hunts, but there are not many hunts that require three overnight stays—two days of flying and then two long days of driving—before you reach your hunting camp. Bob and Tom might have suspected I wanted them along for the sake of companionship, but what I really needed them along for was to play gin rummy.

Around 10 A.M. we set out hunting. Soon we were seeing plenty of sheep—more than eighty ewes and four good bunches of rams. One or two animals had horns over fifty inches. Things were looking good, though we could not get close enough for a shot. We returned to camp for lunch and went out again in the late afternoon. We saw seven good rams of forty inches or more, plus eight smaller rams and twenty-five to thirty ewes. There were certainly plenty of sheep. They were Marco Polo sheep of the subspecies known as Hume argali, though I didn't know it then.

(Left to right) Bob DeWitz, Tom Rubenstein, (I), and our staff are eating breakfast at a local restaurant in Naryn. We flew into Kazakhstan, and it took two days on the road to reach our camp in Kyrgyzstan.

Tom and I set out at 5:30 the next morning for an area where he had seen ibex and I had seen rams. We took the horses to a mountaintop, and from there we could see fifty or sixty ibex on the next mountain. For five or six hours we lay out in the wind watching them, hoping they would begin feeding toward us.

Eventually, Tom's guide, Sultan, set out on horseback to get above the ibex and drive them toward us. I couldn't believe how well the horses managed at that altitude. In barely more than half an hour, Sultan had the ibex moving, and five smaller ones came right by me at a distance of only fifty yards. The animal Tom chose was about three hundred and fifty yards distant and proved up with 46-inch and 44½-inch horns. We left the mountain at dark. Tom was delighted with his trophy. The photos would wait until morning.

Those first two days were a great start. We continued to see many sheep on most days of this hunt, but we gradually realized that our guides were overestimating the horn sizes. I took a ram with a nice tight curl that I had been told would go 54 inches, but it turned out to measure 50 inches; animals that were billed as 56 or 57 inches were also closer to 50 inches. Tom took a ram he was told would go 55 inches, and it turned out to be 46. Alexander now agreed to arrange for me to shoot a second sheep, and he held a high-level conference with our guides.

We moved camp twice, once sleeping out in the mountains at high altitude. It gave me quite a scare when I awoke in the middle of the night and couldn't get my breath. For an hour I sat up and concentrated on breathing deeply before I gradually settled down again in my sleeping bag atop two horse blankets.

The famous Hot Springs camp in Tajikistan is at 14,000 feet, reached via the village of Murgab. The camp leases spots to several outfitters. Ours was Alexander Lisitsin, with whom this would be my seventh hunt.

In parts of that area the terrain was so steep that I had to dismount from my horse and encourage it along. I counted sixteen rams in one band and eighty in another—altogether I counted one hundred and eighteen rams. Two looked to me as if they might go fifty-seven inches, but they proved unapproachable in the time that remained. After Tom and I left, Bob stayed on to hunt ibex for several more days.

I was not happy; I still wanted a big sheep, and I would not have shot the first ram had I known its true size. Still, this was my fifteenth sheep species, and I had certainly seen good numbers of sheep. I was just going to have to come back if I wanted a really big one.

Trying Tajikistan

The next venture took place in 2003. This time I was to hunt Tajikistan, accompanied by Richard Hawkins, and we would not be hunting with Alexander. Sadly, the hunt would qualify as a case study of all that can go wrong. The outfitter's planning was muddled. Richard's travel got scrambled. The airline misplaced my rifle, then found it and promised to ship it onward, but it was so slow to arrive that I had to pay to borrow a rifle.

I had extra downtime at the Gold Dragon Hotel, waiting for the 7mm magnum that never came. On the fourteen-hour drive from Bishkek to our camp, we faced checkpoint after checkpoint, nine or ten altogether, and at some of those we needed to make contributions to the local economy in order to get through. In fairness, I should note that, besides wanting to see our passports, the soldiers at the roadblocks really only wanted food. They were hungry. After independence, Tajikistan suffered a Civil War from 1992 to 1997. Since the end of the war, it has had political stability, but the country has limited natural resources, beyond hydroelectric power and a strategic location. Most of the country has not exactly progressed into the modern era.

Once in the camp, I started to feel a degree of disbelief at what the guides were telling me. For the first few days I saw no sheep at all. We talked to a herdsman in his yurt—a circular, tent-style dwelling—and he said he had seen twelve rams "yesterday." The fellow at the next yurt where we stopped had also seen twelve rams "yesterday." Perhaps the two men had seen the same twelve rams. Or was this just the story they trotted out every time?

We ran across a wolf one morning and shot it, but it stank, so we left it, planning to pick it up later. Wolves were a nuisance to people in the area. Coming close to villages, they would harass and eat their sheep and dogs. This one seemed to be coming from a settlement. By the time we returned for the carcass, someone else had already removed it. The villagers had apparently heard the shot, and we could see where they had dragged the carcass through the snow.

We were told of some small bands of sheep that included good rams, and we found some of those bands, but the rams were much smaller than we had been led to believe. And so on.

Eventually, my guides began telling me that if I wanted a ram with horns measuring more than sixty inches, there were indeed ways to get one. I could shoot any ram and then trade its horns for a much bigger set, the source of which they did not specify. They told me the price for this type of "trophy" would be around three thousand dollars. A day or two later, the price for a nice big set of Marco Polo horns had climbed to five thousand dollars.

We did find a few good-size rams at last, and, as we tried some difficult stalks with the wind carrying our scent to the animals, one of the guides kept begging to take my rifle and shoot the ram for me. He must have asked at least ten times. Eight hours of walking at high altitude had me beat, and then, on our way back to camp, we ran up against a roadblock that held us up longer than any so far.

Richard finally showed up, just in time to leave again. On the drive back there were fifteen or more checkpoints, all creating delays. I began to fear we might miss our flight out. In the end we were able to pick up my errant rifle, and we made it to the airport in time for our flight, but that flight was late, too—and when I reached Houston, the rifle was missing again. I prefer not to think too much about that hunt.

Roof of the World

My third Marco Polo hunt, also in Tajikistan, began on 30 November 2005. I had booked my first Marco Polo hunt in Kyrgyzstan because it had plenty of sheep, and the hunts there were less expensive. For the second try I had chosen Tajikistan because it was producing bigger sheep, but I had chosen the wrong outfitter. Now I was aiming to get both the right country and the right outfitter. I turned once more to Alexander Lisitsin, with whom I had successfully hunted Trans-Caspian and Afghan urial, tur, and snow sheep. This would be my seventh hunt with him.

By now, I knew very well I could expect a taxing journey. Tajikistan and the surrounding region include some of the highest mountains on earth—the Pamir, Hindu Kush, Himalaya, Karakoram, and Kunlun ranges. There is no easy way to get into those inspiring places. I flew eleven and one-half hours from Houston to Milan, another two and one-half hours from Milan to Istanbul, and four hours from Istanbul to Bishkek in Kyrgyzstan. I took another flight to the city of Osh, spent dozens of hours waiting for late planes, and finally made the eighteen-hour drive from Osh to the village of Murgab in Tajikistan, following old Silk Road trails over mountain screen and washed-out river crossings.

With no guardrails or bridges on the roads, you need good drivers. During the Soviet era, I was told, the roads in the region had been in somewhat better shape. My party called our route "the road from hell," though the locals refer to it as the Roof of the World. We had to stop at numerous military checkpoints. Once again, we facilitated passage through each by making gifts of soft drinks and food to soldiers. In Kyrgyzstan Alexander had also retained the services of a retired chief of police, who seemed to know everyone and who could smooth our way through the checkpoints as far as the border of Tajikistan. At that point his driver took him home, and we acquired a new facilitator to help us through the Tajik checkpoints. The purpose of such a person was simply to help smooth the way as a particular need arose, whether it was passing safely through checkpoints or just finding a dozen eggs.

From Murgab the road climbs to the famous Hot Springs Camp, operated by four Tajik brothers, at fourteen thousand feet. I learned the names of two of them: Karim and Atobek Bemurode. The camp leases spots to several outfitters. In the middle of one of the most remote parts of the planet, visiting hunters experience near-luxury camp conditions, with food

Hunters at the Hot Springs camp called the four-wheel-drive truck "Bigfoot." Its massive tires meant it could move hunters through deep snow.

prepared by a chef, an on-site taxidermist to process trophies for the trip home, and a knowledgeable assemblage of hunting guides familiar with every peak and valley of the wrinkled, treeless landscape.

Of all the hunting base camps I've visited, Hot Springs is one of the best organized. Those people know the business they're in, and they are highly successful at it. Almost every visiting hunter takes a trophy Marco Polo ram, generally within a couple of days of arriving at camp. Hunters glassing the valleys and slopes in the area surrounding the camp may see herds of Marco Polo argali numbering in the hundreds. The sheep descend to the valleys from the nearby peaks in Tajikistan and from mountains in Afghanistan and China. There they find light snow and wild grasses in country that is used as the summer range of domestic yak herds.

The cautious sheep also encounter predators—including wolves, snow leopard, and man—and for that reason they are extremely wild and skittish. But there is no other place on earth where hunters can see hundreds of sheep a day and find trophies of such quality. Marco Polo rams possess the most spectacular horns of any *Ovis* species, and in that part of Central Asia really large horns are a possibility. When the stars align, it can be the experience of a lifetime.

Our jet-lagged and road-weary group arrived at the well-provisioned camp at 10 P.M. to hear whispers of great things from satisfied hunters. There was lots of snow, but they were seeing incredible herds of sheep, with the rut in full swing.

The first day out, hunters become acclimated to the high altitude and to temperatures that can dip to minus twenty degrees Fahrenheit. I used part of my downtime to ensure the accuracy of my rifle. From the earlier trips I knew that long-distance shooting was the norm. My 3–10X Leupold scope had been customized with vertical post calibrations indicating 250, 350, 450 and 550 yards. As it turned out, I would need every bit of that. I also had a long talk with my guides, in which I expressed my interest in taking a ram of sixty inches or better. They were positive about helping me achieve my goal.

Our small group consisted of Alexander and native guides Saucha and Kanuch. We left camp at 7:30 the next morning in a four-wheel-drive truck with massive tires, which Hot Springs hunters called "Bigfoot." With wheels that stood almost four feet tall and two feet wide, the vehicle would chug through deep snow to move hunters around. The routine was to drive within three to five miles of a herd of sheep, then use the spotting scope to look for big rams. Younger rams were actively courting hundreds of ewes. Not far from the ewes were the bachelor groups of mature rams. All eyes in the herd were on the lookout for danger.

In late afternoon on the first day, we spotted five rams on my side of the vehicle, standing apart from a group of ewes. When the rams saw us, they immediately began running up the side of a mountain. Alexander gave me the nod to step out of our truck and go for the big ram, which we figured was at least sixty-two inches.

At more than six hundred yards, it wasn't a chip shot. I shot three times, narrowly missing with each shot, before the ram crested the saddle of a mountain. I wasn't mentally or physically prepared for this. It upset me, but there was nothing to do except move on.

We traveled to another valley, where we saw another big group of ewes. From a couple of miles away, our spotting scopes also revealed a group of ten wolves stalking the sheep. Wolves take a toll on the sheep, which often founder in deep snow when pursued by the fleet predators. As we watched, evening began to settle. Going back to camp that night, I considered what I had seen, including scores of sheep and at least one ram of the quality I wanted, and I began to feel good about my chances for success.

In the morning we were greeted by snow flurries. We left camp to check out a new area. The valley revealed a herd of at least five hundred sheep, which almost immediately detected our presence and left the valley. It was an impressive view, the sheep single-filing up a ridge and out of sight. One of my guides suggested we climb to the top to get an idea of where they had fled.

Climbing through the rocks and deep snow wasn't an easy chore. We decided to descend on the other side of the ridge and let Bigfoot pick us up at the base of the mountain. On the way down we spotted plenty of sheep, but there was no cover that would allow us to get close enough to check for the presence of rams.

Back in the vehicle, we made our way to yet another valley. At a turn in the road we spotted a wolf, which saw us around the same time and went into high gear. The driver slammed on the brakes, and I found the wolf in my cross hairs. I took the shot, and the wolf tumbled. The next valley we glassed revealed a big group of ewes to the right and, to the left, a bachelor group of five big boys.

Two hours into the day's hunt, we began a crawling stalk on the five mature rams. As we got close, the sheep saw us and began running up the slope, the big ram leading the group. Near the crest of a ridge, the sheep stopped. A quick reading from Alexander's rangefinder showed a distance of five hundred and fifty yards. It was time for me to trust my shooting ability, rifle, scope, and luck. I put the scope's bottom mark on the sheep and squeezed off a shot.

The rifle boomed, and the 160-grain bullet struck the ram low in the shoulder. The sheep toppled, then righted and made its way over the ridge. In this border region, the other side of the mountain was Afghanistan. The guides knew the shot was good, and they were confident in their ability to pack out the trophy the next morning.

As it turned out, the day's hunt was not yet over. About half an hour out of the camp, on the trail home, two more wolves materialized. One went to the side of our vehicle, and I dispatched it with a quick shot from my 7mm magnum. The other stayed in the road. One more shot, one more wolf.

We headed back to camp with three wolves and fervent hopes that we had a very good ram on the ground. Because wolves prey on sheep in winter and on yaks in summer, there was reason for celebration back at camp. After a couple of vodkas, I was proclaimed the "Wolf King," but I remained nervous about my sheep still out there.

We were up at 6:30 A.M. to see about retrieving the sheep. It was the coldest day yet, with blasts of icy wind. We found the ram's trail leading into Afghan territory over a saddle between peaks. To avoid any risk of political issues, the guides took me back to camp and

In 2005 in Tajikistan, I collected three wolves and took this beautiful Marco Polo ram that broke the 60-inch mark.

went for the sheep without me. They first had to make arrangements with the local Afghan warlord to pay a toll of two hundred dollars and all the ram's meat. The deal done, they drove directly to where the ram had disappeared. They found my trophy Marco Polo ram dead, almost exactly where they had expected.

When the guides arrived back at camp with the trophy, we immediately put a tape on it and saw that indeed it broke the sixty-inch mark. I was one very happy man. Now there really was reason for a celebration.

With the trophy secure and more snowy weather threatening, we decided to head back to civilization a few days early. We began our long backtrack. The trip home was made memorable by flight delays and bargaining to get off waiting lists and onto planes. In Istanbul the airline lost all my bags, including the cape and horns of the Marco Polo ram. A week later, the baggage showed up in New York, where the U.S. Fish and Wildlife Service later cleared my *Ovis ammon polii* trophy. Reclassification since my earlier hunt in Kyrgyzstan meant that my argali taken there was now considered to belong to the Marco Polo subspecies known as the Hume argali, *Ovis ammon humei,* which is typically slightly smaller and has a tighter horn curl than the Marco Polo sheep proper, *O. a. polii*. So, in addition to at last having a fine Marco Polo proper, I had also gained a new trophy species by default.

Few trophy mounts are as gripping as a Marco Polo sheep. The animal is so much larger in body and horn than the familiar North American sheep that it makes people gasp. And once you've been in the thin air and unbelievable mountains where it lives, the setting is unforgettable. Regardless of the travel difficulties, I have only the best things to say about the hunting elements of this trip. I give full credit to the organizational skills of Alexander Lisitsin's Russian Expeditions, as well as to a certain lady who had resumed riding on my shoulder. When I'm looking at a long, difficult shot, I want three things. Give me a good rifle and scope, a good ram, and a wink from Lady Luck.

Fine Times in Other Regions

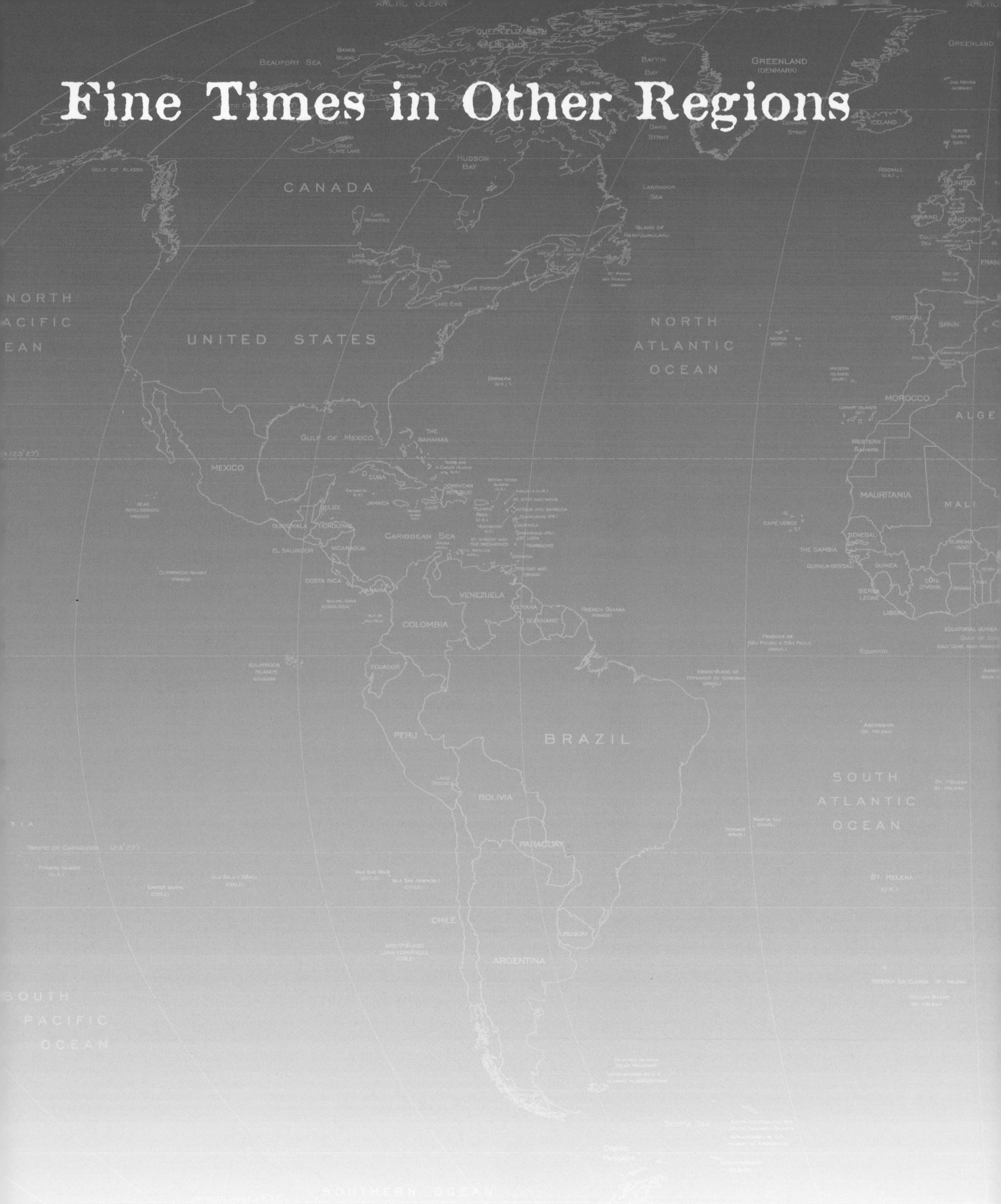

Part 4

Chapter 19

Wild Man of the Chaco

Venezuela and Argentina, 1980s and 1990s

I never wanted to be a movie mogul, but once I fervently wished I had some hot connections in Hollywood. It happened to me in Argentina, where I met a fellow who truly was larger than life.

Argentina is a civilized country, with a rural ranching and agricultural economy that supports the cosmopolitan city of Buenos Aires. Going bird hunting in the hinterlands is quite luxurious, with well-appointed hunting lodges where you don't have to look far for your comforts. This was hardly the kind of country where I expected to find myself sharing meals with a strange character who was living off the land and who seemed to have come straight out of the 1830s.

If there were any mountains where he lived, I suppose I would call him a mountain man. He was making his living from what the country offered, just as the mountain men did—only this was the 1990s, and the part of the country where he lived had no mountains at all. I think of him as the wild man of the scrub, the loco of the Chaco.

Chaco is the word for hunting in the Quechua language. The great plain of the Chaco covers some three hundred thousand square miles, stretching across large areas of Paraguay and Bolivia as well as Argentina. In the less arid sections, some rely on logging the quebracho for wood; others have settled in agricultural communities. Much of the Chaco is still a frontier region. It's hot, semiarid, and sparsely populated.

The area is a source of tannin. It also supplies palo santo wood, whose oil is used as a fragrance for soap. Farmers cultivate yerba maté for tea in the lower Paraguayan part of the Chaco. According to the Nature Conservancy, the biodiversity of the Chaco is impressive. It is home to more than thirty-four hundred plant species, predominantly cactus and thorny shrubs. It has some five hundred bird species (nearly as many as in all of North America), plus one hundred and fifty kinds of mammals, one hundred and twenty species of reptiles, and one hundred species of amphibians.

Besides the white-lipped peccary that I was after, the mammals of the Chaco include monkeys, guanaco, jaguar, puma, giant anteater, and tapir. The region is home to the rare Chacoan peccary, or tagua, a species that was believed to be extinct until its rediscovery in 1974. Birds include the flightless rhea and numerous migratory species that we also see in North America. The area is especially notable as a center of armadillo diversity. There are at least eight species of armadillos in the Argentinean Chaco and ten species in the Paraguayan Chaco. There's even one bearing the charming name "Chacoan fairy armadillo." The Chaco's ecosystems have some of the highest temperatures on the continent. Frequent droughts make for desert conditions, but occasionally there are torrential rains and floods. Generally, the western part of the Chaco is drier than the east.

Bolivia, Paraguay, and Argentina have wrangled repeatedly over who owns how much of the Chaco, so it has been a war zone as well as a frontier. The Trans-Chaco Highway, built in the 1960s, reduced its frontier quality somewhat, and that road was probably the trigger for development of the great ranch where I hunted.

Pablo Gonzalez guided me to a No. 1 tropical whitetail on the plains of Venezuela.

A pup tent was my home for a week in the thickets of the Chaco, Argentina's great northern brush country where every plant tears at your hide.

During other hunts in South America, I had heard about the wildness of Argentina's great northern brush country. It was reputedly the place to go for some exciting hunting for free-ranging white-lipped peccary because it had no luxury lodges or comfortable ranch headquarters.

"If you really want them wild," outfitter Marcelo Sodiro of South America Adventure Safaris told me, "we should head for the Chaco. We'll need to make a camp and get some dogs and a local guide."

Challenge of the Chaco

I knew the Chaco would be a giant expanse of thorny scrub and cactus stretching for hundreds and hundreds of miles, but, even so, I was struck by its vastness. It has few roads. Every plant tears at your hide. The country is level but also rugged, and it's a long way between clusters of civilization. Picture the South Texas brushlands before the advent of barbed wire, and you begin to get the idea.

Like the Texas brush country, the place provided its share of stories. In 1995 we were headed to an area where, I learned, someone had once begun an ambitious cattle operation on an enormous ranch encompassing more than one hundred thousand acres of brush. Cattle ranchers in the region ran mostly Argentine breeds mixed with *zebu*-type cattle adapted to the high temperatures and the less-than-lush forage. These ranchers brought in the cattle and the gauchos, and the place worked out well for a time, but then it came unstuck. For reasons unknown to me—perhaps because it was remote from markets—the ranch had collapsed. The owners had just left.

The lumbering giant among rodents is the capybara. I got a big male in Venezuela with Pablo Gonzalez.

They left behind an assortment of cattle that never did get rounded up out of the intimidating scrub, and those cattle were *wild*. They looked like Brahmas. Thinking about it now, I should have shot one.

We would be hunting peccary on foot, accompanied by a local guide we had picked up in one of the little towns. He brought along his dogs. Marcelo told me they would be a big asset when we ran across a pig.

The guide told us the story of a fellow who lived in the middle of the Chaco thickets all by himself, except for a pack of dogs and a couple of mules. The man lived by catching the wild cattle, corralling them just long enough to subdue them enough to sell them. The guide claimed to have seen the freelance cowman. How on earth he ever got cattle to market baffled me, but that was the story.

We set up our pup tents and started to scout the brush for white-lipped peccary. The endless thorny scrub stretched in all directions. There were few landmarks—nothing much in the way of watercourses to follow or hills to climb in order to get a long view. One day, we found ourselves encountering and talking to the man in the story! Our local guide recognized him. Perhaps the guide had an idea of where the wild man lived and had steered us that way; perhaps our hunt provided the guide with a chance to pay him a visit. I never found out.

To my surprise, the fellow spoke some English. We invited him over to our camp for dinner, and he told us about how he caught wild cattle. The truth is, I quickly found myself as interested in this fellow and his ways as in killing a peccary. He invited us over to see his own modest establishment, where we got a tour of the setup and saw the equipment he employed.

The *loco* had built himself a little lean-to house. As residents of pup tents, we were not exactly in a superior position. It was one of those times when hunting is the great leveler. We were all on the same project, you might say—coming to grips with the Chaco. Cowhide was this man's great standby. Just about everything he had was made of leather. He used cowhide to make the ropes with which he lassoed the wild cattle from the back of one of his mules. He used cowhide to make the heavy chaps he wore to protect himself from the fierce stickers that would otherwise shred the skin or clothes. Each mule also wore a heavy cloak of cowhide draped over it as protection against injury during the hectic capture operations.

He explained his technique to us. He used his dogs to run down and bay a selected animal. Then he would approach on a mule and lasso the victim. Next, he got a rope around one of its back legs, so that if it struggled, it would go down. He would secure the captured animal to a tree with ropes and then hobble it with more ropes. Once he had it firmly tied, so that it could still walk but couldn't run or harm him or the mule, he would drag the animal to a sturdy holding corral he had built. There he held his prizes until they had calmed down enough to be hauled off by a truck that arrived periodically.

You'll agree it sounds like a hard life. There was no help to be had if he or one of his mules were injured. He had to make sure no wild bull or cow got the chance to skewer him on a horn or gore a mule. He had no vehicle, and it was a long, long way to town on foot or on muleback. Even there, medical facilities were limited. Here was a man living essentially in another era, using

Marcelo Sodiro outfitted several South American hunts for me, including one for white-lipped peccary. Far out on the thorny Chaco of Argentina, we hunted on foot with a local guide and his dogs.

The wild man of the Chaco seemed right out of the 1830s when I met him in 1995. He lived by catching and selling wild cattle. Nearly all his equipment was leather, and even his mules wore a cowhide as protection against injury during capture operations.

only the technological conveniences of one hundred years ago, like knives and nails.

He was living out a kind of sturdy, solitary independence that was astonishing for the 1990s. He and his mule looked like something out of a bullfighting poster when they were decked out in their protective leather gear to go out and conquer the wild beasts of the Chaco. I had the urge to bring a Hollywood producer out there and record all this in a movie—the *Crocodile Dundee* of the Chaco.

Why did he stay when the cattle empire collapsed and everyone else simply left? What was his story? Perhaps he had nowhere else to go. Perhaps he had a difficult past, best avoided by keeping to himself at the outer edge of society. Or maybe he just loved the place and felt life would not be worth living if he had to go somewhere else. He appealed to that secret fantasy in all of us—the idea that, if we had to, we could find ways to live off the land, outside all the complications and demands of city life.

I suppose it was not as romantic as it appeared. He didn't have to pay property taxes or auto insurance, but he must have had to cut and haul feed for the captured animals while he held them in his corral. Any that failed to settle down enough to be sold were destined to be converted into meals and leather.

The day he invited us over, he had several wild cattle in his corral. He offered us dinner, but it was not to be beef. Bubbling away in a pot were some wild vegetables he had collected in the thorny scrub, and the meat standing by to accompany the wild greens was armadillo. We had brought along some beer, bread, and soda, which

A ranch hand displays the biggest payara I caught in Venezuela. Two long fangs protruding from the lower jaw are the trademark of this sporting game fish.

looked thoroughly out of place next to his wilderness-style cuisine and the minimal modern conveniences.

He had a colorful way of cooking the armadillo. There's no need to use a pot or a grill when the main course comes in its own handy shell. He simply tossed the armadillo into the cooking fire exactly as it was. When he judged it to be perfectly done, he turned it upside down, as if it were a big bowl, and opened up the underside to eat it! (Would you call that roasted or grilled?) I confess I was not quite ready to join in on a dinner with this as the featured menu item. It looked greasy, and everything that had been inside the armadillo to begin with was still there. I settled for one of the freeze-dried meals I was carrying.

Our host was interested in our peccary hunt and offered the services of his dogs. They would chase cows, pigs, anything, he told us. This was an excellent offer. We planned to go out together the next day. He knew every inch of the terrain like no one else. He knew the water holes where the white-lipped peccary liked to drink and wallow in the mud. He knew their movements and their tracks. We could hardly have hoped for a better arrangement.

We would use no truck or mules on this hunt. There were no roads where we were going. We set off together on foot through the spines and prickles, all of us wearing heavy leggings. Both sets of dogs were on their leashes. Sure enough, we soon ran across some of the wild cattle, but they faced no risk from us that day. The dogs barked, and the cattle swiftly disappeared. While checking a promising water hole, we came across the fresh tracks of a group of peccary moving quite fast. Perhaps our approach had disturbed them.

When we turned the dogs loose, we sprinted through the brush after them. We didn't want them to try to hold the peccary too long, or the peccary might tear them to pieces with their sharp tusks. Within minutes, my arms were ripped and bleeding from the whipping of the cactus and thornbushes. I looked as if I'd been in a knife fight.

As we caught up to the dogs and came upon the melee, we saw that those dogs were smart enough not to attack—they kept up their harrying maneuvers, just out of range of the slashing teeth. There was a whole string of peccary, mostly young ones and females. The big old male dropped behind the group, staying back to fight off the dogs. It was lunging, trying to get its tusks into the barking dogs.

I moved around to one side to avoid any risk to the dogs, and I'm happy to say I dispatched the big peccary quickly and cleanly. We gave the meat to the intriguing wild man of the Chaco, who had been our special stroke of luck. Marcelo had not intended to hunt with this man; our encounter with him had been purely coincidental. I also handed over some gear to thank him, and I asked if there was a way to send him some more after I got home. He gave me a post office box—he went into town about once a month, he said. Visits to the post office were one of his few concessions to contemporary life.

What do you send a guy who seems to need so little? I bought him some sturdy new knives, boots, and pants and shipped them off to the Chaco. No doubt he had understood from my questions that I admired his skills and was fascinated by his extraordinary life. Despite the vast differences between my world and his, for a few hours we were right on the same page, kindred spirits. We were hunters together.

A Little Tropical Whitetail

My first South American hunt was a somewhat experimental venture to Venezuela in June and July of 1987. I was in search of a tropical whitetail and a brocket deer, and I would be the first American to hunt deer on the ranch that was my destination. You could hunt jaguar in Venezuela, but you couldn't bring home the skin. I had already taken a fine jaguar in Mexico in 1980, so the big cat was not on my list.

I flew to Miami and then to Caracas, where my outfitter, Herman Zingg, was based. Like Miami, Caracas is a city of high-rise towers close to the ocean, but Caracas has endless expanses of little concrete houses and shacks climbing the mountains that rise inland from the city. From there I flew northwest to the town of Carora, where my guide, Pablo Gonzalez, met me. He spoke no English, but with him was a fellow named Augusto, who had been to school in Miami and spoke excellent English.

It was hot, perhaps ninety degrees. Our three-and-one-half-hour drive to the ranch on an impressively rough road took us through dry country that looked much like northern Mexico. The hunting ranch was about twenty thousand hectares, or fifty-five thousand acres, at an altitude high enough for the air to cool down at night. In the daytime I was grateful for the comfortable four-wheel-drive Toyota wagon with air conditioning.

The ranch had a gas generator that ran for two or three hours, morning and evening. As we set out on the first morning's deer hunt, many of the several hundred cows were near the headquarters for milking. They were milked by hand in an extended daily round that began around 3:30 A.M. and ran all day long, ending only at dark. You can imagine how the place smelled. Given the limited electricity and the difficulties of refrigeration and refrigerated transport, a fresh milk operation was impractical. Instead, the ranch was in the business of making cheese. Once a week, except when it rained and the roads became impassable, a huge truck struggled over the mountains to haul out the cheese.

It was an hour's drive up to the water hole, or tank, where we would set up our stand. The tank was low, almost dry. We were there by 6:30 A.M. and stayed until 10:30 A.M. We saw lots of doves but no deer. We checked out some other tanks and found plenty of tracks. After lunch and a siesta, we returned to the first tank, again without success.

The next day we tried a different spot that required an hour's walk after an hour of driving. Again we saw lots of tracks, but this time we also saw a dark, turkey-sized bird emerging from the undergrowth. I had no idea what it was, but the guide suggested I take it. I later discovered it was a great curassow—a black bird with white underparts and a striking, frilly crest of curled, dark feathers. Soon afterward we saw a fox, which I think was probably tracking the bird for breakfast. Morning and evening sessions in our blind produced no deer sightings, however.

We tried a third area on the third day, a tank higher up and more remote, but again we saw no deer. This formula was not working. Evidently the deer were visiting the tanks at night, moving around only when it was cooler. We decided to try hunting at night with a spotlight, and this produced my first tropical whitetail, a small one. We went out at night on muleback—three mules, one spotlight. We found a deer and I shot it, but again it was a small one.

By way of a break, we decided to enjoy some of Venezuela's excellent bird shooting before venturing out after brocket deer. The country has large blue rock pigeons and millions of doves, flying very fast with the wind. I shot more than thirty doves in a few minutes.

For brocket deer we would take an extended trip into the mountains, using mules to get to our blind. The mules set out from the ranch ahead of us and met us at the farthest point a vehicle could reach. The country was rough and steep, and I was glad of those mules. Imagine our surprise when, upon reaching the blind, we found a local man and his son installed there. They assured us they were departing just as we were arriving and said there were plenty of brocket deer around.

The brocket deer were not coming in that evening. When we were ready to leave, we ran into another small snag: Our mules were nowhere to be found. Where had they gone in the dark? After a certain amount of shouting for them, we gave up and set off down the mountain on foot. It turned out that the boy minding the mules had simply dozed off and had not heard us calling.

"This is a very good place," I noted in my journal. "Lots of fresh tracks, and it's only a matter of time."

I didn't have quite enough time, though. Another session in the same blind failed to produce a deer, and I was due to leave the following day. We walked all around the tank and saw fresh tracks. It was full moon, and the deer were evidently feeding and drinking late at night.

On my way out, Pablo took me to his home in Carora to see his trophies from Botswana. He had just horns, no mounts; there was no taxidermist in the town. We were already planning my return to Venezuela for a second hunt. The only place to find brocket deer was in the mountains, but there was an alternative if I wanted to try for a better tropical whitetail. He described his own ranch in the Apure area, which he said also had tapir, capybara, puma, and white-lipped peccary. I planned to come back in 1988 during the peak hunting season, January through March.

The return flight to Caracas almost gave me second thoughts. We had a bumpy, scary time of it in a little single-engine Cessna, encountering rough air and clouds over the mountains and the sea. The tower had us fly up to one thousand feet and then way out to sea before they allowed us in. I was highly relieved when we landed safely. Officials then went through my luggage like it had never been searched before. I think they must have been looking for drugs.

I took the pilot out for dinner, judging that I owed him something for having gotten me safely back to Caracas. That night I ate the biggest piece of meat you ever saw. The waiter brought a little grill to the table and grilled the meat for us, slice by slice, right there. It felt as if we had eaten ten pounds of beef; Venezuelans don't seem to realize that too much red meat can be hazardous to your health.

What in the World Is a Jaguarundi?

I booked a second Venezuela trip for ten days, hunting once again with Pablo Gonzalez, but this time I

We were crouched in a blind next to a water hole in Venezuela when this strange, dark, weasel-like animal came to drink. Jaguarundis come in shades from reddish brown to grayish black.

had a nonstop flight to Maracaibo. Pablo's son Oscar and Augusto's son José met me. A pilot would collect me in the morning to fly to Pablo's own ranch in a twin-engine Cessna 310. This time we would travel southwest into the plains, where the country looked a lot like Africa.

The similarity included burning the grass before the rains came, just as in Africa. The rains started in April, transforming the area into a huge swamp. Pablo was waiting. His ranch covered some ten thousand hectares (twenty-five thousand acres), which he had bought at an extremely modest price about twelve years before. He had a pleasant brick ranch house. The wind blew like you've never seen, but it did help offset the stifling heat.

We sighted-in our rifles and went hunting that first afternoon on a neighboring ranch, which we reached by crossing a river by boat. Soon we jumped a big buck and two does. They ran as if the devil were after them, and we couldn't catch up over the rough terrain. The buck was a real wall hanger. We saw several more does that afternoon but no more bucks—until we headed over to a thicket of about two dozen palm trees, and there we found a whole herd of deer. The larger buck and half-a-dozen does ran one way, but a smaller buck fed right in front of us. Pablo wanted me to shoot it.

I hit the buck twice, but not well enough to down it, and we trailed it quite a distance before realizing it had given us the slip in the tall grass and we were trailing only does. We backtracked and conducted a makeshift drive, and, sure enough, that brought out the wounded buck. I dropped it with one long shot.

Then, lo and behold, the drive stirred up the larger buck. We were already busy with congratulatory handshakes over the first buck when, all of a sudden, up

The truck flew across the creek to lodge nose first in the opposite bank—an unexpected crisis on an Argentina dove hunt. Dave Hannah and I and two British hunters were rescued by a passing road grader.

jumped the big boy. It had been hiding in the tall grass, hardly fifteen feet from us, all along! I missed it with my first shot but dropped it with a second. It had a perfect set of eight-point antlers, and we had two deer within two minutes. The larger buck proved up as the No. 1 tropical whitetail in the record book.

The next morning Pablo brought me tea, orange juice, and instructions that we would head out along the river for capybara and ducks. For the most part, what we saw were Indians who lived along the riverbanks. We had left the river and were proceeding near its course in our truck when we suddenly rounded a bend and came upon a group of ten or twelve capybara. Pablo helped me identify a large male, which I collected. That day we saw two more groups of more than a dozen of these odd, lumbering, giant rodents and another couple of dozen tropical whitetail.

To hunt "turkey," as Pablo called them, and tapir, we again set out by boat. When we found two of the birds, we moored the boat and went after them on foot. I missed one but got the other. This one was a crested guan—a dark bird with red legs, a red throat, and a short, bushy crest. We drew a blank on tapir, despite a lot of walking, and wound up coming back downriver in the dark. With the spotlight hooked up, we saw plenty of alligator and capybara.

The boat also ran through a bunch of sporty fish called *payara*, which were jumping all over the place. A big one jumped right into the boat with us, and Pablo quickly dispatched it with a blow to the head. The crew showed me its trademark feature—the *payara* is unmistakable because of the two long fangs that protrude from its lower jaw. These fangs can be as long as four inches, and the fish uses them to prey on piranha. We went out fishing for *payura* the next morning. Some bait produced such a frenzy among the fish that we hardly needed to do more than toss a hook into the water to get them. I also caught about a dozen peacock bass, a pretty, striped catfish with a yellow face, and several other delicious fish. We feasted on them that evening. The local habit was to scale the fish, wrap them in foil with some onions and herb sauce, and toss them in the coals to cook. We never did see a tapir.

Now it was time to fly north to Carora and drive to a mountain ranch to try once more for brocket. We were back to the water hole and blind routine, only this time my guides seemed confident I would have my brocket before noon the next day. We were in the blind just after 7 A.M. Soon after 11:30—before noon, just as the men had said—a big brocket male walked out into the opening around the water hole. Would you believe I missed it? The problem was, I didn't know what I was looking at. Even a big brocket deer is a small animal with very small antlers. It looks rather like a duiker. I thought our visitor was just a spike buck, not worth taking. By the time I understood that it was a good trophy and the guide wanted me to shoot, I had waited too long to shoot.

We planned to go out on foot along the river that afternoon, but no game was moving around. When we wandered into a cattlemen's camp, the gauchos offered us a beer, and it seemed like a good idea to abandon the hunting and get to know these men. They were bursting with curiosity about me, my clothes, and Pablo's scoped rifle.

We jumped another brocket at a lakeside salt lick the next day, but again I failed to get off a good shot. We built a small blind near the lick and stayed until after dark, but the deer and tapir must have been keeping extra-late hours. The lakeshore showed plenty of tapir tracks, as did another lakeshore, where we set up at 6:30 the following morning. I was still hoping for a brocket deer, but the only deer that appeared was a female.

Soon after 9 A.M., however, a strange, dark weasel—a catlike animal with a long tail—came down for a drink. What in the world was this elongated critter?

"Do you want to shoot a jaguarundi? Can you hit him?" asked my guide.

I had never even heard of a jaguarundi. He told me these animals were quite unusual. They came in shades from reddish brown to grayish black and were locally known as *guache*. So I came home with no tapir and no brocket but with a big, black jaguarundi. From the ranch staff to the cowboys, they were all as friendly as could be. I think they felt worse than I did over my going home without a brocket.

The Bird Bonanza of Argentina

Argentina is even more illustrious for bird shooting than Venezuela. The setting for most of my hunts there has been downright luxurious. Starting in the mid-1990s, I went every year. Jeri Booth of the Detail Company in Houston was booking dove hunts there with Carlos Sanchez of Los Ombues Lodge in Entre Rios, about two hundred and fifty miles northwest of Buenos Aires. I had been in the habit of hunting whitewing in Mexico every year, but Jeri told me the dove hunting in Argentina far exceeded what was available in Mexico.

"You can shoot all you want to shoot," she said.

She was right. The doves can produce two or three clutches per year, and the dove hunting is all but unbelievable.

At first, we would go early in the year, January through March, just for doves. The bird is called the eared dove. It is not as large as a whitewing but is larger than a mourning dove and similar to it in appearance. At one time farmers poisoned the legions of doves to contain crop damage, but they eventually realized the birds represented an economic opportunity in themselves. Farmers could sell leases to hunting outfitters whose clients would pay to come in for the tremendous bird shooting.

To give you an example of dove numbers, while based at Carlos's lodge, we went shooting in an area where the game department estimated that one major roost contained more than twenty million doves. This was not counting the year's offspring—and, as mentioned, some

A morning's bag of ducks taken with Carlos Sanchez of the five-star Los Ombues Lodge in Entre Rios, northwest of Buenos Aires. In June, July, and August, hunters can shoot ducks in the morning, go out with dogs for the quail-like perdiz, and then shoot doves in the afternoon.

doves produce more than one clutch per year. No matter how many birds sportsmen shot, we barely made a dent in the number of birds added by the young of the year, let alone in the overall population.

The birds want to eat the grain as it ripens, just before the combines come in. Imagine millions of doves flying into your fields, knocking the grain off the plants and eating it. The farmers beg you to come and shoot them. It's a win-win situation because the farmers get paid, local people get some of the meat, and we get to shoot all the birds we want to shoot. We go in a group of anywhere from fourteen to eighteen.

Eventually, we realized we could have a more interesting time if we went later in the year, in June, July, and August, because then we would also be able to shoot ducks and the quail-like perdiz. We could shoot ducks in the early morning, then go out in the late morning with pointers to flush the perdiz for some really fast shooting. We would come in for lunch, take a siesta, and go out and shoot several hundred doves in the afternoon. There are not as many doves during that season, but you can still take all the doves you want to shoot.

All this was from a base in a five-star lodge, mind you. My party each year is a little different, sometimes including Houston Safari Club friends, sometimes work colleagues and their families. I have yet to take anyone who didn't love it.

Gold-Medal Puma

The range of unfamiliar birds in South America captured my interest, and I began going to different spots to hunt geese. South America has two beautiful geese: the Magellan and the ashy-headed goose. The latter is smaller, less numerous, and breeds in the southern mountains. I also began to grow curious about more of the region's big game.

First, I went out after a puma, or mountain lion, in a southern area of the cattle ranches. This was much like hunting lion in Arizona—you use horses, and you use dogs. But there were some differences. For one, we didn't have to ride over rugged mountains. Puma had been increasing, and at the headquarters of the ranch where I hunted, stock was brought in at night and placed in corrals for safety. The puma were not inclined to come very close to human activity because of the dogs. Instead, the cats would patrol the perimeter areas of the ranch at night.

When a hunt was under way, gauchos would get out on horseback first thing in the morning and conduct their own perimeter patrol, accompanied by dogs on leashes, looking to pick up a fresh cat track. When they hit a track, they turned the dogs loose and got the lion treed or holed up somewhere. Most of the trees were small, scrubby little things that were not much use to a fleeing lion. Then someone would come back to HQ, get the client on a horse, and race over hill and dale to reach the cat.

On my hunt the dogs had the lion cornered in about fifteen minutes. There was no question of riding for hours through the mountains. When I arrived, the men leashed up the dogs so they would not be at risk from untidy shooting, and I was lucky the lion proved to be a large one. I also took introduced red stag. These deer are numerous in the far south of Argentina and seem to make up the main prey base for the puma today.

My outfitter for puma was Marcelo Sodiro, who would outfit several more South American big-game hunts for me. A year later, I went back with Mike Simpson and Dan Duncan of the Houston Safari Club and Dave Hannah of Pittsburgh. I needed two or three animals to finish our "diamonds" for South America in the SCI trophy records, and Mike and Dan each needed four or five. So we all went together and visited several different places. Marcelo arranged for us to cover the spectrum of big-game species. Besides the native deer and puma, the animals available included white-lipped peccary, collared peccary, and some exotics, such as wild boar, mouflon, and axis deer.

Dave and I got our animals first. Mike and Dan were still working on theirs, so Marcelo suggested his driver take us to join two British dove hunters. Dove hunting goes better when there are several hunters out together. It sounded like a fine idea. The last thing we expected was to come close to disaster on a dove hunt. Late in the day, after the hunt, the sky turned ominous. As darkness fell, it began to rain. The dirt roads quickly turned muddy and slippery, and you can be sure there were no guardrails. The only markers were posts planted to show where the road crossed a watercourse. The posts meant "bridge."

All of a sudden, we were out of control, sliding toward a set of those posts. The driver yelled that he couldn't stop, and he couldn't turn, either. Then the truck went sailing into midair. It flew right across the creek and lodged nose first in the opposite bank. I hit the windshield and was out of that vehicle in a second, afraid the truck might slide down into the creek. Dave Hannah was under the dash, in pain, and all the truck doors were jammed. We wrestled the injured men out of the cab and soon realized one of them was going into shock.

Of all things, a road grader coming by turned out to be our rescue party. The driver saw us and picked us up, and we slid for a few miles until we reached the blacktop and made our way to a town with a hospital and a motel, where Marcelo came to retrieve us. The two Brits were the worst off, with head and rib injuries. Dave also wound up needing surgery. I was lucky; all I suffered was a stiff neck.

Perhaps the wild man of the Chaco had the better formula, living without transportation except for his mules. Of all my encounters with the people and the strange animals, birds, and fish of South America, meeting him was by far the most engaging experience. The big white-lipped peccary I shot when his dogs helped bring the quarry to bay is under attack again in my trophy room: I had my puma from Argentina mounted tackling the peccary. Both are gold-medal animals.

Chapter 20

The Far, Far South

Australia and New Zealand, 1980s, 2004

Australia and New Zealand were places I delayed visiting for a long time. Politics and game management were in a stable condition in those countries, as they are today, so the hunting was fairly predictable. I judged that the smart thing to do was make the best of hunting opportunities in other countries while they were open, or when they suddenly opened up. I could always go to the South Pacific. As a result, I did not set foot there until the 1980s.

Little did I know that the South Pacific would hold plenty of excitement for me. It started during a 1982 hunt with Terry Pierson for tahr and chamois at Mount Hutt Station in New Zealand. We were flying over the mountains in a little Bell helicopter, and the situation turned scary in seconds. It was cold at that altitude, and colder yet because the craft's cabin doors had been removed, so we were wearing heavy coats. The oil gauge had a line that came in along the roof of the cabin, and for some reason it broke. Suddenly, the little tube came loose and started snaking about, spraying oil all over the cabin interior, the pilot, and the passenger—me! We could see the oil gauge plunging toward zero. I had no way of judging how dangerous this was, but it didn't look good.

The pilot zoomed down as quickly as possible, found a level spot, landed, and immediately cut the engine. His white coveralls were covered—all right, covered—with oil. With impressive calm, he told me to go and scoop up bunches of grass and use them to clean up the interior of the chopper. I did as he asked, although, frankly, I was wondering how useful it could possibly be to spend time cleaning up the cabin when we apparently had a crippled craft. We were way out in the mountains, and no one knew where we were. How in the world were we going to get out of there?

The pilot had some extra oil and some glue, and he said he was going to make a temporary fix. I cleaned up the chopper while he

My axis deer scored 103¼, well into the record book, and was taken with outfitter Mick Aming of Niall Station in Queensland and guide Bevan Dan. We found the buck on a neighboring ranch.

We had to make a stop to repair the oil line before going back to the Mountain Hutt Station.

glued the broken gauge line. We started out again with some trepidation, heading for the nearest ranch headquarters. I was relieved when we limped in without mishap. Another plane brought us the part we needed, and the temporary repair was declared sufficient to get us back to our base. The pilot said we would fly back to Mount Hutt Station, and he would install the new part there.

Would you believe that after the repair was completed and we were able to set out once more to scout for tahr, the same thing happened again? By then, I assure you I was not eager to have anything more to do with that helicopter. I told Terry I didn't need a tahr *that* bad. Terry is a persuasive fellow, however, and he was not planning to let me go home without my trophies. I went out a third time and got my tahr and chamois.

If you're going to fly all over the mountains in small craft, there are bound to be bad moments. On two Alaskan hunts long before, I'd flown on fixed-wing aircraft that got smashed up. One piled up on its nose when landing on tires, running into soft snow more suitable for a plane on skis. The other was ferrying me in for a sheep hunt when it ran out of runway. Between these and the helicopter incidents, I think I must have used up most of my lifetime quota of near misses. How many times can you expect to walk away from a helicopter oil-gauge failure or an airplane crash? The pilot who saved the day on my hunt in New Zealand was killed about a year later when he flew into the side of a mountain.

Axis and Sandwiches

In 1987 I booked an August-September hunt through Bob Penfold of Hunt Australia, aiming to collect a range of species from a series of places. The hunt did not get off to a promising start. I was supposed to fly from Los Angeles to Auckland, New Zealand, and then on to New Caledonia, but officials turned up a visa snag. Penfold suggested Plan B: Fly on to Sydney, where I could reapply for a visa for New Caledonia, and hunt in Australia for several days until the paperwork materialized.

I overnighted in Sydney and made my application at the French consulate before flying to Brisbane, Queensland, for a night at the beachfront. From there I would charter out to a ranch named Niall Station to hunt axis deer with Mick Aming. My guide was named Bevan.

The main ranch house was sixty years old and looked like something out of a movie. My hosts offered a charming spread of tea and sandwiches before we went out hunting.

The country was extremely dry because it had not had respectable rains in four or five years. The vegetation reminded me of Africa—all burned up. We saw plenty of axis deer that afternoon and kept looking until dark, but we found no good stags except one that was still in velvet.

Mick came in during the evening from working cattle. He had been on this 118,000-acre ranch for eighteen years, and he had just bought the adjacent ranch of 55,000 acres. All told, he had about five thousand head of cattle. Just five men worked them, and they worked pretty well seven days a week, three hundred and sixty-five days a year.

This portion of the hunt was supposed to be easy, but current conditions were poor because of the drought. A plane was coming in for me at noon the next day. Over a beer, Mick and I made new plans. He thought I would have better luck on another ranch about an hour away. Bevan and I would head over there at 5 A.M., taking all my gear, and Mick planned to have the plane pick me up at the second ranch, instead of at Niall.

We arrived at the alternate place just before daylight. This was a ranch of ninety thousand acres, and its main house was more than ninety years old. As at Mick's place, we found only does and small bucks. We did see one fair stag, but it turned out to have one bad horn. Bevan suggested I take the stag anyway because our time was very limited, but I wanted to hold out for a better one.

Conversation died away, and we drove on. I had made the right call. Before long, we spotted another good stag standing on top of a ridge. We made a good stalk, and this time Bevan was perfectly clear.

"Shoot," he told me.

I shot too fast, over the animal, but it just stood there, so I quickly shot again. The second shot hit it in the heart, and it went down. The stag was a fine trophy, with horn length of 29 inches and a score of 103¼; it took a score of about eighty to make the book.

Even after photos, skinning, and caping, there was no need to divert the incoming plane. We had enough time to return to Niall, and, as it turned out, the plane was late because of a heavy headwind.

Sambar and Wombat

Things moved fast that afternoon, taking me from Niall to Brisbane and on to Melbourne, where I was to hunt with another Mick. Mick McCormick was waiting at the airport to take me to his home for supper. We were to start out on a sambar hunt in the morning, leaving before 6 A.M. for an hour's drive to the hunting area. Mick warned that we would probably have about six hours of hilly walking, but the weather was on our side. It was not too cold, and he said the brush was not too thick.

The long day of walking proved fruitless, however. We saw no sambar, though we did come across a wombat. Australia is distinguished for some very unlikely looking wild animals. The wombat appears to have been built by a committee. It reminds me of one

Tom Condon was my outfitter for a free-ranging New Zealand red stag. I took this big 12-point stag at something over 200 yards.

of those split-card games for kids, where you mix and match animal body parts.

"They sure look funny," I noted in my journal. "A wombat has a pig-looking head, with gopher teeth, and a body shaped like a badger's. It weighs forty to sixty-nine pounds, and the claws on its front feet are like bear's."

That first one went its way, but later, on the same hunt, I decided to shoot a wombat to bring home.

Mick's next idea was to head for higher country almost four hundred miles away, where there was a shack we could use as a camp. On the way we ran into quite a snowstorm, which I feared would damage our hunting options. Mick took a different view, pointing out its advantage: The storm and the snowfall should drive the deer lower down. The higher we went, the better the weather became. By the time we reached our new base, the sun was shining, though the chill remained. We had to board up a broken window in the old shack, and we built ourselves a fire and had something to eat to ward off the cold.

By morning, however, the weather had worsened. It snowed and rained on us. We took our gear along because the next stop would be at a different shack. We were now counting on our staying power to cause Lady Luck to smile on us. We spotted a good sambar, a definite improvement, though we were unable to get a shot. Ten minutes later, we saw another, and Mick told me to shoot. I broke the animal's back with a shot at two hundred and fifty yards.

It proved to be a four-point stag, and it just made the book, though the tips of its horns were broken off.

Mick explained that sambar developed a fungus on the horn while in velvet, and then they rubbed down the tips, which made them appear to be broken. We overnighted at the shack before heading back to Mick's home. He caped out the sambar, and I spent the afternoon trying for a few ducks and a couple of kangaroos, which he also skinned out for me.

We were still planning to try for a larger sambar, but Mick wanted to take me on an interesting errand in the meantime. He brought along the meat of my sambar to trade for beef. For this little transaction we went to the ranch where the movie *The Man from Snowy River* was made. Mick introduced me to a fellow he knew well, and I enjoyed learning about the place while Mick boned out the meat. On the wall were photos of Kirk Douglas, who starred in the movie.

The ranch had a large number of horses—about one hundred. It was still running cattle, and the cattle spent the summer in the mountains. The ranchers drove them up in the early spring and brought them down at the end of the season, just as in the movie. Visitors could now enjoy this beautiful ranch on horseback, instead of on the screen. They could take a trail ride all the way up into the high country. There was little risk of getting lost or stranded because the horses all knew the drill. They knew their way back to the headquarters corrals and could be relied upon to bring trail riders safely home.

We were not destined to find a big sambar. We saw only a spike and a bunch of cattle, which spooked and ran. During this hunt I had shot a pretty mountain duck the size of a small goose, as well as a red fox, a large kangaroo, and a spiny echidna, a little marsupial that looks like a cross between a porcupine and a hedgehog. When we picked up my skins from the local taxidermist, I left the echidna with him for mounting. I figured he knew the animal and would probably do a better job than a taxidermist across the globe might do. The echidna is often a talking point in my trophy room (see chapter 7).

I had to delay my visit to New Caledonia, but I worked things out with Mick to return the following year to try for a bigger sambar and then go to New Zealand for red deer, wapiti, and fallow deer.

Goat, Lamb, and Potatoes

In March 1988 I was back on the long-haul flight from Los Angeles via Hawaii and Auckland to Melbourne, where Mick was waiting for me. We drove to his home, and his wife, Sheryl, provided a welcome cup of tea. Mick's daughter, Elizabeth, had spotted two goat on their place that morning, and we walked along a steep riverbank to look for them, but they had evidently moved on.

That evening I was included in a fine Australian lamb barbecue to celebrate the twentieth birthday of a niece of Mick and Sheryl. I was nursing a sore throat on top of jet lag, and they rounded up a doctor friend to give me a penicillin shot. The lamb and the shot both probably helped prepare me for a predawn start to our hunt. We were to get up early, Mick told me, because it was about an hour's drive to the potato patch where we would be trying for a big sambar.

I can't claim to remember much about the journey. When we got there, we set ourselves up to watch for sambar coming into the patch to feed. Before long, a good one came in. After the failures of the year before, I was impatient—I took too long a shot. I thought I had hit the animal, and we searched for it, but we could not find it. The patch was surrounded by thick forest, and the sambar had retreated into this heavy cover, where searching was difficult. We eventually abandoned the effort.

We switched to going out after a goat the next day, and I got a handsome white one with black legs. It scored 75⅛ inches and proved to be No. 4 in the book.

Then we packed up to head for a cabin from which we would continue looking for sambar. Mick said he had seen a big stag in a tangled area of blackberries about an hour's walk away. As we approached the spot, we jumped a stag and a doe, but they took off before we could see them well enough to shoot. The only sambar we saw clearly during a lot of walking along the river bottom that day was a very young one. Mick wanted to catch it but restrained the impulse.

We walked some more blackberry thickets in the morning, slept in the afternoon, and went out later to search. It was fruitless—unless you count the blackberries. The day after that, following the same routine, we returned to where we had jumped the first two deer, and for a second time we spotted two deer but were unable to get a good shot. I did shoot, but I missed. I just could not seem to get this deer. Perhaps the planets were misaligned or the hunting gods were unhappy. It was while out on this hunt that I heard my dad had died of a heart attack.

Stewart Island

It was time to set out for New Zealand. Mick and I flew into Christchurch on the South Island and on to Invercargill, where we would shop for food and then take a charter over to Stewart Island. Invercargill is the jump-off point for the enormous Fiordland National Park, which covers the southwestern section of the South Island. The large Stewart Island is the southernmost part of New Zealand. We set out in a small plane at 5 P.M.—at that latitude it would remain light well into the evening. Was there a landing strip on the island? If so, it was nowhere near the place where we were headed. Our plane was going to land on the beach while the tide was out—a new experience for me. I crossed my fingers, hoping the sand was firm enough.

We got down safely enough and unloaded our gear. As the pilot revved up and started his takeoff, the little plane slowed and got stuck in the sand. The pilot jumped out and began moving the muck, digging out a track in front of the tires so he could try another run. This was another new experience. I've had my share of helping dig out stuck vehicles, but I usually don't have to worry about the tide coming in. Suddenly, that plane looked very vulnerable indeed. I had visions of darkness closing over us with the craft still stuck and the tide washing in to sweep it away forever. Then it began to rain.

Eventually, the pilot was satisfied with his sand-moving operations on the beach and was ready to give his makeshift runway a go. He climbed into his seat, and, out in the rain, Mick and I positioned ourselves so that we could each lift and push on a wing for a little extra horsepower. It worked. The plane roared to life, its wheels found enough traction to get moving, and the pilot lifted off and disappeared into the weather.

Now the wind was blowing, and rain was coming down so hard that we could barely see. We had intended to put up a tent, but Mick said there was a cabin about a mile away, which seemed a much better option in the downpour. We carried our gear over to it, and after three or four sodden trips, we had everything inside the cabin. We built a fire, put on some dry clothes, and went to bed. It rained and blew all night long, but we sure slept well after all the digging and hauling.

Mick cooked up a big breakfast to start the day right. The fellow with whom we would later be hunting red deer and fallow was hunting the next block over, and he came to pay us a call. He and a client had been there for a few days already, but they had seen only does. As we headed out to scout, the wind was still blowing like crazy, and it rained off and on. We saw lots of sign but no deer. This area is among the very few that have free-ranging whitetail, and that was the species we were after.

After lunch at the cabin, we spent part of the afternoon watching a promising opening and then walked back to camp along the oceanside sand dunes. Mick favored beach patrols because, he said, the deer came out onto the beach to eat kelp. But two beach walks of an hour and a half each still yielded no deer.

It rained and blew all night. I was beginning to think it would never quit. This is a temperate rain-forest ecosystem, and it *rains*. To be honest, I found it a miserable place. Deer with any intelligence were presumably sheltering wherever they could—with one exception. From our own shelter in the cabin, Mick

I hunted banteng in 2005 in Arnhem Land, in the Northern Territory of Australia, with guide Max Davidson. Max was right when he said the bull was good—it was No. 1 in the book for a time.

looked out the window and spotted a doe right there, sharing the opening with us.

On the last day, when the weather eased a little, we hunted all day, hiking the inland hills. Only twenty feet from us, we saw a small six-point jump another young animal. On the way back we saw three sheep that had apparently gone wild. We also jumped a fawn that still had its spots, but the trophy animals must have been attending to business elsewhere. That night the moonlight in the dunes was so bright that we could have read a newspaper.

After all the walking on the beach, my gun was as gritty with sand as I was. I was looking forward to a shower, once we were back on the mainland. The pilot of the plane that picked me up turned out to be a young woman, scarcely more than a girl. I'll admit I was taken aback, recalling the incident on the beach a few days before, but she knew what she was doing behind the controls.

Wapiti, Fallow Deer, and Red Deer

Before heading to Te Anau, about two hours' drive north, to hunt wapiti with Richard Hayes, we had a break in town. We met a helicopter pilot who told us all about the commercial hunting and trapping of red deer.

Australia's tropical coast is a fisherman's paradise, famous for giant queenfish. Elizabeth was thrilled to catch a big one.

Settlers had introduced all of the dozen big-game species of New Zealand. Red deer originally released in New Zealand came from good bloodlines in some famous English herds, and, in the rich environment of the far south, their trophy quality soon far exceeded anything to be found in Britain. The animals also proliferated to an alarming extent, seriously damaging the habitat for native species. Control efforts by government hunters got rolling as early as the 1930s, with deer cullers taking out enormous numbers of animals every year.

Still, deer numbers remained high until helicopter gunships entered the picture. The next step in the evolution of the issue was live capture for a fledgling deer-farming industry. Free-ranging deer are now much harder to find than they once were, and most of the trophy hunting occurs on private land. The pilot told us his crew live-trapped only females, and they sold the meat from the stags.

Mick and I had plenty of time to talk, and the more we talked about it, the more we thought it might be a good idea to look again for the sambar I had shot in the potato patch. We had searched for it at the time because I thought it had been hit, but now we decided perhaps we had given up too soon. Mick said the animal had been running in a strange way, and it had also broken the fence on its way out. If it had not been injured, it would have been able to jump that fence easily. He called home and asked Sheryl and Elizabeth to go out and mount another search for the sambar. Later, when he called Sheryl back, sure enough, they had found my trophy, about eighty yards into the woods. It had a nice 25-inch set of horns.

We had hoped we might be able to return to Stewart Island, but rough weather was predicted for several more days, taking that possibility off the table. We decided hunting on the mainland would be more productive. We drove to the small town of Te Anau, the gateway to the wilderness of Fiordland. On the first morning at Richard's place, we went out into the hills and shot a nice 11-point wapiti just before midday.

Next, we set out early for a long drive north to the town of Timaru on the Pacific coast, where we were to meet Kenny O'Rourke and go out after fallow deer. We first stopped at his taxidermy shop to drop off the wapiti skin and horns, which the shop would pack for me. Reaching our camp around noon, we had a light lunch and went hunting. We climbed some very steep hills, glassing until dark, and saw about three dozen fallow deer.

Our timing was good. The bucks were in the rut, or the roar, as they call it in New Zealand. Mick stayed in camp the next day, and I set out with Kenny to walk the hills. We went down one hill and up another, then down that one and up the next. All day we climbed. This was the most climbing I had done in some time, and my feet

My son Jason joined me on a hunt with Simon Kyle-Little in Arnhem Land, where I took a wild ox.

were feeling it. We jumped one buck but couldn't get a clean shot, and then, as we were returning to our camp, we saw another good one. We decided to go back to camp for a quick bite and then go after it.

At 6:15 P.M. we were on top of a ridge and just starting our stalk when we realized that two bucks were moving up the hill toward us. The second was a good one, and I took it with a successful neck shot as it was running away. We were back at our cabin by 7 P.M., triumphant.

It was raining on and off as we skinned out the fallow and hauled it to town to be packed up with the wapiti. We now drove to Christchurch for a flight to Auckland, on the North Island. We would spend the night there before flying on to Taupo to hunt Sika in the Ripia River area with outfitter Tom Condon. His wife picked us up at Taupo and—you guessed it—took us home for tea. The Ripia camp was about two hours' drive away, but we still had enough afternoon left for some scouting. My guide, Steve, and I found a young buck and a doe, and we used the daylight still remaining after supper to scout for another hour or so. This time we saw lots of deer.

We planned to hunt a large valley nearby after breakfast. Soon we spotted a doe and a fawn, and then we heard a stag roar. Steve gave a couple of convincing grunts, and next we saw the stag coming right down toward us, only about twenty-five yards away. One shot in the neck did it. By 9:30 P.M., we were headed back, Steve carrying the buck out whole.

Three generations of hunters are pictured here—Grandpa, Jason, and Jason's son JR, who was one year old. JR is all smiles over his grandpa's water buffalo. Jason and Tiffany shot great buffalo as well.

We devoted the remainder of our hunt to getting a good red stag. We returned to Taupo, and a helicopter took me into the next hunting area. Tom and I went out scouting that first afternoon and saw two cows (or hinds, as they are locally called) and a good stag. I could see that the place had fine trophy animals.

We headed out around 6:30 A.M., ready for a long day of mountain walking. We saw a hind early on, and Tom did some calling. He brought in a stag, but the vegetation was too thick for us to see its horns. We waited and watched. As the stag began moving off again, we finally got a good view of it and saw that it was a small eight pointer—not the trophy I wanted. We climbed up and down three more mountains without seeing or hearing any other sign of deer. Rain drove us back toward headquarters. In late afternoon we went out again. We spotted six hinds but no stag.

We planned to return in the morning to scout some more where we had seen the six hinds. This proved to be sound strategy. Before even reaching the area where the hinds had been, we spotted a beautiful, big 12-point stag going up the side of a hill. I jumped out of the vehicle and took off after it, getting a shot at a little over two hundred yards. I hit the stag with the first shot, but it took off running. It took two more shots to anchor the stag. It was one of the best red deer shot in the wild in a long time, a great way to finish the hunt.

I returned to the far south for rusa deer in New Caledonia in 1989, and I have been back to Australia several times for water buffalo, banteng, and fishing. As we stalked the banteng in Arnhem Land on a hunt out of Darwin in the Northern Territory, my guide, Max Davidson, was a model of Australian understatement. He said only that the bull we were after was a good one. It turned out to be very good indeed—it was No. 1 in the book for a time.

In June 2004 my family joined me in Arnhem Land. I was now traveling with a party of six: Elizabeth; her daughter, Tiffany; Jason; his wife, Jan; and my one-year-old grandson, JR. Jason and his family were living in Beijing, China, at the time, so his ten-hour flight to Australia was nothing in comparison to our forty-eight hours of traveling from the United States.

We hunted with Simon Kyle-Little of Australian Big-Game Safaris. This camp was downright luxurious, as far as outback hunting goes, but Jan and Tiffany weren't so sure. Tiffany dragged her Louis Vuitton luggage through the dirt, and Jan's eyes were as wide as saucers as she clutched baby JR. It was quite a sight. Simon brought along his wife, Elspeth, and their two small children, Dylan and Allison, as entertainment for JR. The children were well versed in the dangers of the outback and warned us, "See over there, it's a cane toad. If you look at it, it'll spit poison in your eyes!"

While we were out on a family drive to see wild mustang and numerous buffalo, Simon suggested I take a trophy bull we had spotted. Simon and I made the stalk while the family stayed back in the truck. A short time later, we were photographing three generations of "hunters" around the bull. JR had just turned one year old the month before, so we propped him up by letting him hold onto the bull's horns. I thought his mother was going to die when he bent down and began chewing on them.

Jason and Tiffany shot great buffalo, as well as wild pig. I was also fortunate enough to take a wild ox, a descendant of a breed of short, stubby red cattle that were once used as draft animals to haul out water buffalo hides. We all enjoyed some fabulous fishing at camp, and Elizabeth and I took our own overnight fishing trip with Simon on Australia's tropical coast. Sleeping in a tent by the gorgeous turquoise waters of the ocean meant we could get up in the morning and be fishing within minutes of opening our eyes. It was a fisherman's paradise. The only little problem was that we sometimes had to cut a line when a fish went down to hide in the coral. We caught ten different kinds of fish, including the famous giant queenfish. Simon grilled our catch right there on the sandy beach, and the meal was accompanied by fine Australian wines.

From Australia's desert and open woodlands and the picture-perfect tropical coast of Queensland to the heavy rain forest and the high, scenic, and challenging mountains of New Zealand's South Island, the countries down under are beautiful in very different ways. But don't let anyone tell you that hunting in Australia and New Zealand is easy, just because people speak English and you are served tea and sandwiches in the genteel comfort of farmhouse living rooms. On some of the deer hunts you also need to be born waterproof, be willing to climb until you drop, and be ready to help dig out a stuck airplane.

Chapter 21

Loyalty Pays Off

Europe, 1982–2006

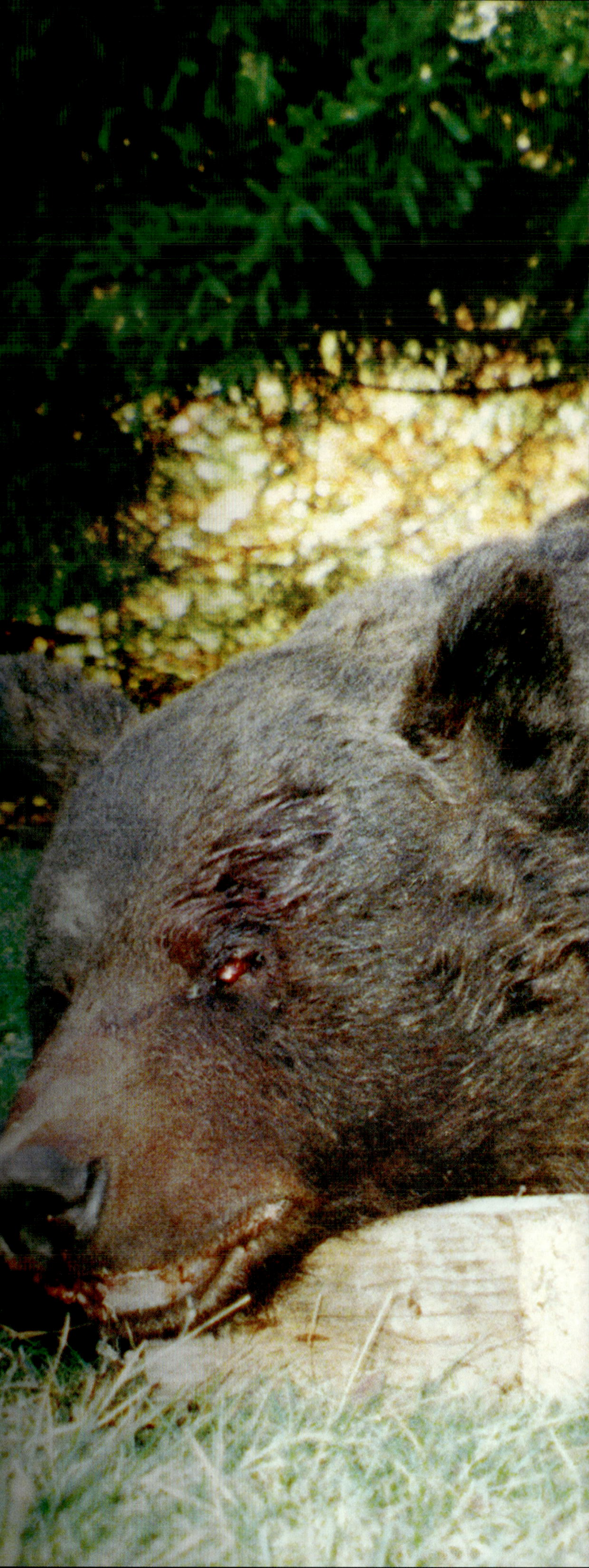

My fellow passengers told me where to step off the train, and I found myself at a tiny railroad siding with no office, no building of any kind, and certainly no telephone. There was not another soul in sight. I stood beside the track with my duffel bag, the rails stretching away into the pleasing countryside of Merrie England. Was I at the right place? What was I supposed to do now?

My destination was the Duke of Bedford's estate at Woburn Abbey, famous in deer conservation circles for retrieving the Père David deer from the brink of extinction. I don't suppose too many visitors arrived quite the way I did. I had flown in from Houston, taken a train from the airport into London, and made a couple of transfers to catch a train that passed close to Woburn.

Coping with my gear on trains was awkward—bags did not all have wheels in 1989. Nor did everyone carry cell phones in those days. I had no phone number for

My gold-medal Eurasian brown bear was taken with one shot from a cozy stand beside a moonlit clearing. The bears in Romania are mostly nocturnal.

the place, anyway. Someone was supposed to be at the railroad siding to meet me, but, after waiting fruitlessly for almost an hour, it seemed like a better idea to set off on foot and see if I could find anyone who knew which way I should walk.

A truck stopped, and I asked the driver if I was in the right vicinity. Oh, yes, he told me, Woburn Abbey was just a few miles down the road. I was relieved when the next vehicle that pulled up proved to contain Mike and Travis Simpson of the Houston Safari Club—and you can guess why they were late. They had been out hunting. We were to hunt at Woburn for four species: Sika, Père David deer, Chinese water deer, and Reeves muntjac. The muntjac and water deer came out at dusk to feed, and the others could be hunted in the daytime.

We stayed at a nearby bed-and-breakfast and were welcomed to Woburn by none other than the distinguished deer stalker Kenneth Whitehead. He was a founder and officer of the British Deer Society, and his interest in deer was among the factors that led to the passage of the 1963 British Deer Act, which prohibited deer hunting with shotguns because they tended to cause wounds from which the animals did not recover. When we met him, he was in his mid-seventies, though he looked much younger. He said the health secret that made him so spry and chipper was that he ate a banana every morning, without fail. (Whitehead died in 2004 at the age of ninety-one.)

Top Ten

As Old World hunts go, my solo arrival at Woburn by rail was the exception because nobody arrives alone by train. Later, I hunted in England three times with outfitter Kevin Downer, who supplied full-scale hunting plus sightseeing service. He arranged bed-and-breakfast accommodations, knew where the fine restaurants were, and could adjust the touring schedule according to how the hunting went. Two of those trips were in the fall, one of them a hunt for red stag with Houston Safari Club companions Mike Simpson and

Kenneth Whitehead, founder of the British Deer Society, was there to welcome us to Woburn Abbey, where I took a gold-medal Sika in 1989.

Dan Duncan. We were all trying to get additional species to reach SCI's diamond level with our European animals.

For a good roe-deer trophy, Kevin said I needed to hunt in the summer. Roe deer are to the Europeans what white-tailed deer are to Texans: Year after year, hunters go out searching for that monster buck. There's certainly a lot more antler on a whitetail. The stalkers may decide against shooting a good roebuck in the hope that if they save it for next year, its antlers will be even better. I hated to go that far to shoot just one animal, so I suggested Elizabeth come with me and we take in some history as well.

The first morning we were there, Elizabeth decided to sleep in. Kevin and I set out hunting, and at one point he pulled up beside a fence and told me about the big driven-pheasant shoots in the area. The fence bordered an enclosure where there were brooder houses. A gamekeeper lived there to watch over the raising of one thousand or more pheasant chicks. The fence was low, and as soon as they were old enough to fly, the birds could get out into the surrounding countryside. The gamekeepers continued to place feed out in the paddock for them to discourage them from moving too far away. They often returned to the feeder to eat, which ensured successful driven-pheasant hunts in season.

As Kevin was describing all this to me, I glanced over to one side and suddenly saw a little head and horns sticking out of the lush grass. There was a roebuck right there, across a field from us! Kevin declared it a top gold-medal deer. It seemed to be lying in the grass; we could see only the head, quite low down. Which way did the body go? Should I shoot to the left or to the right? I didn't want to shoot the buck in the head.

"He's watching us," said Kevin. "And when he gets up, he's going to take off. Can you shoot him in the throat?"

I wasn't sure—a roe deer does not supply much of a target to begin with. At my shot, the buck went down. We ran over, and then we realized the buck had been at the crest of a small rise. It had been standing up, but the terrain dropped away behind it, which explained why we had seen only its head.

It was indeed a beautiful deer, in the top ten in the book, with heavy gnarling on its horns. We had a fine time showing the trophy to people who had shot dozens of roebuck but who had rarely seen one that good.

All this was before breakfast. By the time we reconnected with Elizabeth, the hunt was over, and our history tour could begin. We went into London for a day, visited the dramatic ancient stone circle at Stonehenge, and went to see the Roman relics in the beautiful city of Bath. Kevin gave us a fascinating tour of the original Roman public bath and its sophisticated piping systems, including underfloor heating.

Getting the Hang of Europe

My first European hunt was in Spain in 1982. I had hunted Africa three times by then, and I realized that if I were going to try for the Weatherby Award, I needed to collect some trophies in Asia and Europe, too. At that early stage only a handful of outfitters were operating in Spain, among them Ricardo Medem of Cazatur and Felix Lalanne of Safari Brokers. Safari Club International then recognized only one kind of ibex, called the Spanish ibex, so I went over to get ibex, fallow deer, red stag, and mouflon—my first non-North American sheep.

The real blessing of that trip was getting to know Felix. He knew how to assemble a whole package, with choice places to stay and historical tours arranged comfortably around the edges of a hunt. I would go back to Spain several times and would enjoy hunts with Felix in Bulgaria and Romania as well. His efficiency showed me that loyalty to a reliable outfitter can get you a long way. After that 1982 hunt with Felix, I set about trying

I was looking at a pheasant-breeding enclosure when a fine roe buck with heavily gnarled horns appeared. It made the top ten in the SCI record book.

Elizabeth, outfitter Kevin Downer, and I celebrated my roe deer at a great restaurant in the historic city of Bath.

to get all the different kinds of ibex and chamois Europe had to offer, a project in which he played a key role over a period spanning more than twenty years.

My second European hunt was in Austria. It was part of my 1984 grand tour with Ed Armania, which might be called Eurasian Antiquities 101. It began with a hunt in Nepal, outfitted by T. J. Thapa. During a pause at Tiger Tops lodge, I rode an elephant, watched a tiger from a blind, and saw several Asian rhino. A portion of our stay also involved going by boat to a wilder camp, which we explored on foot. We saw several rhino there.

I flew on to Delhi, India, where the traffic consisted largely of bikes, motorbikes, and odd three wheeled carts. We saw temples and stunning ivory carvings. We visited Agra to see the Taj Mahal (1631–1653) and the Agra Fort (1565–1573) from the Moghul era. We saw the deserted Red Sandstone City (1569–1585) en route to Jaipur, the "pink city." In Jaipur I tried a real Indian dinner.

"The food is as hot as in Mexico. Never again," I vowed in my journal. "I've had enough curry for a lifetime."

I saw the palace known as the Amber Fort, built in 1727. Its walls, punctuated with seven gates, were eighteen feet high and nine feet thick and ran for five miles around the city. The builder of this palace had twelve queens, and he built their rooms around a large courtyard. I rode up to the palace on the back of an elephant.

On the way to Greece I discovered that several pieces of jewelry had been filched from my baggage, and my rifle bolt, removed by the airline, did not show up, either. From the hotel I looked out over the intense blue of the Aegean Sea. I was relieved to be back in a land of more familiar food. The roast pork was out of this world, and it was great to be able to eat salad without fear.

I visited the Apollo Temple at Delphi (300 BC); Corinth and Mycenae; and the Acropolis in Athens. The Greek temples were very much older—the Temple of Poseidon dated to 3,000 BC. The palaces were on the mountaintops, with the old towns below. On 22 November 1984 I was enjoying a Thanksgiving turkey dinner in Athens. British Airways eventually found and delivered the rifle bolt I thought I would never see again, which was fortunate, because I still had some hunting to do.

My final round of antiquities was in Istanbul, Turkey, where I saw the famous Blue Mosque (1609–1616) and the sultan's palace, called Topkapi, which had been home to six thousand people at its peak of operations. The kitchen tour alone took twenty minutes. The place had unbelievable collections of gold and gemstones, including an eighty-six-carat diamond. In Istanbul I caught up with Mike Simpson, Russell Selle, and Cecil Hopper of Houston, and, following an excellent Turkish lunch of goat and lamb cooked three different ways, we flew to Anatolia. We stayed in a pleasant hotel during our hunt.

We left at 4:30 A.M. for the check station, where we were assigned our guides. Russell got his ibex by 9:30 A.M., and I spotted two very good ibex, but they were outside our hunting area. That afternoon we glassed as the ibex started to move out to feed after their siesta. We spotted a good one still lying down and waited for it to get up so we could move toward where it was feeding. As we moved closer, the guide spotted the ibex crossing a clearing, and I got off a long shot from three hundred yards, just as it was entering some brush. We found a blood trail, followed it, and finished off the animal. I had a very good 36-inch ibex, and we had an ibex dinner that evening.

My next objective was the alpine ibex, offered in Austria at the estate of Count Otto Herberstein. I flew from Istanbul to Vienna and then to Graz, where the count had arranged to pick me up for the forty-five-minute drive to the hundred-room castle. It was one thousand years old and was still in the same family. I had a large bedroom and bathroom with a fireplace in each!

Over breakfast the count instructed my guide, who did not speak English. On the morning's hunt we saw several ibex, plus mouflon and fallow deer. At lunch the guide went over what we had seen, and the count offered some more advice. During the afternoon, I collected my ibex, which proved to be eleven years old and had only three teeth left on one side of its jaw. On the way back I shot a mallard. Mike Simpson had taken an ibex that scored 180 points and made the top spot in the record book. Mine turned out to be very heavy, with 35-inch horns, scoring 190 points. Hunting staff are not always proficient at caping, so I oversaw the caping operation myself. I was not confident about this process because so many Europeans simply mount the horns. The quality of that trophy definitely called for a celebratory drink with the count.

The guide then took me out to look for mouflon. Soon after setting out, we saw a sheep, and the guide told me to shoot it. I shot and missed, and the ram fled straight upward. We went after it and jumped it a second time, but I could not get off a shot. We heard some rock falling, but it turned out this was caused by ibex bolting across an opening, not by my mouflon. Then we saw some mouflon females with the big ram. This time my shot was good, and I had my ram. We were back at the castle for lunch, and once again I kept an eye on the skinning work.

The forty-five-day around-the-world marathon in 1984 made me even more appreciative of the logistical and linguistic ease that Felix Lalanne brought to the experience of hunting in Europe. I roped him in on most of the remaining chamois and ibex species I wanted.

Balkan Chamois in Bulgaria

In 1996 I went to Bulgaria for chamois but failed to get one. I scheduled a return match for October 2002. I left Houston for Paris on my way to Sofia, Bulgaria. After that, I planned to proceed to Romania and Turkey for more chamois species and then go to Iran for Armenian and Esfahan sheep (see chapter 17). Felix had arranged for a driver and a woman interpreter to meet me at Sofia and help get my Bulgarian gun permit.

We drove approximately three hours to the lodge from which we hunted chamois. The government had

I got this Alpine ibex in Austria on the estate of Count Otto Herberstein. The animal was eleven years old and had 35-inch horns.

built comfortable lodges in the mountains and supplied local guides. We arrived with enough daylight left to spend three hours in a high stand that same afternoon, hoping for wild boar. None appeared.

Felix and I were to set out at 7 A.M. for chamois. We were hunting in a mountain area of heavy woodland—not what I thought of as typical chamois country. We did see a lot of chamois, but I could not get a shot. Eventually, we moved to more open country where we could glass the slopes, and we saw another twenty to forty chamois. I tried a long shot of around three hundred yards, but I missed. We continued hunting until dark but saw only one more chamois, and I could not get a shot at it.

On the second day we hunted a different area with similar results. We saw chamois, I missed a shot, and again we hunted until dark. With only one day left, we decided to go back to where I had taken the long shot—that was where we had seen chamois in the greatest numbers. This time we approached from a different direction, and, sure enough, we soon found the animals, including a number of females and young. They were across a valley from our position. We had to do a lot of walking to get closer to them and jumped a female in the process.

I was conscious that I was on the verge of leaving Bulgaria without a chamois on my second try. In the afternoon, with less than four hours left to hunt, we found a group of five males. We had a good vantage point with plenty of cover to mask our presence and supply good shooting rests. Our hope was that the males would gradually feed closer to us, or that other chamois might come out to feed in an opening one to two hundred yards away. The minutes ticked into hours. At last, as the light was beginning to fade, a chamois did walk out and start to feed.

At first I could not shoot because there were tree branches in my way. I waited for about fifteen minutes as the feeding chamois slowly moved to one side, where I could see it better. It turned broadside. I had a great rest and got off what I thought was a good shot, but the chamois turned and ran downhill. I shot again, and then the animal was gone. I could not believe it. Could I have missed? What were we to do now?

I wanted to follow the animal, but it was a long way back up the mountain to our vehicle, and the guide wanted to start back. His English was not good, so negotiating was tricky. I eventually understood that he was directing me to set off for the vehicle while he went down after the chamois. He would see if he could find a blood trail and track the animal in the small amount of light remaining. I started up the mountain, and he set off downward.

After a time, I heard a shot—a hopeful sign. I was almost to the top of the ridge by then, and it was almost dark. I pulled out my flashlight and flashed it to signal my location. Apparently, the guide saw my signal, because he hollered in response. Then, sure enough, up he came with my chamois. My first shot had hit the animal in the shoulder, and the second had broken one of its back legs. It was almost done for when the guide finished the job.

I'm not sure which of us was the happier man at that point. Now I could see that the problem was the bullets, not the shooter. My bullets had gone right through the animal without mushrooming. I was not using my usual 160-grain Remington load, and the substitute bullets were too hot. We still had a long walk, and it was utterly dark in that forest; I thanked goodness for my little light. I carried my backpack and both rifles, while the guide carried the chamois on his back.

The ride back to the lodge sure felt good. Everyone turned out to welcome us, shooting movies and bringing out the beer and wine to celebrate. We had a dinner of fresh trout from the river that ran past the front of the lodge. It was after midnight when I retired, and we were to leave for Romania at 5 A.M.

Bulgarian chamois were a challenge—I nearly failed on two visits there, connecting at last only late on the day before we were leaving.

Romanian Railroad Hunt

At one time, logging trains had run on narrow tracks alongside the creek, all the way up into the mountains. At one place the line tunneled right through a mountain so loggers could haul out logs on the other side. By the time I walked along the railroad bed with Felix, the tracks and ties were long gone. The terrain was so steep that we struggled to imagine what the logging operations must have been like.

Felix said Houstonians Dan Duncan, Irvin Barnhart, and Mike Simpson had all shot Carpathian chamois right from the railroad bed. He showed me the points in question as we walked. We rounded a curve, and I was taking pictures of the place where the route passed beside a sheer cliff near the river when we saw a chamois right on top of that very cliff.

"That's a good one," said Felix. "Shoot."

I shot, and the chamois disappeared. Felix thought I had hit it, and so did I, but the local guide said I had missed. The terrain was too treacherous for anyone to go up and check, but Felix insisted he was sure the animal had been hit, and he declared that, even if no one else was going up there, he was going.

We looked at him in disbelief. This was not a mountaineering expedition. Nowhere is it written that hunting outfitters shall also be proficient climbers. Here

Felix Lalanne was the outfitter who coordinated most of my chamois and ibex hunting. Pursuing Carpathian chamois in Romania took us along an old logging railroad grade complete with tunnels. Felix distinguished himself with some cliff-climbing heroics to retrieve my trophy.

was a side of Felix I had not had occasion to see before. While the rest of us waited and wondered uselessly at the bottom of the cliff, Felix took some rope and somehow got himself up that impossible-looking face. When he got all the way to the top of the cliff, he found my chamois lying there, stone dead. The only way to get it down was with the rope, so he put the rope around it, slipped it over the side, and cautiously lowered my trophy down to us.

When we got back to the lodge and word got around, Felix became something of a hero among the local game scouts. I felt more than vindicated in my belief that it was important to have a committed outfitter as well as the local guides working for me. He surely earned his keep that day, with his climbing skills, his faith in my shooting, and his confidence in his own judgment that it was worth the effort of climbing the cliff. I got some of the fallout benefits as well. A game official who heard about the adventure dropped in to ask if I would like to shoot a Eurasian brown bear.

I told him I'd heard about those hunts. You sit in a stand, they tell you which animal to shoot, and the bigger the bear, the more it costs. I declined, telling him a stand hunt did not really interest me. I had been caught short on such a hunt in Poland, when the game warden told me an animal was in a certain price range, and I took it. The trophy proved considerably larger than his estimate, and its price was several thousand dollars more than he had quoted.

We talked about the Romanian game-conservation program. The Romanians have lots of bear and manage them intensively, shooting only boars. The game scout's full-time job includes knowing the number of bear in an area and their sizes. By attracting the bear to baits, game scouts conduct counts in the fall, before the animals go into hibernation. In spring, when the bear wake up, they often return to the sites of good meals they enjoyed before hibernating. When the game department gets ready to sell the permits, officials know just how many bear they have in each size and price range.

Most of the monitoring takes place from the same comfortable stands as the hunting. These are not your

The Duke of Bedford's estate at Woburn Abbey is renowned for Père David deer.

typical Texas deer stands. Each is more like a well-appointed playhouse on stilts, with a stove and thick walls for warmth, carpet on the floor to muffle sound, double-glass windows all the way around, and couches and soft chairs inside. The game official said he had seen a good one during his fall check. He also said the stand hunting was not as easy as it might sound because the shooting was at night, by moonlight. He encouraged me to come out and spend a few hours at the stand, just to get the feel of it.

Four of us agreed to go out there after dinner, and we stayed most of the night, grateful for the stove and comfy seating. A vehicle had killed a white horse on the road, and that was the current bait. Sure enough, the bear showed up and began eating it. As I watched, the official told me the price, which I declined to pay, though I did enjoy watching the bear. The next day the same official caught up with us and again tried to persuade me, this time with a slightly better price. Because they charge by the size range, he couldn't give me much of a discount, but I had to give him full marks for persistence. This time I agreed.

Moonlight Bear

That night we went back into the cozy stand. I would be shooting Felix's .300. We shed our shoes to be extra quiet. I fell asleep in a chair until someone shook me awake. The bear had arrived.

"Be careful," said the guide.

He handed me the rifle and told me to ease it out the window.

I could not see the bear well, despite the moonlight and the whiteness of the horse. Perhaps I was also not yet fully awake. At any rate, I eased the rifle into place, but then I hit the outer glass with my rifle barrel! No one had told me there were two windows. The bear, of course, was instantly gone. Now I was upset—I wanted that bear.

I collected this bezoar ibex in Anatolia, Turkey, in 1984. The horns are 36 inches long.

"You didn't tell me about the second window," I complained.

Everyone else was upset, too—I had scared off the bear.

I fell asleep again. An hour or so later, someone woke me—the bear was back. Carefully, I set up the rifle and opened the window. I waited until the bear turned; then I shot. I thought it was a good shot, but, once more, the bear was gone.

We were not about to start looking around for a wounded bear with a torch in the middle of the night. All present agreed that doing so would be too dangerous, and we should instead come back at first light. We got back to the lodge around 4 A.M., and the kitchen staff was waiting up for us because we had had no dinner. We had a hell of a dinner at that hour, and we lay down for a couple of hours.

At first light, back in the clearing, we found that bear not twenty feet from the horse, shot right through the heart—a perfect one-shot kill. It was a good, big bear. I was glad the official had talked me into it. Without a spotlight, the moonlight hunt had been more exciting than I had expected.

From that point on, things proceeded in the same organized way. A tractor arrived, lifted up the whole bear, and hauled it off in a trailer. Reflecting on the hunt, it is striking that in a mostly rural country, where one would assume people just wanted to be rid of all brown bear, the people and the bear coexisted a good deal more smoothly and calmly than they have ever been able to do in North America. The Romanians managed their brown bear well as a source of revenue. The bear were mostly nocturnal, and, as best I could tell, the farmers and villagers did not seem to want them all dead.

Failed Mission in Turkey

I arrived in Istanbul in midmorning on Turkish Air. My guide for Anatolian chamois, Riza Gozluk of Kaan Karakaya's Shikar Safaris, awaited me when I emerged from customs. He wanted to take me out sightseeing, but I was tired after two fractured nights in the bear stand. I spent a lazy day in the hotel, and we left the following morning for Erzurum, on the far eastern side of Turkey, north of Syria and the Iraq border. It was about a three-hour drive.

We followed a narrow road along a river up into the mountains, stopping for lunch in a village called Yusufeli, where we had some excellent grilled lamb with rice. I could not believe how the people lived—houses hanging off the edges of hills and food crops growing on every scrap of lowland, to the very edge of the river. People here have been living this kind of marginal existence for hundreds of years.

Our base was a lost little village called Altiparmak. The local game warden, fifty-three-year-old Mustafa Pehlivan, invited us to stay in his guesthouse, which had four bedrooms and a sitting room, rather like a bed-and-breakfast. There I met an interesting Australian fellow who was backpacking across Turkey. He did not speak Turkish and was traveling alone, riding local buses. Apparently, he was getting along fine using sign language.

We, on the other hand, would run into a snag the next day. As we set off through the village at 6:30 A.M. with our local guide, forty-eight-year-old Mahmut Todak, the mayor stopped us, informing us we could not go hunting. Even though we had our license and all the required papers, he ran this village. The guides and the driver tried to tell him everything was in order, but he simply gave them a flat no, and they were all afraid to cross him. After all, they had to live with him.

They consulted by phone with a more senior game official, who must have had a word with the mayor. We waited for two hours, and then word came that we could go hunting. We drove for about an hour to the base of a mountain and started walking. The terrain was steep, but it was crisscrossed with cattle and sheep trails that made for relatively easy going. After climbing for about two hours, we reached an area of old summer camps for cattle and sheep, located just at the timberline. Herders had formerly stayed there all summer.

The structures were interesting. Each had lower walls built of rocks that were stacked up to support the wooden floor and walls of an upper story. The lower level partly cut into the slope, so that one could have walked directly into the upper story from higher up the slope. The livestock spent the night within the rock walls, and the herding family slept in the room above. I saw ten or twenty of these structures, which had been out of use for about ten years because the young men were no longer interested in that kind of life. They were heading to the cities to find work. At one time, I was told, there were some three hundred cattle and fifteen hundred sheep in these mountains during the summer, but now there was just a handful of milk cows.

We started to climb, pausing periodically to glass, but we saw no chamois. About halfway up the mountain, the sole of one of my boots came off. Riza had some string, and we tried to tie the boot back into walkable condition. After a few hundred yards, it came apart again, and the sole of my other boot started to separate. We all had a good laugh about these fancy, expensive hunting boots falling to bits before our eyes, and Riza took some photos of my sorry footgear.

The guides were wearing little rubber shoes, like rain overshoes, and wanted to give them to me. They said they could walk in their socks. We still saw no chamois, so, after several more glassing pauses, we decided to head back down. Soon I had to give up on my left boot altogether; it simply would not stay on. I accepted one of the rubber

This is the abandoned hut where we stayed on my failed chamois hunt. Notice how the lower level is built into the mountain and how it supports the upper level. Herders would sleep in the upper-level structure and put their animals in the lower structure for safety.

shoes and came down the mountain wearing one little rubber shoe and one flapping, tied-together boot—*shwip-shwoop, shwip-shwoop.*

Fortunately, my gear did include a second pair of boots. We set off again at 6:30 the next morning, this time without encountering a challenge from the mayor. We went to the same general area and tried a different mountain. We saw a single chamois far away. It was a long climb, and once we accomplished it, the chamois had evaporated. One guide went out scouting for it while the rest of us stopped for lunch, but he couldn't find the animal.

Together again, we went on. We eventually saw our chamois again, but it was so far away that we had no chance of reaching it in the remaining afternoon hours. I now had only two hunting days left, and I proposed bringing food and sleeping bags the next day to give us the option of staying out in the mountains. In this way we could avoid losing four or five hours getting out and back in again. The guides were reluctant; it was cold at night and snowy at the higher elevations. As a compromise, we agreed to stay in one of the abandoned herders' huts if I did not yet have a chamois.

First, we went back to where we had seen the lone animal, but we didn't see it. We tried a second mountain, again with no luck. The local guides took a scouting foray and saw seven chamois on a third mountain, so we retreated to our selected hut and got a roaring fire going in the old fireplace. We planned to go after the group of seven chamois in the morning.

We set out at 6 A.M. Five hours after we had spotted the animals, we topped out on the ridge we had chosen as an approach, and the chamois were gone. The wind had changed while we were on our way up, and I think they winded us. We had another gourmet meal of bread and cheese, identical to our lunch fare every day. Riza and the local guide wanted to climb to another high point to scout, but I was disheartened by now and stayed put.

Wouldn't you know it, an hour later, Riza came running down and told me they had walked right into the chamois at the top. The animals had just stood and looked at them. The chamois came into view on the top—keeping tabs on us, I suppose—and we watched them for a while. We were out of time to try another climb. On the hike down we saw another three chamois, but they were about five hundred yards away—too far away to shoot. Again, we just watched them. It was close to dark when we reached our vehicle, after more than ten hours of climbing. I could not remember when I had last hunted so hard for four days in a row with nothing to show for it.

Wild Boar and Golf in Morocco

Casting a backward glance over these European hunts, I think the message they carry is that when you find an outfitter who feels right, the smart thing to do is to stick with him. Frank Green booked my early

Before leaving Morocco, we went hunting for wild boar, using a makeshift riverside blind.

African safaris. The Klineburgers arranged most of my North American hunts and those in difficult places like Russia and Mongolia, where they had the right connections. To collect all the many species available in South Africa, I mostly stuck with Chappie Scott. Felix booked me almost everywhere in Europe and accompanied me himself on most of my chamois and ibex hunts. He is a good guide and also a good judge of animals. His presence meant I was not completely dependent on the local guides.

Felix did a great job of putting together guided tours along with the hunts. I did take one trip to Spain without him, when several of us from Houston went on a red-legged partridge hunt with Cazatur. For the rest, Felix was my man. In Mallorca, when I hunted Balearean goat, he arranged for us to see the pearl factory, eat lobster, and play some golf. In Spain we visited the Pyrenees, stayed at lovely hotels and castles, toured the cities, spent time at beaches or on his boat, and dined at fine restaurants he knew. In 2005 I was

Felix spent a little time hunting golf balls with me in Morocco when Elizabeth and I added a stop in Marrakesh to our itinerary.

back in Spain for southeastern Spanish ibex and Beceite ibex. In March 2006 I was back again for a Ronda ibex but failed to get one. My hunt got scrambled when fog destroyed visibility and then turned to rain for the duration of my permit. Extending the hunt was not workable because Elizabeth was with me, and we were booked to go on to Marrakesh in Morocco. There Felix had us stay in a beautiful five-star hotel right on an eighteen-hole golf course.

From there he took us to the exotic Casbah, or market, where throngs of people were buying from hundreds of small stalls in the narrow streets and alleys. Snake charmers plied their art. Vendors spread out their wares, offering everything from fruits and nuts to textiles and metalwork. Somewhere in that fascinating rabbit warren of Old-World commerce, Felix guided us through heavy twelve-foot-high wooden doors in an unpromising mud wall that looked as if nothing of interest could possibly be behind it.

We found ourselves inside a quiet, dark, and stylish restaurant, utterly unexpected after the surrounding bustle and melee of the Casbah. As we settled down on big pillows on the restaurant floor, a bottle of wine appeared. And the food! There was no need for us to figure out what to order because Felix had pre-ordered a sampling of all the local specialties for us. While we were feasting, belly dancers began to perform. Eventually, out came unfamiliar and delicious local desserts. The place was so elegant and plush that one did not do anything as undignified as offering to pay before leaving. We simply got up and departed. Felix would receive the bill later and see to it. When we stepped back into the hubbub on the street, a car was waiting to sweep us back to our hotel.

One of the attractions in Morocco was that we had planned some wild boar hunting. I am a big fan of the roast suckling pig listed on Spanish menus, but the Muslim people of Morocco do not get along well with pigs. Late in the day Felix took me to a makeshift blind at a nearby river, and we sat inside, waiting for the pigs to come out to feed. They usually appeared just before dark. The first evening we saw only a lot of young animals, and I was not inclined to shoot. The following day our local guides put out some gooey, fermenting bait, a mixture of dates and corn, which brought in a good-size boar that evening. I shot and hit it. We could not find the trophy that night, but the local guides later found it in a nearby field and sent me the tusks.

Having missed getting my Ronda ibex on the March hunt because of weather, I returned to Spain in November–December 2006 and collected a very good one. Riza wants me to go back to Turkey for another try for Anatolian chamois. I have all the chamois except that one, but the country where it lives is tough, and there are no horses to ease the way. There is nowhere else to collect this trophy where the going is smoother. The only way to get one is on your own two feet. Will I go back? I think the Anatolian chamois of the Turkish mountains are probably safe from me.

Chapter 22

Wrap Up

SCI International Hunter Award, 2001; Conklin Award, 2003

When I started big-game hunting in the 1960s, I was not so much chasing trophies as chasing experience. I was burning to see Alaska and Africa for myself. If an animal was native to Africa, that was where I wanted to shoot it. Later, when I had begun to focus more on the awards that drive trophy hunting, Dr. Jim Conklin told me he thought he was the only recipient of the Weatherby Award who had never shot an exotic animal as a trophy.

That sharpened my perspective. I wanted to be the second. I have nothing against hunting exotics—it's just that for a long time I didn't want to go that way. To some extent I suppose that sentiment is still operating inside me. At any rate, the springbok certainly typifies the Eastern Cape, and that was what I brought home from the Tams' superb hunting operation in 2008.

Dr. Bob Speegle also offered me some guidance.

"You keep your nose clean, and you're going to win the Weatherby," he told me, "because you've got good-quality trophies."

Those two pieces of advice have stood me in good stead, and I'm grateful.

After I received the North American 27 Award in 1980 and the Weatherby Award in 1991, I was honored

Some hunting in the twenty-first century is from comfortable lodges like Irvin Tam's in South Africa, a far cry from my mobile Kenya safari in 1976.

in 2001 with SCI's International Hunter Award and in 2003 with the Conklin Award. High-mountain expeditions earned me the Ovis World Slam for twenty of the world's wild sheep species and the Capra World Slam for twenty of the world's goat species. These are all gratifying acknowledgments of the effort I have devoted to hunting over many years.

But things change; the world moves on. Only a handful of people received the North American 27 before requirements shifted to reflect current conditions. At the time I earned the Weatherby, you needed about two hundred trophy animals to be in the running, and Safari Club International had only about three thousand members. Today, the competition is tougher—SCI has more than fifty thousand members, and it hosts a myriad of contests. The Conklin Award was created to emphasize fair chase more than quantity. You've got to be good to earn that one. I was proud to be the second person to receive the Conklin Award—the first was Don Cox. By now, there are now several other hunters who have received all three major awards—the Weatherby, International Hunter, and the Conklin Award.

At one time or another I have had fifteen No. 1 world-record animals, and other hunters have since

Elizabeth took a dart hunt for white rhino with Tam Safaris in 2008, and Jason and JR joined us in the Eastern Cape.

superseded most of them. There's a pang in losing a No. 1 spot, though it's also gratifying to know hunters are still taking excellent trophies. Several of my records, however, still stand at the time of writing: nilgai, jaguar, tropical white-tailed deer, and Blanford urial. In some places I was lucky and came along at the right time. My nilgai is unlikely to be challenged, only because it is no longer possible to hunt nilgai in the wild in Nepal. In fact, I shot two when I was scarcely aware of what a really good one looked like. The guide told me one "blue bull" was very good, and it turned out to be the No. 1 animal. Closings have likewise complicated the picture for species like jaguar, polar bear, and walrus, and even for whole countries, most notably Kenya. Alongside closings have come openings. Being among the first people to go into a new hunting area is one of the greatest thrills one can experience as a sportsman. This happened to me in Sudan, Pakistan, Venezuela, the Amazon, and Iran.

Looking back through my journals, I am struck by how much space is devoted just to the business of getting to far places. Logistics, difficulty, and uncertainty are the overriding realities at the time. Will the plane come? Will the weather hold? But these details are of no lasting importance and soon disappear from memory. What stays with you, years after any hunt, are the moments of triumph and the bouts of serious hazard—getting a really fine trophy, or getting a scare at a military checkpoint.

My trophy room includes three distinct rooms—Africa, North America, and the other four continents. I have many full-size mounts of bear, muskox, lion, sheep,

Jason also darted a rhino on this family safari. Thirty or forty years ago, who would have dreamed that we would be using darts to hunt?

and various other species not mentioned in this book. My abiding love for bird hunting is also underexposed in this memoir, as is the fabulous bird shooting in Argentina (chapter 19). When I was a kid, the limit on pheasant in South Dakota was twenty-five birds a day. Much of my earliest hunting was for birds, and I still love to hunt them every year. I have chased ducks and geese from Hudson Bay to Costa Rica and Venezuela, and I'm a lifetime member of Ducks Unlimited. The birds in my trophy room include most of the North American game species, Magellan and ruddy-headed or Ashland goose; rosy-billed pochard; silver, Chilean, and Brazilian teal; masked duck; white-cheeked and brown pintail; red shoveler and Muscovy; plus rock pigeon, perdiz, and green parrot.

My record in Argentina was the day I shot seven hundred and twenty-five dove in one morning. I came in for lunch and decided to see if I could bust one thousand, so I went out that afternoon and shot another five hundred and fifty. These days I'm satisfied with two to four hundred. I bring all the dove home. One year, meat shipments were shut down because of a disease scare, but then they opened up again. Both the birds and the bird-hunting operations seem to be multiplying in Latin America.

Then there's fishing. I like to go fishing from time to time, too. Ken Fanning, my guide for the 1987 glacier bear that opens this book, took Elizabeth and me out fishing from Yakutat in late July 1994, as I was en route to Russia for snow sheep. We got mighty wet in rough seas, and I caught six kings. Elizabeth was not happy;

JR was proud of the copper springbok his grandfather took in South Africa. In turn, Grandpa was delighted to have been able to share his many hunting camps with his son and grandson.

Peter Tam (right) guided Jason to his lion, and JR, Elizabeth, and I were there to help celebrate.

she was seasick. The next day we floated a river—much calmer—and caught about fourteen fish. The third day out was the highlight. We went halibut fishing, and Elizabeth caught the biggest fish, a hundred-pounder—mine weighed only seventy pounds. She hauled the fish fillets home while I hunted in Russia.

The chief purpose of my travels has always been hunting, but the benefits extend far beyond the trophies. Fascinating people cross your path of adventure; hunting is just the reason to be there. The greatest rewards are invariably the experiences, just as I thought in the first place. It now seems hard to believe that I once had to sleep in a Russian army camp or that I spent nervous hours listening to the gunfire of rebellion in Sudan. And experiences can change your perspective. I enjoy horses, but my feeling for mules went up several notches when the wild man of the Chaco said he favored mules because "a horse is too flirty." Horses probably could not have survived the hard life he had chosen.

Some of my more hair-raising adventures have taken place on other continents—Africa, with all its chaos; Asia, with all its militarism. Yet, in terms of hunts where you really have to climb and work hard, there is little to touch North American sheep hunting. Just look at the amount of time it took me to get really good trophies of all four species: an average of more than three weeks for each. Although I was anxious to get Jason and JR to Africa, my childhood feeling for the mountains and the North remains close to the surface. Big-game hunting in North America is still some of the toughest hunting to be found in all the world.

Odds and Ends

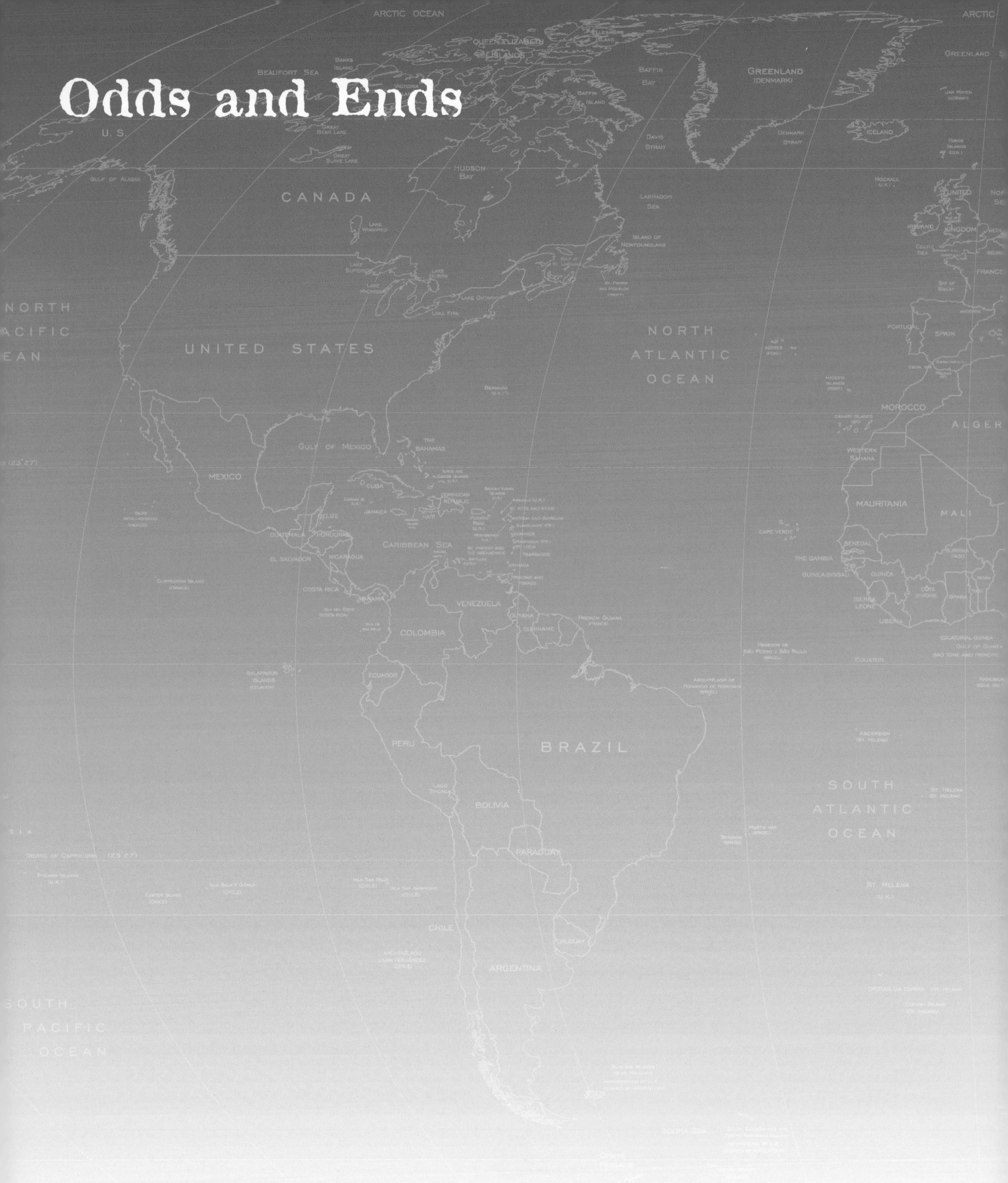

Part 5

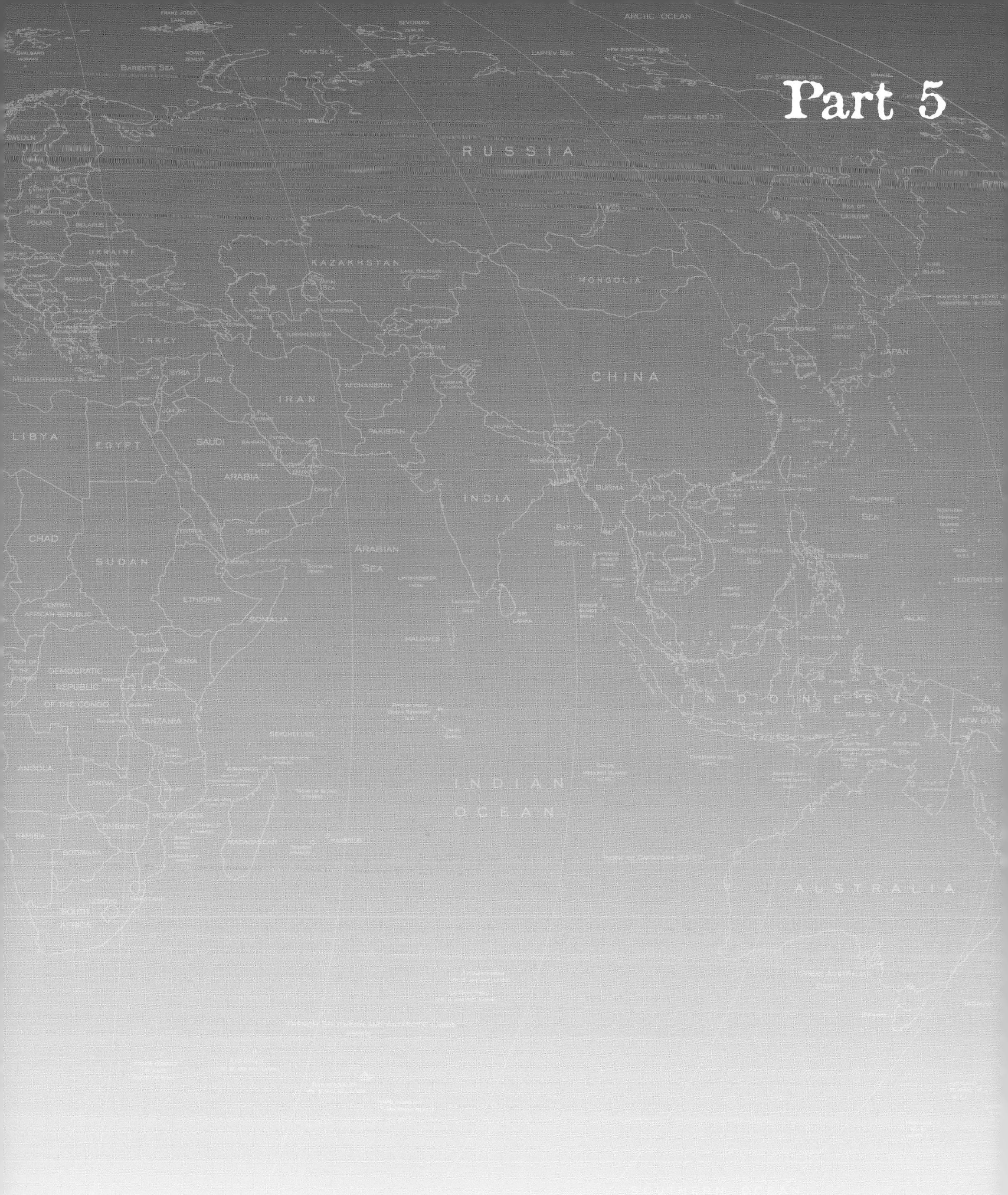
ARCTIC OCEAN
BARENTS SEA
KARA SEA
LAPTEV SEA
EAST SIBERIAN SEA
RUSSIA
POLAND
BELARUS
UKRAINE
ROMANIA
BLACK SEA
TURKEY
GREECE
MEDITERRANEAN SEA
SYRIA
IRAQ
JORDAN
KAZAKHSTAN
MONGOLIA
UZBEKISTAN
TURKMENISTAN
KYRGYZSTAN
TAJIKISTAN
AFGHANISTAN
IRAN
PAKISTAN
CHINA
NORTH KOREA
SOUTH KOREA
SEA OF JAPAN
JAPAN
YELLOW SEA
EAST CHINA SEA
NEPAL
BHUTAN
BANGLADESH
INDIA
BURMA
LAOS
THAILAND
VIETNAM
CAMBODIA
PHILIPPINE SEA
PHILIPPINES
SOUTH CHINA SEA
LIBYA
EGYPT
SAUDI
ARABIA
QATAR
OMAN
YEMEN
CHAD
SUDAN
ETHIOPIA
SOMALIA
ARABIAN SEA
BAY OF BENGAL
ANDAMAN SEA
SRI LANKA
MALDIVES
CENTRAL AFRICAN REPUBLIC
UGANDA
KENYA
DEMOCRATIC REPUBLIC OF THE CONGO
TANZANIA
SEYCHELLES
INDONESIA
PALAU
ANGOLA
ZAMBIA
COMOROS
MOZAMBIQUE
ZIMBABWE
NAMIBIA
BOTSWANA
MADAGASCAR
MAURITIUS
SOUTH AFRICA
INDIAN OCEAN
AUSTRALIA
GREAT AUSTRALIAN BIGHT

Chapter 23

Hunting Chronology

1962 Completed college

1963 Alaska—moose/caribou; Minnesota—deer; Wyoming—antelope

1964 Alaska—Dall sheep/moose/black bear/caribou; Minnesota—deer; Canada—moose

1965 Alaska two-week horseback hunt—moose/black bear/mountain goat

1966 Colorado—elk; Canada—moose

1967 Colorado—elk; Mexico—duck

1968 Colorado—elk; Wyoming—deer

1969 (Hurricane Camille destroyed author's Mississippi home, postponed African safari)

1970 Colorado—elk; Mexico—geese/cranes; Canada—geese; Alaska—black bear; Alabama—deer

1971 Alaska—Dall sheep/caribou/black bear

1972 Alaska—polar bear/wolves; Arizona and Nevada—mountain lion

1973 British Columbia—caribou (failed on Stone sheep); Utah—mountain lion; Alaska—barren-ground caribou/moose

1974 Alaska—brown bear; British Columbia—Stone sheep/mountain goat; Baja California, Mexico—desert bighorn

1975 Alberta—Rocky Mountain bighorn (completing Grand Slam)/elk; Alabama—deer

1976 Kenya—Thirty-five-day first African safari, thirty-six animals (twenty-seven species); Nunivak Island, Alaska—Greenland muskox; Wood River, Alaska—Dall sheep; Texas—bison; New Mexico—pronghorn antelope; Arizona—Coues deer with Marvin Glenn; Oregon—Columbia black-tailed deer; more than one hundred days hunting

1977 Kotzebue, Alaska—arctic grizzly (March); St. Lawrence Island, Alaska—Pacific walrus (March); Mexico—birds; Sudan—elephant/bongo/plains game; more than sixty days hunting

1978 Canada (Newfoundland)—Quebec-Labrador caribou/woodland caribou (September); Colorado—mule deer; New Mexico—elk (November); Central African Republic—elephant/plains game; Mexico—birds; more than seventy-five days hunting

1979 British Columbia (September)—moose/mountain goat; Wyoming—mule deer

1980 Mexico and Costa Rica—ducks; Guadalajara, Mexico—jaguar (March); Cameron, Louisiana—alligator; British Columbia—mountain caribou (October); Wyoming—mule deer (October); New Mexico—pronghorn antelope (November); Utah—Shiras moose (November, completing North American 27); Alaska—wolf/red fox/wolverine; Ireland—pheasant; Mexico—dove; more than ninety days hunting

1981 Namibia—African safari; Mongolia—argali/ibex/black-tailed gazelle; Russia (August)

1982 Red Sea Hills, Sudan (January); Spain—fallow deer; Utah—moose; Australia /New Zealand

1983 Baku, Russia—tur; Zambia/Zimbabwe—leopard (October, sixteen species); Mexico—big game/dove

1984 South Africa (June); Dhorpatan, Nepal—blue sheep (November); "Around the World," India/Greece/Turkey/Austria/Germany/Holland (October–December); California—Roosevelt elk; Russia, Mongolia—Altai argali/ibex/wolf/roe deer; more than seventy-five days hunting

1985 Ethiopia (February–March); Tajikistan—Afghan urial (November–December); Rajbiraj, Nepal—nilgai/sloth bear/axis deer/barking deer (November–December); more than fifty days hunting

1986 Pakistan—Blanford urial (February); South Africa (June); China—blue sheep

1987 Yakutat, Alaska—glacier bear (May); Venezuela (June); Australia/New Zealand (August–September); Northwest Territories, (September); Utah (October); Coppermine/Spence Bay/Northwest Territories, Canada (November); more than seventy days hunting

1988 Venezuela (March); Australia/New Zealand (March–April); South Africa (June); Russia—saiga (September); Northwest Territories; Utah

1989 Liberia (December 1988–January 1989); Russia; Australia/New Caledonia; Venezuela; England

1990 Tanzania (September–October); Argentina—birds

1991 China—blue sheep (September); Argentina—birds; Poland; Weatherby Award

1992 Nepal; Kazakhstan; Russia

1993 Russia—Transcaspian urial (October–November); Mexico—mule deer; Argentina—birds

1994 Russia—snow sheep (August); Bulgaria/Turkey (October–November); Alaska—fishing; Mexico—birds; Argentina—birds

1995 Russia—snow sheep (August); Kyrgyzstan (Khirgizia)—Marco Polo argali/ibex (September); Argentina—mountain lion/white-lipped peccary/birds

1996 Northwest Territories—arctic caribou/muskox; Minnesota—pheasant; Argentina—brocket deer/ water buffalo/birds; England; Austria; South Africa—family safari; Spain—birds

1997 Mexico—ocellated turkey; Iceland—reindeer; Spain; Argentina—birds

1998 Tajikistan—Afghan urial (October–November); Argentina birds

1999 Tajikistan—Afghan urial (February–March); Russia—chamois; Zimbabwe; Spain—birds; Argentina—birds

2000 Australia/New Zealand; Bulgaria; Romania; North Carolina—swan; Argentina—birds

2001 Colorado—elk; Texas—red sheep; Argentina—birds; SCI International Hunting Award

2002 Bulgaria/Turkey/Iran—chamois/Esfahan mouflon (October–November); Argentina—birds

2003 Kamchatka (Russian Federation)—snow sheep (August–September); Tajikistan—Marco Polo argali (October–November); England; Paraguay; Argentina—birds; Conklin Award

2004 Kamchatka (Russian Federation)—snow sheep; Argentina—birds; Australia—buffalo/pigs/oxen/offshore fishing

2005 Tajikistan—Marco Polo argali/wolves (November–December); Spain—ibex; Montana—mule deer; Argentina—birds

2006 Spain—ibex; Morocco—wild boar; Texas—sheep/birds; Montana—mule deer; Argentina—birds

2007 Australia; Texas

2008 South Africa; Colorado—mule deer

2009 Colorado—antelope

Chapter 24

Hunting Biography

Gary Ingersoll was born 6 September 1939, in the small town of Austin, Minnesota.* He was literally "born to hunt," as his father was a professional trainer of champion bird dogs. Hunting was in his blood.

Among Gary's first traveling big-game hunts was one for polar bear in Alaska. Not knowing what to expect on a guided hunt, he took up the challenge with great enthusiasm. His reward was a polar bear of more than ten feet. This was quite a lucky start!

Subsequently, Gary expanded his hunting adventures in North America and went on to take most of Alaska's big game, as well as elk, mule deer, and pronghorn antelope, besides yearly Colorado elk hunts. When another hunter in camp asked if he had a Grand Slam of North American wild sheep, Gary did not know what this was and quickly learned that very few hunters at that time had attained this achievement.

Gary has always been a tireless goal-oriented person. He takes his relentless work ethic with him to the mountains, woodlands, and jungle. In his mind, a challenge had been made. He secured a Dall, Rocky Mountain bighorn, and Stone sheep, but could not seem to get a break with the desert bighorn. His luck came in the form of a north Baja tag and a desert ram that turned out to be a B&C head. His goals became loftier as Gary went on to become one of the first few hunters to obtain the vaunted North American 27 game species (a set since expanded by Safari Club International). In the process of accomplishing this feat, Gary was fortunate enough to harvest a walrus and the number one Mexican jaguar.

He expanded his hunting horizons with a 35-day Kenya safari in the summer of 1976. During this trip, Gary was able to take 27 different species, including lion, leopard, Cape buffalo, and black rhinoceros.

Several more hunts came and went, and at a hunting convention Dr. Jim Conklin approached Gary about his future hunting aspirations. For the first time in a long time, Gary had no goal. Dr. Conklin suggested he apply for the Weatherby Hunting and Conservation Award. Although he liked the idea of this new challenge, Gary wanted to win this most coveted award on his own terms. He refused to "pad" his hunting resume with non-fair chase species. He discussed this issue several times with Dr. Conklin, who said he agreed and had done the same during his own Weatherby run. A solid friendship was born from this mutual respect.

The highest peaks, darkest jungles, and densest forests became Gary's backyard and he left few wild spots on earth untouched. He hunted the far corners of the world, taking many magnificent trophies such as the Mongolian argalis, two blue sheep, two Marco Polos, several ibex and chamois, and the No. 1 and 2 Blanford urial. He was continually off to Africa in search of the toughest and rarest game, including the bongo, mountain nyala, Nile lechwe, and forest elephant, and he put down tracks in Europe and the South Pacific.

*From the program for the second annual Conklin Award presentation, 2003.

His wild sheep collection soon numbered more than twenty, and he had several world records to his credit, including at least one from every continent. Gary felt he was finally ready to apply. In 1991, in only his second year of application, Gary was bestowed the Weatherby Award he had worked so hard to obtain. And in 2001, Gary was presented SCI's highest hunting honor, the International Hunting Award. He is still expanding his collection of native game and to date has obtained virtually every fair chase inner circle and slam that SCI offers.

Throughout his life, Gary has been an ardent supporter of hunting and conservation organizations. Through volunteering and financial support, he has an enviable record of giving back to the hunting community. He is a longtime supporter of the Foundation for North American Wild Sheep, Grand Slam/Ovis Club, Houston Safari Club, Safari Club International, Ducks Unlimited, and the Rocky Mountain Elk Foundation. He has underwritten conservation projects in the United States, Asia, and Africa. His trophy room is a constant source of entertainment for grade school children, and each year he volunteers as a guest guide for underprivileged and urban youth who are given the opportunity to take their first hunt in Texas at the Double D Ranch.

Like Dr. Jim Conklin and the 2002 recipient, Mr. Donald G. Cox, Gary is indeed another "Tough Guy." The Conklin Foundation is proud to present the 2003 Conklin Award to Mr. Gary Ingersoll.

Chapter 25

Bibliography

Anonymous. "With a Little Help from Lady Luck," n.d.

Conklin Foundation, The. Program of the Second Annual Presentation of the Conklin Award. Reno, Nevada, 24 January 2003.

Byford, David. "Close-Call Leopard," n.d.

——. Gary Ingersoll: 1991 Weatherby Award Winner," 24 August 1992.

——. "Should a Hunter Settle for Second Best?" 12 August 1986.

——. "Who Said a Family Fun Hunt Can't be Productive?" 12 August 1986.

Byford, David, and Charles Tischler. "The Adventures of Gary Ingersoll in Pakistan, 1986," n.d.

Ingersoll, Gary R. Conklin Foundation Award, Acceptance Speech, 24 January 2003.

——. Hunting Journals, 1984–2004.

——. "Super Slam Blue Sheep," n.d.

——. Weatherby Award Acceptance Speech, 10 December 1991.

Klineburger, Bert. *International Hunter: 1945–1999, Hunting's Greatest Era.* Kerrville: Sportsmen on Film, 1999.

Nichols, Randy. *Beyond the Horizon.* Houston: Houston Safari Club, 1996.

Nicholson, Frank M. "The 'Grand' Finale," n.d.

——. Gary Ingersoll: "A Different Drummer," n.d.

Pires, Adelino Serras, as told to Fiona Claire Captsick. *The Winds of Havoc: A Memoir of Adventure and Destruction in Deepest Africa.* New York: St. Martin's Press, 2001.

Tischler, Charles. "Gary Ingersoll Profile," n.d.

——. "Gary Ingersoll on Safari," n.d.

——. "The Taking of a Bear," 1 June 1988.